Tꞓ

A Practical Student's Guide: Programming in Java and MATLAB

Ka Lok Man
Kaiyu Wan
Tomas Krilavičius

A Practical Student's Guide: Programming in Java and MATLAB

This book is designed to be used in a programming course using the Java or MATLAB languages

LAP LAMBERT Academic Publishing

Impressum/Imprint (nur für Deutschland/ only for Germany)

Bibliografische Information der Deutschen Nationalbibliothek: Die Deutsche Nationalbibliothek verzeichnet diese Publikation in der Deutschen Nationalbibliografie; detaillierte bibliografische Daten sind im Internet über http://dnb.d-nb.de abrufbar.

Alle in diesem Buch genannten Marken und Produktnamen unterliegen warenzeichen-, marken- oder patentrechtlichem Schutz bzw. sind Warenzeichen oder eingetragene Warenzeichen der jeweiligen Inhaber. Die Wiedergabe von Marken, Produktnamen, Gebrauchsnamen, Handelsnamen, Warenbezeichnungen u.s.w. in diesem Werk berechtigt auch ohne besondere Kennzeichnung nicht zu der Annahme, dass solche Namen im Sinne der Warenzeichen- und Markenschutzgesetzgebung als frei zu betrachten wären und daher von jedermann benutzt werden dürften.

Coverbild: www.ingimage.com

Verlag: LAP LAMBERT Academic Publishing GmbH & Co. KG
Dudweiler Landstr. 99, 66123 Saarbrücken, Deutschland
Telefon +49 681 3720-310, Telefax +49 681 3720-3109
Email: info@lap-publishing.com

Herstellung in Deutschland:
Schaltungsdienst Lange o.H.G., Berlin
Books on Demand GmbH, Norderstedt
Reha GmbH, Saarbrücken
Amazon Distribution GmbH, Leipzig
ISBN: 978-3-8443-9855-7

Imprint (only for USA, GB)

Bibliographic information published by the Deutsche Nationalbibliothek: The Deutsche Nationalbibliothek lists this publication in the Deutsche Nationalbibliografie; detailed bibliographic data are available in the Internet at http://dnb.d-nb.de.

Any brand names and product names mentioned in this book are subject to trademark, brand or patent protection and are trademarks or registered trademarks of their respective holders. The use of brand names, product names, common names, trade names, product descriptions etc. even without a particular marking in this works is in no way to be construed to mean that such names may be regarded as unrestricted in respect of trademark and brand protection legislation and could thus be used by anyone.

Cover image: www.ingimage.com

Publisher: LAP LAMBERT Academic Publishing GmbH & Co. KG
Dudweiler Landstr. 99, 66123 Saarbrücken, Germany
Phone +49 681 3720-310, Fax +49 681 3720-3109
Email: info@lap-publishing.com

Printed in the U.S.A.
Printed in the U.K. by (see last page)
ISBN: 978-3-8443-9855-7

Preface

This book has two primary objectives: to teach the basic principles of programming in Java and MATLAB as outlined in curriula at many leading universities, and to teach the basic constructs of the Java language and the MATLAB language. In addition, this book is designed to be used in a programming course using the Java or MATLAB languages.

The concept of "learning by example" has been stressed throughout this book. Each chapter contains many examples, exercises and programs. These programs also demonstrate the general software engineering concepts and principles of good programming style.

During the preparation of this book, numerous individuals have provided us with suggestions, points of interest and other help. We wish to thank our colleagues from Xi'an Jiaotong-Liverpool University (China) and University of Liverpool (UK) for the many stimulating and helpful discussions we have had with them on the topics covered in this volume. We extend a special thanks to Bailing Zhang for providing us with his teaching materials in Java programming, which inspired our preparation of the Java chapter in this book. This book could not have been written without his support and contribution in particular, and that of our other colleagues in general.

ii

Contents

Preface   i

1   **Java Programming**   **1**
   1.1   Introduction 1
       1.1.1   Using Java Step by Step 2
       1.1.2   Basic Elements of a Java Program 3
       1.1.3   Java Application Execution 6
   1.2   Fundamental Programming Concepts in Java 7
       1.2.1   Syntax and Semantics 7
       1.2.2   Constructs of Java Language 7
       1.2.3   Data Conversions 14
       1.2.4   Classes and Objects 15
   1.3   Programming Statements 21
       1.3.1   Conditional Statement 22
       1.3.2   Repetition Statements 30
       1.3.3   Operators 41
       1.3.4   Branching Statements 45
   1.4   Programming with Methods 50
       1.4.1   Static Methods 50
       1.4.2   Recursive Methods 55
   1.5   Class and Object 59
       1.5.1   Introduction to Class and Object 59
       1.5.2   Declaring Classes and Objects 61
       1.5.3   Instantiation 64
       1.5.4   Setting Classes to Work 70
       1.5.5   Some Important Classes 78
   1.6   Array 90
       1.6.1   Basic Concepts of Array 90
       1.6.2   Advanced Topic of Array 95
   1.7   Some Advanced OOP Topics 101
       1.7.1   Encapsulation 101
       1.7.2   Java Access Modifiers 101
       1.7.3   Passing Object to Methods 104
       1.7.4   The This Reference 105
       1.7.5   Class Composition 106
       1.7.6   Inheritance: Extend Class 107
       1.7.7   Controlling Inheritance Through Visibility Modifier 112
       1.7.8   Overriding Methods 113
       1.7.9   Abstract Class 115
       1.7.10   Dynamic Method Binding 116
       1.7.11   Interface 118
   1.8   Lab Exercises 121

1.8.1   Lab 1 - Elementary Programming 121
1.8.2   Lab 2 - Input/output, Programming Statement 123
1.8.3   Lab 3 - Control Statements (if , if-else, switch), Repetition Statements (while)125
1.8.4   Lab 4 - More on Control Statements (while/do-while/for) 132
1.8.5   Lab 5 - Programming with Static Methods 139
1.8.6   Lab 6 - Further Exercises with Static Methods 144
1.8.7   Lab 7 - Introduction to Classes and Objects 149
1.8.8   Lab 8 - More on Classes and Objects 158
1.8.9   Lab 9 - String and Array 167
1.8.10 Lab 10 - More on Array 175
1.8.11 Lab 11 - Advanced OOP Topics 184

2   MATLAB Programming   **193**
2.1   Introduction 193
      2.1.1   Main Components of the MATLAB System 193
      2.1.2   How to Start 194
      2.1.3   MATLAB Desktop 194
      2.1.4   Help 195
      2.1.5   MATLAB Language 196
      2.1.6   Simple Operators 196
      2.1.7   Variables and Expressions 197
      2.1.8   MATLAB Workspace 198
      2.1.9   Arrays and Matrices 199
      2.1.10 Basic Mathematical Functions 205
2.2   Plots 207
      2.2.1   Single Plot 207
      2.2.2   Multiple Plots 207
      2.2.3   Customizing Plots 208
2.3   Programming in MATLAB 209
      2.3.1   Function Files 209
      2.3.2   Control Statements 210
      2.3.3   Simulink 225
2.4   Problems and Answers 235
      2.4.1   Introduction, Sect. 2.1 235
      2.4.2   Arrays and Matrices, Subsect. 2.1.9 237
      2.4.3   Plots and Programming in MATLAB, Sect. 2.2 and 2.3 241
      2.4.4   Control Statements, Subsect. 2.3.2 243
      2.4.5   Answers for Problems from Polynomials in MATLAB, Sect. 2.3.2.5 248
      2.4.6   Answers for Problems from Linear Equations in MATLAB, Sect. 2.3.2.6 . . 254

Bibliography   **254**

Chapter 1

Java Programming

1.1 Introduction

There are types of programming languages as shown below.

- *Machine languages :* they are strings of numbers giving machine specific instructions. Each type of CPU has its own specific machine language. For example,

$$+1300042774$$

$$+1400593419$$

$$+1200274027$$

The code is used to indicate the operations to be performed and the memory cells to be addressed. This form is easier for computers to understand, but is more difficult for a person to understand.

- *Assembly languages :* they are English-like abbreviations, which are translated via assemblers. These assembly languages represent elementary computer operations. Each architecture of a computer has its own assembly language. For example,

LOAD BASEPAY

ADD OVERPAY

STORE GROSSPAY

Assemblers translate these codes to machine languages at the intermediate level. Although they are descriptive, they basically follow the machine instructions.

- *High-level languages :* in high-level languages, programmers write program instructions called statements that resemble a limited version of English. e.g., the statement "value = value + delta". These languages are portable, in the sense that they can be used on different types of computers without modifications. Compilers translate those statements to machine languages. Examples are FORTRAN, PASCAL, COBOL, C, C++, JAVA, BASIC, etc. These high-level languages can be classified into two types:

  - *Procedural languages:* traditional languages where statements are a sequence of instructions executed in sequence. PASCAL, C, BASIC and FORTRAN are such procedural languages.

1

  – *Object-oriented languages:* in Object-oriented languages, objects contain data and the
    methods to work on those data. These languages may involve extensive use of message
    passing. They are good for large projects thanks for the concepts such as encapsulation
    and inheritance. C++, C# and Java are such object-oriented languages.

As you may know, ultimately a computer can only run programs at the machine code level.
A program written in a high-level language such as Java cannot be executed directly on a computer. Such programs must be either compiled or interpreted. Compiled languages are completely
converted to machine languages before execution. In this case, conversion happens only once.
In contrast, interpreted languages are converted to machine language *on the fly*, therefore the
languages must be converted every time when codes are executed.

Java [1–3] is a programming language originally developed by James Gosling at Sun Microsystems (which is now a subsidiary of Oracle Corporation) and released in 1995 as a core component
of Sun Microsystems' Java platform. The language derives much of its syntax from C and C++
but has a simpler object model and fewer low-level facilities. Java applications are typically compiled to byte code (class file) that can run on any Java Virtual Machine (JVM) regardless of
computer architecture. Java is a general-purpose, concurrent, class-based, object-oriented language that is specifically designed to have as few implementation dependencies as possible. It is
intended to let application developers "write once, run anywhere". Java is currently one of the
most popular programming languages in use, and is widely used from application software to web
applications [7].

Java is a general purpose object-oriented language along the lines of C++ while it is particularly
designed to interface with Web pages and to enable distributed applications over the internet.
The Web is becoming the dominant software development arena, which drives Java as the best
supported, most widely taught language. Even outside the Web, e.g. in scientific computing, Java
is as good as all other languages. Java has several features as shown below to make it become an
important language.

- The Java Language has several good design features such as secure, safe, object-oriented,
  etc.

- Java has a very good set of libraries covering many things from commerce, multimedia,
  images to mathematical functions.

- Java has the available electronic and paper training and support resources, growing labor
  force trained in Java.

- Java is rapidly getting the best integrated program development environments.

1.1.1   Using Java Step by Step

Different from VC++ programs, Java applications are in a nutshell. That is, all Java programs
are written into a file with a *.java* extension. Applications are *.java* files with a main method
which is executed first. There are two ways of compiling and running a Java application (via
byte-codes):

- One way: run the compiler on a .java file:

$$javac\ MyProgram.java$$

  then produce a file "MyProgram.class" of Java byte-codes.

- The other way: run the interpreter on a .class file:

$$java\ MyProgram$$

This executes the byte-codes.

In both of the above approaches, the commands *javac* and *java* are part of Java Development Kit (JDK). Example 1 shows the simplest java application.

Example 1

```
class HelloWorld  { /* each program is enclosed in a class definition */
/*------------------- main function begins ---------------*/
public static void main (String[ ] args) /*main() is the first method that is run*/
{
     System.out.println("Hello World!");
  /*the notation class.method or package.class.method is to refer to a public method*/
}
}
```

Since Java is object-oriented, programs are organized into modules called classes, which may have data in variables and subroutines called methods.

Next we introduce basic steps of installing and using Java.

- Download and Install Java : download from JDK web-site

  (http://download.java.net/jdk6/binaries) and choose: Windows Offline Installation, Multi-language JDK file.

  After installation, suppose you are working in the Windows environment, you need add environment variables: Suppose JDK has been automatically put into folder :

  C:\Program Files\Java\jdk1.6.0_18

  then add C:\Program Files\Java\jdk1.6.0_18\bin at the end of path in the environment variables.

- Creating Java Programs : the "source code" for a java program can be written on any word processor or text editor and saved in text format, with a "java" file extension. Examples of text editor are : Notepad, Wordpad (in Microsoft window accessories), WinEdit (http://www.winedit.com/), and Programmers text editor:

  (http://www.med-editor.com/indexus.html).

  EditPlus is recommended as a text editor, HTML editor and programmers editor for Windows. While it can serve as a good Notepad replacement, it also offers many powerful features for Web page authors and programmers (Website : http://www.editplus.com/).

1.1.2 Basic Elements of a Java Program

Basic elements of a Java program include *basic structures* such as *Classes and Methods, Comments, Identifiers, Reserved Words, White Space* and *Statements*. Next we introduce each of these elements with examples.

- *Basic structure (skeleton):* in the Java programming language, a program is made up of one or more classes; A class contains one or more methods. A method contains program statements. A Java application always contains a method called main. Example2 shown below is a simple Java application, which prints "Welcome to the Introduction to Programming in Java" message on the screen after execution.

Example 2

```
public class Welcome
{
  /*------------------- prints the welcome message---------------*/
```

```
public static void main (String[ ] args)
{
     System.out.print ("Welcome to");
   System.out.println("the Introduction to Programming in Java");
   /* println is another method provided in the System.out object*/
}
}
/*------------------- main method ends ---------------*/
```

- General Java Program Structure :   the structure includes class header and class body as shown in Figure 1.1.

- Comments :   comments in a program are also called inline documentation. They explain the purpose of the program and describe the steps. They do not affect how a program works though. Java comments can take two forms:

(1) "//" this comment runs to the end of the line.

(2) "/* this comment runs to the terminating symbol, even across line breaks */".

You should develop good commenting practises and follow them habitually. Figure 1.1 shows an example where the main method in an application is where the processing begins, and the main method must always be defined using the reserved words like public, static and void (for now).

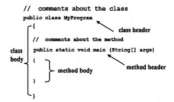

Figure 1.1: General Java program structure

- Identifiers : identifiers are the names of variables, methods, classes, packages and interfaces. In the Welcome program shown in Example 2, *Welcome, String, args, main, print* and *println* are identifiers. An identifier can be made up of letters, digits, the underscore character _, and the dollar sign $. Identifiers may only begin with a letter, the underscore or a dollar sign. They CANNOT begin with a digit. Java is case sensitive, therefore Total and total are different identifiers. Sometimes you choose identifiers when writing a program (such as Welcome program). Sometimes you use another programmer's code, so you use the identifiers that they have chosen. Often you use special identifiers called reserved words that already have a predefined meaning in the language (e.g., class, public, static and void). A reserved word cannot be used in any other ways.

- Java Reserved Words: Java keeps some reserved words, therefore you should avoid using these words when you write your own program. Reserved words are listed in Table 1.1:

- White Space: spaces, blank lines and tabs are collectively called white space. White space is used to separate words and symbols in a program. Extra white space is ignored when the program runs. Programs should be formatted to enhance readability using consistent indentation. For example, among Example 3, Example 4 and Example 5, Example 3 has the best presentation because of the nice white space.

Table 1.1: Java reserved words

abstract	default	goto	operator	synchronized
boolean	do	if	outer	this
break	double	implements	package	throw
byte	else	import	private	throws
byvalue	generic	inner	public	transient
case	extends	instance of	rest	true
cast	false	int	interface	try
catch	final	long	short	var
char	finally	native	static	void
class	float	new	super	volatile
const	for	null	switch	while
continue	future	protected	return	

Example 3

```
//**********************************************************************
// Lincoln.java          Author: Lewis/Loftus
//
// Demonstrates the basic structure of a Java application.
//**********************************************************************
public class Lincoln
{
    //-----------------------------------------------------------------
    public static void main (String[] args)
    {
        System.out.println ("A quote by Abraham Lincoln:");
        System.out.println ("Whatever you are, be a good one.");
    }
}
```

Example 4

```
//**********************************************************************
// Lincoln.java          Author: Lewis/Loftus
//
// Demonstrates a poorly formatted, though valid, program.
//**********************************************************************

public class Lincoln{public static void main (String[] args){
System.out.println("A quote by Abraham Lincoln:");
System.out.println("Whatever you are, be a good one.");}}
```

Example 5

```
//**********************************************************************
// Lincoln.java          Author: Lewis/Loftus
//
// Demonstrates another valid program that is poorly formatted.
//**********************************************************************

        public class
```

```
        Lincoln
    {
                        public                           ·
     static
          void
      main
            (
String
                      []
         args                    )
     {
            System.out.println (
"A quote by Abraham Lincoln:"                )
        ;     System.out.println
                (
            "Whatever you are, be a good one."
            )
       ;
     }
       }
```

- Statements :   a statement is a basic building block in many computer programs because
  it specifies an action. A statement in Java is terminated with a semicolon. For example,
  $intsum = num1 + num2$;. Statements can be grouped together in a block by enclosing
  them in curly brackets, i.e. $\{\dots\}$. A method is a collection of statements that is grouped
  together in a block to perform specific tasks. Statements can be divided into three types (or
  constructs):

    - *Simple Sequence* is one simple command after another.

    - *Selection* decides which step to be taken depending on some conditions, e.g. if state-
      ment.

    - *Iteration* repeatedly executes a command or a block of commands until some predefined
      conditions occur, e.g., while loops and for loops.

1.1.3   Java Application Execution

To execute a Java program, the application must be either compiled or interpreted first. Java
applications can be interpreted and executed. The Java compiler translates Java source code into
bytecode (somewhere in between source code and machine language). It is a file with the extension
.class . Another software tool, called an interpreter, translates bytecode into machine language
and executes it. The Java compiler is not tied to any particular machine. Java is considered to
be architecture-neutral.

Java applications can be compiled and executed. A Java program is "compiled" into Java
bytecode by doing this in a "command window", using the "javac.exe" (Java compiler) file. We
work in the directory (folder) where the Java program is saved, e.g., D:\⟩ javac Welcome.java.

In a summary, steps involved in creating a stand-alone Java program are :

1. Type code by using an appropriate text editor.

2. Compile source code by using the Java compiler.

3. Execute the class file by using the Java interpreter.

1.2 Fundamental Programming Concepts in Java

1.2.1 Syntax and Semantics

- Syntax and Semantics : programming languages differ from ordinary human languages in being completely unambiguous and very strict about what is and what is not allowed in a program. The rules that determine what is allowed are called the syntax of the language. The *syntax* rules of a language define how you can put symbols, reserved words and identifiers together to make a valid program. A syntactically correct program is one that can be successfully compiled or interpreted; programs that have syntax errors will be rejected. The *semantics* of a program statement defines what that statement means, in other words, statement's purpose or role in a program. A program that is syntactically correct is not necessarily semantically correct.

- Errors : a program can have three types of errors as shown below:

    - Compile-time errors : a compiler finds problems with syntax and other basic issues. If compile-time errors exist, an executable version of the program cannot be created.

    - Run-time errors: a problem can occur during program execution, for example, trying to divide by zero, which causes a program to terminate abnormally.

    - Logical errors: a program may run, but produces incorrect results.

- Development Environments : there are many development environments which can develop Java software. For example: Sun Java Software Development Kit (SDK), Borland JBuilder, Microsoft Visual J++, etc. Though the details of these environments differ, the basic compilation and execution process are essentially the same.

- Styles of Programming : all programs are built with statements that act on data. For efficiency and to enable the modeling of real world problems, statements and data must be organized in some ways. In traditional or procedure oriented programming, statements are organized with actions or tasks. In Object Oriented Programming (OOP) the whole program is organized with objects (or groups of data). OOP offers more scopes for modeling real world problems.

- Java Program Structure : the "container" that all Java programs are built inside is a class. Within that class there is at least one method, which performs some specific tasks. All Java programs have a "main" class with a "main" method where the tasks start. Statements are the building blocks with which methods are built.

1.2.2 Constructs of Java Language

- Variables : variables are used to store data (e.g. numbers and letters). They can be thought as containers, which hold things like number and letters. A variable has its own value. A variable must be declared, specifying the variable's name and the type of information that will be held in it, as shown in Figure 1.2. Data type determines what kind of value the variable can hold. A variable declaration tells computer what kind of data the variable will hold in order to store and retrieve the value of the variable in different ways. Multiple variables can be created in one declaration. Memory usage is necessary for all operations. A variable is a name for a location in memory.

    There are some rules and guidelines for naming variables:

    - A variable name (or an identifier) should be as concise as possible but long enough to suggest its meaning.

    - Variable names can be made up of elements such as letters, digits, the "_" or the "$" character.

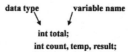

int total;
int count, temp, result;

Figure 1.2: A variable example

- A variable name cannot start with a digit number.
- Java reserved words cannot be used for variable names.
- Java is case sensitive, therefore uppercase and lowercase letter are considered to be different.

A variable can be given an initial value in the declaration as shown below:

```
int sum = 0;
int base = 32, max = 149;
```

A primitive type variable may have some default value, and it makes your program clearer to explicitly give the variable a value. An easy way to avoid an uninitialized variable is to initialize it within the declaration. When a variable is referenced (or used) in a program, its current value is used. Example 6 shows variable declaration.

Example 6

```
class Add2Integers1{
    public static void main (String[] args) {

        int sum;
        int n1 = 1;
        int n2 = 2;

        //calculate the sum
        sum = n1 + n2;

        //display the sum
        System.out.println("The sum of 1 and 2 is " + sum);
    }
}
```

The compiling and executing command for the above program as well as the execution result are shown in Example 7.

Example 7

```
Javac Add2Integers1.java
Java Add2Integers1
Result : The sum of 1 and 2 is 3
```

- Assignment : an assignment statement changes the value of a variable. The assignment operator is the "=" sign. In the example below,

```
total=55;
```

The expression on the right is evaluated and the result is stored in the variable on the left. Therefore after executing the above statement, the value that was in "total" is overwritten. You can only assign a value to a variable that is consistent with the variable's declared type, as shown in Example 8.

Example 8

```java
public class Geometry
{
    //------------------------------------------------------------
    //  Prints the number of sides of several geometric shapes.
    //------------------------------------------------------------
    public static void main (String[] args)
    {
        int sides = 7;  // declaration with initialization
        System.out.println ("A heptagon has " + sides + " sides.");

        sides = 10;  // assignment statement
        System.out.println ("A decagon has " + sides + " sides.");
        // "+" in the "println" statement is used as string concatenation.

        sides = 12;
        System.out.println ("A dodecagon has " + sides + " sides.");
    }
}
```

The execution of the geometry program is shown in Example 9.

Example 9

```
Javac Geometry.java
Java Geometry
Result : A heptagon has 7 sides.
A decagon has 10 sides.
A dodecagon has 12 sides.
```

- Constants : a constant is an identifier that is similar to a variable except that its value will never change. The compiler will report an error if you try to change a constant. In Java, you can use the reserved word "final" to declare a constant, e.g., $final\ double\ PI\ =\ 3.14159;$. To prevent accidental errors, you may give names to constant numerical values, e.g.

$circ\ =\ 3.14159 * diam;$. Example 10 illustrates how to use the constant PI.

Example 10

```java
class Area{
    public static void main (String[] args) {

        final double PI = 3.14159;
        double area;
        double radius = 3;
```

```
        // calculate the area
        area = PI*radius*radius;

        // display the sum
        System.out.println("The area of the circle is " + area);
    }
}
```

The compiling and executing of the Area application is as follows:

```
Javac Area.java
Java Area.javac
The area of the circle is 28.274309999999996
```

- Primitive Data Types : there are eight primitive data types in Java. Four of them represent integers including *byte, short, int and long.* Two of them represent floating point numbers including *float, and double.* One of them represents characters such as *char*, and one of them represents boolean value such as *boolean.* The difference between various numeric primitive types is their size and therefore the values they can store are shown in Table 1.2.

Table 1.2: primitive types and sizes table

Type	Storage	Min Value	Max Value
byte	8 bits	-128	127
short	16 bits	-32,768	32,767
int	32 bits	-2,147,483,648	2,147,483,647
long	64 bits	$< -9 * 10^{18}$	$> 9 * 10^{18}$
float	32 bits	$+/- 3.4 * 10^{38}$ with 7 significant digits	
double	64 bits	$+/- 1.7 * 10^{308}$ with 15 significant digits	

The precision of a floating-point number is the number of digits after the decimal. Therefore the float data type is a single precision data type. It stores 7 digits after the decimal point. Also, the double data type is a double precision data type and stores 14 digits after the decimal point. The boolean data type is used for logical testing and can store only one of the two values (true or false). The character data type char is used to store single characters.

- Characters : a char variable stores a single character from the Unicode Character Set. Each character is stored as a binary number. The Unicode Character Set uses sixteen bits per character, allowing for 65,536 unique characters. It is an international character set, containing symbols and characters which are used by many programing languages. Character literals (or actual values) are enclosed by single quotes: 'a', 'X', '7', '$', ',', '\ n'. Characters are listed in Figure 1.3 and Figure 1.4.

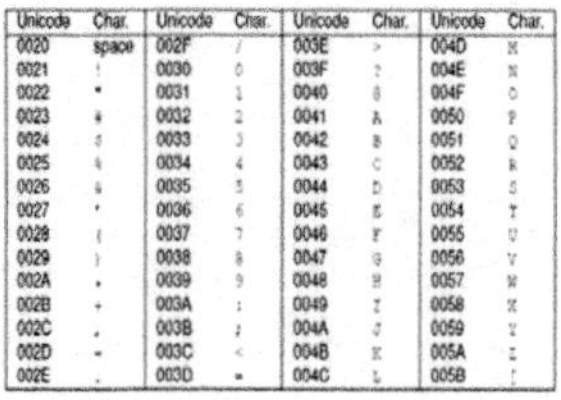

Unicode	Char.	Unicode	Char.	Unicode	Char.	Unicode	Char.
0020	space	002F	/	003E	>	004D	M
0021	!	0030	0	003F	?	004E	N
0022	"	0031	1	0040	@	004F	O
0023	#	0032	2	0041	A	0050	P
0024	$	0033	3	0042	B	0051	Q
0025	%	0034	4	0043	C	0052	R
0026	&	0035	5	0044	D	0053	S
0027	'	0036	6	0045	E	0054	T
0028	(	0037	7	0046	F	0055	U
0029	)	0038	8	0047	G	0056	V
002A	*	0039	9	0048	H	0057	W
002B	+	003A	:	0049	I	0058	X
002C	,	003B	;	004A	J	0059	Y
002D	-	003C	<	004B	K	005A	Z
002E	.	003D	=	004C	L	005B	[

Figure 1.3: Characters in Java

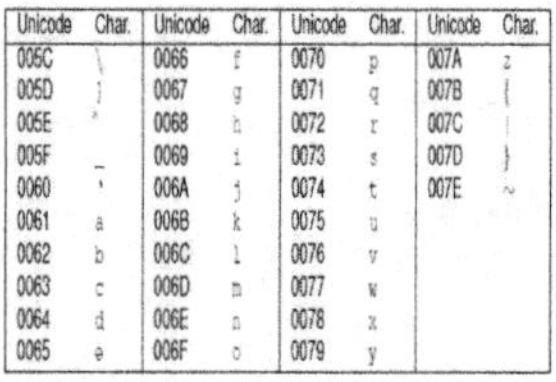

Unicode	Char.	Unicode	Char.	Unicode	Char.	Unicode	Char.
005C	\	0066	f	0070	p	007A	z
005D	]	0067	g	0071	q	007B	{
005E	^	0068	h	0072	r	007C	|
005F	_	0069	i	0073	s	007D	}
0060	`	006A	j	0074	t	007E	~
0061	a	006B	k	0075	u		
0062	b	006C	l	0076	v		
0063	c	006D	m	0077	w		
0064	d	006E	n	0078	x		
0065	e	006F	o	0079	y		

Figure 1.4: Characters in Java

The ASCII character set is older and smaller than Unicode, but is still quite popular. The ASCII characters are a subset of the Unicode character set, including the following shown in Table 1.3:

Table 1.3: ASCII characters

uppercase letters	A, B, C, ...
lowercase letters	a, b, c, ...
punctuation	period, semi-colon, ...
digits	0, 1, 2, ...
special symbols	&, |, \\, ...
control characters	carriage return, tab, ...

- Boolean : a boolean value represents either a true or false value. A boolean can also be used to represent any two states, such as a light bulb being on or off. The reserved words "true" and "false" are the only valid values for a boolean type. Example 11 shows the boolean numeric primitive data.

Example 11

```java
public class DataTypeEx {
    public static void main(String args[]){
        boolean x,y,z;
        int a=12,b=24;
        x=(a>b);
        y=(a!=b);
        z=(a+b==36);
        System.out.println("x="+x);
        System.out.println("y="+y);
        System.out.println("z="+z);
    }
}
```

The expected output of the program is as follows:

```
x = false
y = true
Z = true
```

- Arithmetic Expressions : an expression is a combination of operators and operands. Arithmetic expressions compute numeric results and make use of the arithmetic operators shown in Table 1.4. If any operand associates to an arithmetic operator is a floating point number, after evaluating the arithmetic expression, the result of such an expression will be a floating point number.

Table 1.4: Arithmetic operators

Addition	+
Subtraction	-
Multiplication	*
Division	/
Remainder	%

- Division and Remainder : if both operands associate to the division operator (/) are integers, the result is an integer and the fractional part is discarded. For example, 14/3 equals 4 while 8/12 equals 0. The remainder operator (%) returns the remainder after dividing the second operand into the first. The remainder operation takes two arguments, x and y, and is defined as $x - y * n$, where n is the integer nearest the exact value x/y. For example, 14%3 equals 2.

- Operator Precedence : operators can be combined into complex expressions. As an example,

---

```
result = total + count/max - offset;
```

Operators have a well-defined precedence determining the order in which they are evaluated. For instance, multiplication, division and remainder are evaluated prior to addition, subtraction and string concatenation. Arithmetic operators with the same precedence are evaluated from left to right. Parentheses can always be used to force the evaluation order. Figure 1.5 illustrates the operator precedences.

Figure 1.5: Operator precedences example

- Assignment : the assignment operator has a lower precedence than the arithmetic operators. In case the right and left hand sides of an assignment statement can contain the same variable, the assignment operator will be executed after the arithmetic operator. Example 12 illustrates the application of the assignment operator.

Example 12 *Computes the Fahrenheit equivalent of a specific Celsius value using the formula $F = (9/5)C + 32$*

```
public class TempConverter
{
    public static void main (String[] args)
    {
        final int BASE = 32;
        final double CONVERSION_FACTOR = 9.0 / 5.0;

        int celsiusTemp = 24;  // value to convert
        double fahrenheitTemp;

        fahrenheitTemp = celsiusTemp * CONVERSION_FACTOR + BASE;

        System.out.println ("Celsius Temperature: " + celsiusTemp);
        System.out.println ("Fahrenheit Equivalent: " + fahrenheitTemp);
    }
}
```

- Literals : a literal is the source code representation of a fixed value. Literals are represented directly in your code without requiring computation. Integers are normally 32 bits long but long integers are 64 bits long. For example:

1.2. FUNDAMENTAL PROGRAMMING CONCEPTS IN JAVA

```
a= 2;
// here 2 is a 32 bit integer literal.
```

Another example :

```
a = 2L;
// here 2 is a 64 bit integer literal. L here represents long data type.
```

Integers can be expressed in hexadecimal or octal. Floating point number can be any number with a decimal point, for "real number" in mathematics. Literal numbers with a decimal point are assumed to be double unless a 'f' suffix is used. For example,

$float \ vatRate \ = \ 17.5f;$.

In the decimal number system, each digit has a place value of 1, 10, $100 = 10^2$, $1000 = 10^3$. 10 therefore is called base. For example,

```
int decVal = 26;
// the number 26 is in decimal
```

In the octal number system, base is 8, values are prefixed with an 0. For example,

```
b = 055;
// the variable b is set to 45, i.e., (( 5* 8)+ 5).
```

In the hexadecimal number system, base is 16, and prefixing a value 0x or 0X. For example,

```
int hexVal = 0x1a;
// the number 26 is in hexadecimal
```

Floating point values can also be expressed in exponential form, which is very common in scientific computing. You can append a trailing e or E to represent the exponent value. For example,

$a \ = \ 2.0E1; sets \ a \ to \ 2*10^1$, which is equal to 20.

$a \ = \ 2.0E2; sets \ a \ to \ 2*10^2$, which is equal to 200.

Example 13 and 14 show DataTypeEx1 and DataTypeEx2 programs.

Example 13

```
public class DataTypeEx1 {
    public static void main(String args[]) {
        byte x=054;  // octal number
        byte y=54;   // decimal number
        byte z=0x54; // hexadecimal number
        System.out.println(" x converted to decimal number: "+x);
        System.out.println(" y converted to decimal number: "+y);
        System.out.println(" z converted to decimal number: "+z);
    }
}
```

In this example, octal number is 054; decimal number is $5*8+4 = 44$;, hexadecimal number is $0x54$; and decimal number is $5*16+4 = 84$. The execution and output of the program is :

```
javac DataTypeEx1.javac
java DataTypeEx1
```

The output of the program is: x converted to decimal number: 44 y converted to decimal number: 54 z converted to decimal number: 84

Example 14

```
public class DataTypeEx2 {
    public static void main(String args[])
    {
        int x,y,z;
        x=12;
        y=35;
        z=x*y;
        System.out.println(x+"*"+y+"="+z);
    }
}
javac DataTypeEx2.javac
java DataTypeEx2

output: 12*35=420
```

In summary, Declarations can appear anywhere in code. Variables must be initialized before being used. All operators are assigned precedence. When statements are evaluated, higher precedence operations are evaluated first. Brackets alter precedence.

1.2.3   Data Conversions

Sometimes it is convenient to convert data from one type to another. For example, you may want to treat an integer as a floating point value during a computation. Conversions must be handled carefully to avoid losing information. Widening conversions are the safest because they tend to extend from a small data type in size to a larger one (such as from an int to a double). Narrowing conversions can lose information because they tend to restrict from a large data type in size to a smaller one (such as from a double to int). Java will automatically convert any numeric type to a more general numeric type demanded by context. The primitive numeric types in increasing order of generality are as follows:

$byte \rightarrow short \rightarrow int \rightarrow long \rightarrow float \rightarrow double$.

The conversion of a primitive usually occurs in following situations: assignment, arithmetic promotion, and method call. Example 15 shows some legal and illegal conversions.

Example 15 *The following code is legal,*

```
int i;
double d;
i = 10;
d = i;   // legal
```

While the following code is illegal.

```
double d;
int i;
d = 1.2345;
i = d;   // illegal
```

There are general rules for data conversion. A non-Boolean data may be converted to another non-Boolean type, provided the conversion is a *widening conversion*, in which a value is changed to a type that accommodates a wider range of values than the original type that can accommodate. A non-Boolean may NOT be converted to another non-boolean type, if the conversion would be a *narrowing conversion*.

Casting occurs when the type is put in parentheses in front of the value being converted. Both widening and narrowing conversions can be accomplished by explicitly casting a value. For example, if num1 and num2 are integers and average is a double, we can achieve this by casting:

$average = (double)(num1 + num2)/2;$

Another example: if mark1 and mark2 are doubles, then result is an integer:

$result = (int)(mark1 + mark2);$

Arithmetic promotion conversions happen within arithmetic statements. Four conversion rules for binary operator are listed below:

- if one of the operands is a double, the other operand is converted to double;

- else if one of the operands is a float, the other operand is converted to a float;

- else if one of the operands is a long, the other operand is converted to a long;

- else both operands are converted to int.

Example 16 shows the arithmetic promotion conversions. The type of the expression on the right side of an assignment operation can be safely promoted to the type of the variable on the left.

Example 16

```
public class IdentifierUse1 {
    public static void main ( String[] args ) {
    // type conversion in assignment operations
        int myInt;
        byte myByte = 127;
        myInt = myByte; // byte -> int

        System.out.println("myInt=" + myInt);

        // type conversions in arithmetic operations
        myByte = 127;
        myInt = myByte + myInt; // myByte operand is converted to int

    System.out.println("myInt=" + myInt);
    }
}
```

1.2.4   Classes and Objects

1.2.4.1   System Class

Initially, you can think of an object as a collection of data values with access to services that can be performed. The services are defined by methods in a class that defines the object. In Figure 1.6, the println method of the System.out object is invoked .

The System class contains several methods for printing texts on the screen:

println() //cursor moves to new line

print() //cursor stays on same line

Example 17 prints three lines of output.

Example 17

System.out.println ("Life wasn't meant to be easy.");

Figure 1.6: System.out object

```
public class CountIn
{
    public static void main (String[] args)
    {
        System.out.print ("One... ");
        System.out.print ("Two... ");
        System.out.print ("Three... ");
        System.out.println ("Four... ");
        System.out.println ("She was just seventeen");
        System.out.println ("If you know what I mean.");
    }
}
```

The output of the program is as follows:

```
One ... Two ... Three ... Four ...\\
She was just seventeen \\
If you know what I mean.\\
```

The Keyboard class is NOT a part of the Java standard class library. We provide the Keyboard class to make reading input from the keyboard easily. The Keyboard class contains a set of methods for reading data from the keyboard/screen as shown below:

```
readInt()      // read integer data from the keyboard
readFloat()    // read float point data from the keyboard
readDouble()   // read double data from the keyboard
readChar()     // read character from the keyboard
readString()   // read a string from the keyboard
```

Example 18 shows an application of Keyboard class.

Example 18

```
public class Quadratic {
    // determines the roots of a quadratic equation.
    public static void main (String[] args)  {
        int a, b, c;  // ax^2 + bx + c
        System.out.print ("Enter the coefficient of x squared: ");
        a = Keyboard.readInt();
        System.out.print ("Enter the coefficient of x: ");
        b = Keyboard.readInt();
        System.out.print ("Enter the constant: ");
        c = Keyboard.readInt();
        // use the quadratic formula to compute the roots
```

```
    // assumes a positive discriminant
    double discriminant = Math.pow(b, 2) - (4 * a * c);
    double root1 = ((-1 * b) + Math.sqrt(discriminant))/(2 * a);
    double root2 = ((-1 * b) - Math.sqrt(discriminant))/(2 * a);
    System.out.println ("Root #1: " + root1);
    System.out.println ("Root #2: " + root2);
  }
}
```

The output of the program is as follows:

```
Enter the coefficient of x squared: 1
Enter the coefficient of x: 2
Enter the constant: 1
Root #1: -1.0
Root #2: -1.0
```

The program presented in Example 19 takes a number in centimeters from the command line and converts it to inches, which illustrates another application of Keyboard class.

Example 19

```
public class Cm2in {
    public static void main (String[] args) {
        double cm, in;
        System.out.print ("Enter the value of centimeters: ");
        cm = Keyboard.readDouble();
        in = cm / 2.54;
        System.out.println(in + " inches");
    }
}
```

The output of the program is as follows:

```
Enter the value of centimeters: 10
3.937007874015748 inches
```

Example 20 shows the program that takes a number in inches from keyboard and converts it to centimeters.

Example 20

```
public class In2cm
{
    public static void main (String[] args)
    {
        double inch;
        System.out.print ("Enter the value of inches: ");
        inch = Keyboard.readDouble();
        double cm = inch * 2.54;
        System.out.println(cm + " centimeters");
    }
}
```

Example 21 shows the program that reads two numbers from keyboard and outputs the total pay due, with one number indicating the amount of hours that an employee worked and another number indicating their basic pay rate.

Example 21

```
public class Payday {
    public static void main (String[] args) {
        double hours, rate, pay;
        System.out.print ("Enter the hours: ");
        hours = Keyboard.readDouble();
        System.out.print ("Enter the rate: ");
        rate = Keyboard.readDouble();
        pay = rate * hours;
        System.out.println("The paycheck is " + pay + " yuan.");
    }
}
```

The output of the program is as follows:

```
Enter the hours:  8
Enter the rate: 10
The paycheck is 80.0   yuan.
```

Example 22 shows a program that accepts a price on the command line and prints out the appropriate tax and total purchase price based on the assumption that sales tax is 7.25%.

Example 22

```
public class Salestax {
    public static void main (String[] args) {
        final double TAXRATE=0.0725;
        double price, salestax;
        System.out.print("Enter the price: ");
        price = Keyboard.readDouble();
            salestax = price * TAXRATE;
        System.out.println("Sales tax is " + salestax);
    }
}
```

The output of the program is as follows:

```
Enter the price: 35
Sales tax is 2.5374999999999
```

1.2.4.2   Escape Sequences

Escape sequences are used to print a double quote character. The following line would confuse the compiler because it interprets the second quote as the end of the string.

```
System.out.println("I said "Hello" to you.");
```

Special text formatting tasks are performed by escape sequences. An escape sequence consists of a backslash (\) followed by an escape character which is treated in a special way. Therefore, the above code can be revised as follows:

```
System.out.println("I said \"Hello\" to you.");
```

Table 1.5 lists some Java escape sequences:

Table 1.5: Java escape sequences

Escape Sequence	Meaning
\b	backspace
\t	tab
\n	newline
\r	carriage return
\"	double quote
\'	single quote
\\	backslash

Example 23 shows how to use escape sequence.

Example 23

```
public class Roses
{
    // Prints a poem (of sorts) on multiple lines.
    public static void main (String[] args)
    {
      System.out.println ("Roses are red,\n\tViolets are blue,\n" +
        "Sugar is sweet,\n\tBut I have \"commitment issues\",\n\t" +
        "So I'd rather just be friends\n\tAt this point in our " +
        "relationship.");
    }
}
The result is : \\
Roses are red,
        Violets are blue,
Sugar is sweet,
        But I have "commitment issues",
        So I'd rather just be friends
        At this point in our relationship.
```

1.2.4.3 String Class and Methods

The difference between classes and objects can be concluded as follows : A class is the basic building block for Java programs. It is a container for groups of methods which perform related tasks. An important role for many Java classes is the creation of "objects". An object can be considered as a collection of data values with access to services that can be performed on its contents. The data values describing each object are called attributes. For example, each "String" is an object that is a collection of characters. For the Strings Class, *Strings* are objects rather than primitive data types. Each string object is a member of the String class. Since strings are so common, Java has a simple way to create them:

$title = "Java is fun"$;

The string object is the variable *title* and its content is the string literal "Java is fun".

All examples of strings (or literals) are written inside double quotation marks. The string concatenation operator (+) is used to append one string to the end of another, e.g.,

"Java programming is" + "lots of fun".

It can also be used to append a number to a string, e.g.,

"Java programming is" + 2 + "much fun".

A string literal cannot be broken across two lines. Example 24 illustrates how to concatenate strings.

Example 24

```
public class Facts
{
    // prints various facts.
    public static void main (String[] args)
    {
        // strings can be concatenated into one long string
        System.out.println ("We present the following facts for your "
                            + "extracurricular edification:");
        System.out.println ();
        // a string can contain numeric digits
        System.out.println ("Letters in the Hawaiian alphabet: 12");
        // a numeric value can be concatenated to a string
        System.out.println ("International dialing code for Anarctica: "
                            + 672);
        System.out.println ("Year in which Leonardo da Vinci invented "
                            + "the parachute: " + 1515);
    }
}
```

The plus operator (+) is used both for string concatenation and arithmetic addition. The function performed by the + operator depends on the context. If both operands are strings, or if one is a string and another is a number, the + operator performs string concatenation. If both operands are numeric, it adds them, as shown in Example 25. The + operator is evaluated from left to right but parentheses can be used to change the operation order.

Example 25

```
public class Addition
{
    // concatenates and adds two numbers and prints the results.
    public static void main (String[] args)
    {
        System.out.println ("24 and 45 concatenated: " + 24 + 45);
        System.out.println ("24 and 45 added: " + (24 + 45));
    }
}
```

The output of the program is as follows:

```
24 and 45  concatenated: 2445
24 and 45 added: 69
```

Once a string object has been created, you can use the dot operator to invoke its methods, e.g.,

```
title.length()
```

The String class has several methods that are useful for manipulating strings. Some of the methods return a value, such as an integer or a new string object. The characters in a string are located by a position number beginning at zero.

Several useful String methods are:

int length( ) returns the number of characters in a string;

char charAt(int index) returns the character at specified index;

For example:

```
String name = "Fred" name.length()          //returns the value 4
name.charAt(1)          // returns the character 'r'
```

1.2.4.4 Other Concepts Related to Class

- Class Libraries : a class library is a collection of classes that you can use when developing programs. There is a Java standard class library that is a part of any Java development environment. The System class and the String class are the part of Java standard class library. Other class libraries can be accessed by importing them into your program.

- Packages : the classes of the Java standard class library are organized into packages. Some of the packages in the standard class library are shown in Table 1.6.

Table 1.6: Java packages

Package	Purpose of the package
java.lang	General support
java.applet	Creating applets for the web
java.awt	Graphics and graphical user interfaces
javax.swing	Additional graphics capabilities and components
java.net	Network communication
java.util	Utilities

- The Import Declaration : when you want to use a class from a package, you could use its fully qualified name, e.g. *java.applet.Applet*. You may also import the class, then just use the class name : *import java.applet.Applet*; To import all classes in a particular package, you can use the * wildcard character,e.g. *import java.applet.**;. All classes of the java.lang package are automatically imported into all programs, e.g., System, String or Math classes.

- Class Methods : some methods can be invoked through the class name, instead of through an object of the class. These methods are called class methods or static methods. The Math class contains many static methods, providing various mathematical functions, such as absolute value, trigonometry functions, square root, etc.

- The Math Class : math methods (and some stored constants) are accessed by writing the class name followed by the 'dot' operator. Some useful Math class methods are:

  Math.sqrt(number) method returns the square root value of the argument. If argument value is less than zero, it will return NaN value. e.g. num2 = Math.sqrt(num1);

  Math.pow(double a, double b) method returns the value of the first argument raised to the power of the second argument. e.g. num2 = Math.pow(num, 3);

1.3 Programming Statements

Programs consist of statements. Unless indicated otherwise, statements in a method are executed one after the other in the order that they are written. Some programming statements modify that order though, allowing you to decide whether or not to execute a particular statement, or perform a statement repetitively. The order of statement execution is called the flow of control. Below are those statements that can define the flow of control of your program.

1.3.1   Conditional Statement

A conditional statement lets you choose which statement will be executed next. Therefore they are sometimes called *selection statements*. Conditional statements in Java are *the if statement*, *the if-else statement* and *the switch statement*.

1.3.1.1   The If Statement

The if statement has the following syntax shown in Figure 1.7:

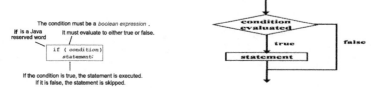

Figure 1.7: Syntax of if statement   Figure 1.8: Logic of if statement

Below is an example. In this example, first, the condition is evaluated. Its value is either true or false. If the condition is true, the println statement is executed. If it is not, the println statement is skipped.

```
if (mark > 50)
   System.out.println (mark + "pass");
```

Example 26 reads the user's age and prints comments accordingly. This example shows the application of if statements.

Example 26

```
public class Age
{
   //---------------------------------------------------------------
   //  Reads the user's age and prints comments accordingly.
   //---------------------------------------------------------------
   public static void main (String[] args)
   {
      final int MINOR = 21;

      System.out.print ("Enter your age: ");
      int age = Keyboard.readInt();

      System.out.println ("You entered: " + age);

      if (age < MINOR)  System.out.println ("Youth is a wonderful thing. Enjoy.");

      System.out.println ("Age is a state of mind.");
   }
```

```
}
```

Figure 1.8 shows the logic of the if statement.

A condition often uses one of Java's *equality operators* or *relational operators*, which return Boolean results. Table 1.7 lists these operators. Equality and relational operators have precedence lower than the arithmetic operators.

Table 1.7: Boolean operators

==	equal to
≠	not equal to
>	less than
<	greater than
≤	less than or equal to
≥	greater than or equal to

1.3.1.2 The If-Else Statement

An else clause can be added to an if statement to make it become an if-else statement:

```
if ( condition )
    statement1;
else
    statement2;
```

If the condition is true, statement1 is executed; If the condition is false, statement2 is executed. Either of these two statements will be executed, but not both.

The program in example 27 asks the user about the Java course and prints comments.

Example 27

```
public class Love1
{
    //-----------------------------------------------------------------
    //  Asks the user's about the Java course and prints comments accordingly.
    //-----------------------------------------------------------------
    public static void main (String[] args)
    {
        System.out.println ("A GREAT 2nd YEAR SUBJECT ");
        System.out.print ("Are'nt you glad you're here?  Reply n for No or y for Yes : " ) ;

        char answer ;
        answer = Keyboard.readChar();

        if (answer == 'y') System.out.println("\n\t It's great that you entered: " + answer) ;

        else  System.out.println("\n\t I guess youd rather be somewhere else too" ) ;

        System.out.println ("\t\t HAVE A NICE DAY ");

    }
}
```

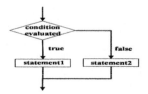

Figure 1.9: Logic of if-else statement

Figure 1.9 shows the logic of the if statement.

Several statements can be grouped together into a *block statement*, delimited by braces {...}. For example, in an if-else statement, the if portion, the else portion or both of the portions, could be block statements, as Example 28 shows.

Example 28

```
public class Guessing2
{
    public static void main (String[] args)
    {

        int answer = 7;

        System.out.print ("I'm thinking of a number between 1 and 10."
                        + " Guess what it is: ");
        int guess = Keyboard.readInt();

        if (guess == answer)
            System.out.println ("You got it! Good guessing!");
        else
        {
            System.out.println ("That is not correct, sorry.");
            System.out.println ("The number was " + answer);
        }
    }
}               // note the indentation in this program
```

1.3.1.3   Nested If Statement

Nested if statements means to use the if statement inside another if statement. An else clause is matched to the last unmatched if statement. Using indentation helps to clarify the logic in the nested ifs. Example 29 shows an application which reads the user's age and prints comments accordingly. Example 30 is a program that accepts two integers and determines which is larger. Example 31 is a program that accepts three integers and determines which is largest. Example 32 is a program that accepts a percentage of the examination mark and determines the grading. All these examples illustrate several applications of nested if statements.

Example 29

```
public class Age2
{
```

```
//-------------------------------------------------------------
//  Reads the user's age and prints comments accordingly.
//-------------------------------------------------------------
public static void main (String[] args)
{

   System.out.print ("Enter your age: ");
   int age = Keyboard.readInt();


   if (age <18)  System.out.println ("Youth is a wonderful thing. Enjoy.");
      else
         if (age<30) System.out.println ("Old enough to have fun,"
               + "young enough to get into trouble.");
         else
               System.out.println ("Life gets tedious don't waste it.");
   }
}
```

Example 30

```
public class Larger    // determines the larger of 2 numbers
{
  public static void main(String[] args)
  {
     System.out.println("Enter a number:");
     int num1 = Keyboard.readInt();
     System.out.println("Enter another number:");
     int num2 = Keyboard.readInt();
     if (num1 > num2)  System.out.println(num1 + "is the larger");
     else  if (num2 > num1)
               System.out.println(num2 + "is the larger");
           else System.out.println(num1 + "is equal to" + num2);
  }
}
```

Example 31

```
public class Largest1        // determines the largest of 3 numbers
{
   public static void main (String[ ] args)
   {
      int num1, num2, num3, max;

      System.out.println ("Enter three integers: ");
      num1 = Keyboard.readInt();
      num2 = Keyboard.readInt();
      num3 = Keyboard.readInt();

      max = num1;

      if (num2 > max)
            max = num2;
      if (num3 > max)
            max = num3;
```

```
        System.out.println ("Maximum value: " + max);
    }
}        // this is called the 'Bubble sort algorithm'
```

An alternative solution might be :

```
public class Largest2
{
  public static void main(String[] args)
  {
      System.out.println("Enter a three numbers:");
      int num1 = Keyboard.readInt();
      int num2 = Keyboard.readInt();
      int num3 = Keyboard.readInt();

      if (num1 > num2)        // cond1
        if(num1 >num3)        // cond2
            System.out.println(num1 + "is the largest");  // true, true
        else
            System.out.println(num3 + "is the largest");  // true, false
      else
          if (num2 > num3)        //cond3
            System.out.println(num2 + "is the largest");  // false, true
          else
            System.out.println(num3 + "is the largest");  // false, false
  }
}
```

Example 32

```
public class ExamGrade1 {
    public static void main (String[] args) {
        String  grade;
        int mark;
        System.out.println("Enter exam mark:");
        mark = Keyboard.readInt();

        if (mark>=80) grade="HD";

        if ((mark>=70) && (mark<80)) grade="D";

        if ((mark>=60) && (mark<70)) grade="C";

        if ((mark>=50) && (mark<60)) grade="P";

        if (mark<50) grade="N";

        System.out.println("Result:\t" + mark + "\t" + grade );
    }
}
```

An alternative solution is as follows:

```
class ExamGrade2
{
```

```
static void main(String[] args)
{
String grade;
System.out.println("Enter exam mark:");
int mark = Keyboard.readInt();

if (mark>=80)      grade="HD";                // true
else
    if (mark>=70) grade="D";        // false, true
    else
        if (mark>=60) grade="C";        // false, false, true
        else
            if (mark>=50) grade="P";// false, false, false, true
            else grade="N";        // false, false, false, false

System.out.println("Result:\t" + mark + "\t" +grade );
}
}
```

To combine if statements, you can use either of the following syntax:
Multiple ifs:

```
if(condition1) action A;
if(condition2) action B;
if(condition3) action C;
```

or Nested ifs :

```
if(condition1) action A;
else
    if(condition2) action B;
    else
    action C;
```

Some issues related to Nested Ifs

- *Properties of Nested If statements :* For any statement to be executed, it must be preceded by a unique set of truth values. If the first 'condition' is True, the next statement will be executed and the flow of control will jump to the end of the nested if statements. For each condition after the first, you may have some prior knowledge about the possible value of the variable(s).

- *Comparing Characters :* You can use the relational operators on character data. The results are based on the Unicode Character Set. The uppercase alphabet (A-Z) and the lowercase alphabet (a-z) both appear in alphabetical order in Unicode Character Set. The following condition is true because the character 'A' comes before the character 'J' in Unicode:

```
if ('A' < 'J') System.out.println ("A is before J");
```

- *Comparing Strings :* A character string in Java is an object. Therefore you cannot use the relational operators to compare strings. Later in this chapter we will use the *equals* method and the *compareTo* method for comparing two strings. The *equals* method tells if two strings are equal and the *compareTo* method tells if one string comes before another alphabetically. At this stage, you can use the *charAt()* method to extract a character from each of two strings and compare in this way: e.g., $str1.charAt(0) > str2.charAt(0)$.

- *Comparing Floating Point Values :* When comparing two floating point values for equality, you should rarely use the equality operator (==). In many situations, you might consider two floating point numbers to be "close enough" even if they are not exactly equal. To determine the equality of two floats, you may use the following technique:

```
if (Math.abs (f1 - f2) < 0.00001)   System.out.println ("Essentially equal.");
```

- *Ternary Operator :* Java provides a ternary operator that operates like the if-else structure. A ternary operator needs three operands, and it is called an operator because it returns a value. The syntax of ternary operator is $Boolean - exp$? $value1$: $value2$. The Boolean expression is evaluated and the control is transferred to either $value1$ or $value2$ depending on whether the result of Boolean expression is true or false. $Value1$ will be returned if the Boolean expression is true. $Value2$ will be returned if the Boolean expression is false. The evaluated value is returned by the operator and can be assigned to a variable if needed. As shown in Example 33, the output of the below code will be that the variable max will be assigned to the value 20.

Example 33

```
int max, a =10, b=20;
max = a>b? a:b;
System.out.println(max);
```

1.3.1.4   The Switch Statement

The switch statement provides another means to decide which statement to execute next. The statement evaluates an expression, then attempts to match the result to one of several possible cases. Each case contains a value and a list of statements. The flow of control transfers to the statement list associated with the first value that matches. The switch logic is shown in Figure 1.10. The general syntax of a switch statement is shown in Figure 1.11.

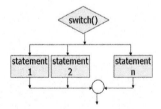
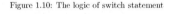
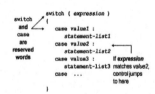

Figure 1.10: The logic of switch statement   Figure 1.11: The general syntax of a switch statement

Often a break statement is used as the last statement in each case's statement list. A break statement causes control to transfer to the end of the switch statement. If a break statement is not used, the flow of control will continue into the next case. Each 'case' in the switch statement must contain an integer or a character. Example 34 shows a program that reads a grade from the user and prints comments accordingly.

Example 34

```
public class GradeReport {
    public static void main (String[] args) {
        int grade, category;
        System.out.println ();
        System.out.print ("Enter a numeric grade (0 to 100): ");
        grade = Keyboard.readInt();
        category = grade / 10;
        System.out.print ("That grade is ");

        switch (category)
        {
            case 10:
                System.out.println ("a perfect score. Well done.");
                break;
            case 9:
                System.out.println ("well above average. Excellent.");
                break;
            case 8:
                System.out.println ("above average. Nice job.");
                break;
            case 7:
                System.out.println ("average.");
                break;
            case 6:
                System.out.println ("below average. You should see the");
                System.out.println (lecturer to clarify the material "
                                    + "presented in class.");
                break;
            default:
                System.out.println ("not passing.");
        }
    }
}
```

Usually the case statement in switch is intended to implement a logic set of alternatives that are mutually exclusive, just like the way the **if** ... **else if** combination is used. This requires the use of the break statement to avoid the fall through from one case to the next. In contrary, the break statement prematurely terminates the execution of the block, therefore all subsequent statements are skipped. This means that a switch statement can be more closely resemble the related if statement. Example 35 provides two solutions to decide what is current season from the user input month.

Example 35

First solution:

```
if (month==11 || month==12 || month==1)     season = "Winter";
else if (month==2 || month==3 || month==4)  season = "Spring";
else if (month==5 || month==6 || month==7)  season = "Summer";
else if (month==8 || month==9 || month==10) season = "Autumn";
else season = "Bogus Month";
```

Second Solution :

```
n = ((y+10)%12)/3+1
```

Table 1.8: Rationale for the second solution

month	season
2-4	1(spring)
5-7	2(summer)
8-10	3(fall)
11-1	4(winter)

```
switch (n)
{
   case 1:
      System.out.println ("Spring!");
      break;
   case 2:
      System.out.println ("Summer!");
      break;
   case 3:
      System.out.println ("Fall!");
      break;
   default:
      System.out.println ("Winter!");
      break;
}
```

The rationale for the second solution is shown in Table 1.8.

n is computed with the following formula: $n = ((y + 10)\%12)/3 + 1$.

In summary, the value that is used in the *switch* can be an expression, such as $grade/10$ or $((y + 10)\%12)/3 + 1$. Values associated with the cases must be distinct, sometimes they can be constant expressions. After each colon there can be a list of statements. No {} are needed. This list can be empty. Statements are executed from the first statement after the label whose value equals that of the expression, and continues until either a break is encountered, or the terminating } is encountered.

1.3.2   Repetition Statements

Repetition statements execute a block of statements numerous times while some condition remains true. The condition that controls a loop is a Boolean statement. Types of repetition statements include *the while loop, the do loop* and *the for loop.*

1.3.2.1   The While Statement

The while statement has the following syntax:

```
while ( condition )
   statement;
```

while is a reserved word; If the condition is true, the statement is executed. Then the condition is evaluated again. The statement is executed repetitively until the condition becomes false. If the Boolean expression is false, the loop body is not executed even once.

The logic of a while loop is shown in Figure 1.12. The loop body is repeated while the controlling Boolean expression is true. If the condition of a while statement is false initially, the statement is never executed. Therefore, the body of a while loop will execute zero or more times. Example 36 shows an application that prints integer values from 1 to a specific limit. The logic of the application is shown in Figure 1.13. Example 37 shows an application that prints the first 10

powers of 2. The logic of the application is shown in Figure 1.14. Example 38 shows an application
that computes the average of a set of values entered by the user. The running sum is printed as
the numbers are entered. The logic of the application is shown in Figure 1.15.

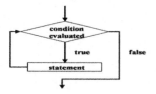

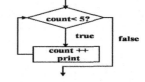

Figure 1.12: The logic of while loop   Figure 1.13: The logic of counter code

Example 36

```
public class Counter
{
    public static void main (String[] args)
    {
        final int LIMIT = 5;
        int count = 1;
        System.out.println();

        while (count <= LIMIT)
        {
            System.out.print ("\t" + count);
            count = count + 1;
        }

        System.out.print ("\tDone");
    }
}
```

The output of the program is :

```
1        2        3        4        5        Done
```

Example 37

```
public class PowerOfTwo
{
    public static void main (String[] args)
    {
        final int  LIMIT = 10;
        int count = 1, power = 1;
        while (count <= LIMIT)
        {
            power = power *2;
            System.out.print (power + "\t");
            count = count + 1;
        }
        System.out.println("All done. ");
    }
}
```

The output of the program is :

2	4	8	16	32	64	128	256	1024

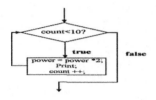

Figure 1.14: The logic of PowerOfTwo Code

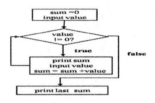

Figure 1.15: The logic of the average class

Example 38

```
public class Average {
   public static void main (String[] args) {
      int sum = 0, value, count = 0;
      double average;
      System.out.println();

      System.out.print ("\tEnter an integer (0 to quit): ");
      value = Keyboard.readInt();

      while (value != 0)
      {
         count=count+1;

         sum += value;
         System.out.println ("\tThe sum so far is " + sum);

         System.out.print ("\tEnter an integer (0 to quit): ");
         value = Keyboard.readInt();
      }

      System.out.println ();
      System.out.println ("\tNumber of values entered: " + count);

      average = (double)sum / count;
      System.out.println ("\tThe average is " + average);
   }
}
```

One possible outputs of the program is shown below :

```
Enter an integer (0 to quit):6

The sum so far is 6

Enter an integer (0 to quit):7

The sum so far is 13
```

```
Enter an integer (0 to quit):8

The sum so far is 21

Enter an integer (0 to quit):9

The sum so far is 30

Enter an integer (0 to quit):6

The sum so far is 6

Enter an integer (0 to quit):0

The sum so far is 0

Number of values entered:4

The average is 7.5
```

The body of a while loop must eventually make the condition false. If not, it is an infinite loop, which will execute until the user interrupts the program. This is a common type of logical error. You should always double check to ensure that your loops will terminate normally. Example 39 shows an infinite loop.

Example 39

```
public class Forever {
    public static void main (String[] args)
    {
        int count = 1;

        while (count <= 25)
        {
            System.out.println (count);
            count = count - 1;
        }

        System.out.println ("Done"); // the statement will never be reached!
    }
}
```

1.3.2.2 Nested Loops

Similar to nested if statements, loops can be nested as well. That is, the body of a loop could contain another loop. Each time through the outer loop, the inner loop will go through its entire set of iterations. Example 40 shows a Java program that prints multiplication tables shown in Table 1.9. In the example, the loop body is repeated while the controlling boolean expression is true. The logic of the program is shown in Figure 1.16. A palindrome is a word or phrase that can be read in the same way in either direction. Example 41 shows an application checking strings to see if they are palindromes.

Example 40

```
public class Multiply
{
   public static void main (String[] args)
   {
       final int SIZE = 10;
       int x = 0;
       while  (x < SIZE)
       {   x++;
          int y=0;
          while (y < SIZE)
          { y++;
             int z = x*y;
             if (z<10) System.out.print(" ");
             if (z>100) System.out.print(" ");
             System.out.print(" ")+z;
           }
         System.out.print();
       }
   }
}
```

Table 1.9: Multiplication tables

1	2	3	4	5	6	7	8	9	10
2	4	6	8	10	12	14	16	18	20
3	6	9	12	15	18	21	24	27	30
4	8	12	16	20	24	28	32	36	40
5	10	15	20	25	30	35	40	45	50
6	12	18	24	30	36	42	48	54	60
7	14	21	28	35	42	49	56	63	70
8	16	24	32	40	48	56	64	72	80
9	18	27	36	45	54	63	72	81	90
10	20	30	40	50	60	70	80	90	100

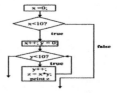

Figure 1.16: Logic of the multiply program

Example 41

```
public class PalindromeTester
{
   public static void main (String[] args)
   {
     String str, another = "y";
```

```
    int left, right;

    while (another.equalsIgnoreCase("y")) // allows y or Y
    {
        System.out.println ("Enter a potential palindrome:");
        str = Keyboard.readString();
        // Keyboard.readString() reads a string from the Keyboard

        left = 0;
        right = str.length() - 1;
        // str.length() gives the length of the string

        while (str.charAt(left) == str.charAt(right) and left < right)
        {
            left++;
            right--;
        }

        System.out.println();

        if (left<right)
            System.out.println ("That string is NOT a palindrome.");
        else
            System.out.println ("That string IS a palindrome.");

        System.out.println();
        System.out.print ("Test another palindrome (y/n)?");
        another = Keyboard.readString();
    }
  }
}
```

Sample output :
    Enter a potential palindrome:
    java
    That string is NOT a palindrome.
    Test another palindrome (y/n)? y
    Enter a potential palindrome:
    radar
    That string IS a palindrome.
    Test another palindrome (y/n)? n

1.3.2.3   The Do-While Statement

The do-while statement has the following syntax:

```
do
{
    statement;
}
while ( condition )
```

do and while are reserved words. The statement is executed once initially, then the condition is
evaluated. The statement is repetitively executed until the condition becomes false. A do-while
loop is similar to a while loop, except that the condition is evaluated after the body of the loop
is executed. The logic of the do-while statement is shown in Figure 1.17. With a do-while loop,

the loop body is always executed **at** least once even if the boolean expression starts out false.
However, with a **w**hile loop, shown in Figure 1.12, the loop body might be executed zero times.

Figure 1.17: Logic of do-while

Example 42 prints integer values from 1 to a specific limit. Example 43 prints the first 10
powers of 2 using do-while. Example 44 shows a program that finds out the possible number of
chicken and rabbits, given a total number of the legs of chicken and rabbit. Example 45 reverses
the digits of an integer mathematically. All these examples use do-while loops.

Example 42

```
public class Counter {
    public static void main (String[] args){
        final int LIMIT = 5;
        int count = 0;

        do
        {
            count = count + 1;
            System.out.println (count);
        }
        while (count < LIMIT);

        System.out.println ("Done");
    }
}
```

Example 43

```
public class PowerOfTwo2 {
    public static void main (String[] args){
        final int LIMIT = 10;
        int count = 1, power =1;

        do
        {
            power = power*2;
            System.out.print (power + "\t");
            count = count + 1;
        }
        while (count <= LIMIT);

        System.out.println ("Done");
    }
}
```

Example 44

```
public class ChickenRabbitLegs {
public static void main (String[] args){
int c, r=0, legs;
System.out.print("Enter #Chicken and Rabbit legs:");
legs = Keyboard.readInt();

System.out.print(" Chicken  Rabbit");

do{
    c = (legs-4*r)/2;
    System.out.print("      "+c);
    System.out.print("         "+r);
    r++;
}
while( 4*r <= legs);
}
}
```

Example 45

```
public class ReverseDigit {
public static void main (String[] args){
int number, lastDigit, reverse = 0;
System.out.print ("Enter a positive integer: ");
number  = Keyboard.readInt();
do
{
    lastDigit = number % 10; // determine the digit in the 1s position

    reverse = (reverse * 10) + lastDigit;
    // add the digit in 1s position into the reversed number

    number = number / 10;
    // truncates that digit from original number using integer division
}
while (number > 0);
System.out.println ("That number reversed is " +  reverse);
}
}
```

The output of the program is :

```
Enter a positive integer:  102
That number reversed is 201
```

1.3.2.4 The For Statement

The syntax of the for statement is shown in Figure 1.18. Example 46 shows a very simple program using the for statement. Example 47 shows a generating function , e.g., $f(x) = x^2 + x + 41$. The logic of this program is shown in Figure 1.19. In this example, the x is declared in the loop header, it exists only inside the loop body and can not be referenced elsewhere.

Example 46

```
final int LIMIT = 5;
for(int count=1; count <= LIMIT; count++)
    System.out.println(count);
System.out.println("Done");
```

Example 47

```
public class Example {
  public static void main(String[] args)
  {
    for (int x =0; x<10;x++)
    //declare a variable in the loop header (when it is not needed outside);
    {
        int y =x*x + x +41;
        System.out.println("\t" + x + "\t" + y);
    }
  }
}
```

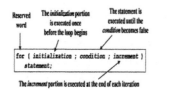

Figure 1.18: The syntax of for statement   Figure 1.19: The logic of the generate function

A for loop is equivalent to the following while loop structure:

```
initialization;
while ( condition )
{
    statement;
    increment;
}
```

In the for statement, the increment code executes after the loop body even though it is in the header.

Example 48 is a program that computes the average of a set of values entered by the user. The running sum is printed as the numbers are entered.

Example 48

```
double x;   double sum =0;
for (int i=0; i<5; i++) {
  System.out.print("Enter your number to be added:");
  x = Keyboard.readDouble();
  sum = sum + x;
  System.out.println("\tx= " + x + "\t\tsum = "+ sum);
}
```

For the previous multiple table example shown in Table 1.9, the program can be rewritten with the for statement as shown below.

Example 49

```
public class Multiply
{
    public static void main (String[] args)
    {
        final int SIZE = 10;
        int x = 0;
        while (x<SIZE)
        {   x++;
            int y=0;
            while (y<SIZE)
            {   y++;
                int z = x*y;
                if (z<10) System.out.print(" ");
                if (z>=100) System.out.print("  ");
                System.out.print(" " +z);
            }
            System.out.println();
        }
    }
}
```

Like a while loop, the condition of a for statement is tested prior to execute the loop body. Therefore, the body of a for loop will execute zero or more times. It is well suited for executing a specific number of times that can be determined in advance. Note that there is no semicolon after the closing parenthesis at the beginning of the loop. Example 50 shows a program that prints multiples of a user-specified number up to a user-specified limit.

Example 50

```
public class Multiples {
    public static void main (String[] args) {
        final int PER_LINE = 5;
        int value, limit, mult, count = 0;

        System.out.print ("Enter a positive value: ");
        value = Keyboard.readInt();

        System.out.print ("Enter an upper limit: ");
        limit = Keyboard.readInt();

        System.out.println ("The multiples of " + value + " between " +
                            value + " and " + limit + " (inclusive) are:");

        for (mult = value; mult <= limit; mult += value)
        {
            System.out.print (mult + "\t");

            count++;
            if (count % PER_LINE == 0)
                System.out.println(); // print a specific number of values per line of output
        }
    }
}
```

Figure 1.20: Asterisk triangle

The result of the program is as follows:

```
Enter a positive value:    10
Enter an upper limit:    100

The multiples of 10 between 10 and 100 (inclusive) are:
10   20   30   40   50
60   70   80   90   100
```

If you want to use a for loop that prints out just the even numbers between 2 and 20, i.e., 2, 4, 6, 8, 10, 12, 14, 16, 18, 20. There are several ways to do this. Example 51 presents three different solutions, showing how even a very simple problem can be solved in many ways.

Example 51

Solution 1: There are 10 numbers to print. Use a for loop to count 1, 2, ..., 10. The numbers we want to print are 2*1, 2*2, ..., 2*10.

```java
for (N = 1; N <= 10; N++) {
    System.out.println( 2*N );
}
```

Solution 2: Use a for loop that counts 2, 4, ..., 20 directly by adding 2 to N each time through the loop.

```java
for (N = 2; N <= 20; N = N + 2) {
    System.out.println( N );
}
```

Solution 3: Count off all the numbers 2,3,4, ..., 19, 20 , but only print out the numbers that are even.

```java
for (N = 2; N <= 20; N++) {
    if (N%2==0) // is N an even number
        System.out.println( N );
}
```

Like if and while, for statement can be nested. Example 52 shows a program that prints a triangle shape using asterisk (star) as shown in Figure 1.20.

Example 52

```
final int MAX_ROWS = 10;
for (int row = 1; row <= MAX_ROWS; row++) {
      for (int star = 1; star <= row; star++) {
                      System.out.print ("*");
      }
      System.out.println();
}
```

Note: only when the inner loop complete then does the outer loop execution start.

For the reversed triangle, the program is shown in Example 53.

Example 53

```
final int ROW=10;
final int COL =10;
int i,j;

for (i=0; i<ROW; i++)
{
    for (j=i; j<COL; j++)
        System.out.print("*");

    System.out.println();
}
```

A for loop can contain multiple initialization actions separated with commas. It is illegal to combine multiple type declarations with multiple actions. To avoid possible problems, it is suggested to declare all variables outside of the for statement. A for loop can contain multiple update actions, separated with commas. Also it is even possible to eliminate the loop body with multiple update actions. However, a for loop can contain only one boolean expression to test for ending the loop. To allow two or more variables to control a for loop, Java permits you to include multiple statements in both the initialization and iteration portions of the for statement. Each statement is separated from the next by a comma. Example 54 shows two solutions for the same problem which prints values of a and b when a is less than b. The second program is more efficiently coded.

Example 54

```
int a, b;
b = 4;
for(a=1; a<b; a++)
{ System.out.println("a = " + a);
  System.out.println("b = " + b);
  b--;
}

int a, b;
for(a=1, b=4; a<b; a++, b--)
{ System.out.println("a = " + a);
  System.out.println("b = " + b);
}
```

1.3.3 Operators

1.3.3.1 Logical Operators

Boolean expressions can be combined using the following logical operators shown in Table 1.10:

Table 1.10: Logical operators

!	Logical NOT
&&	Logical AND
||	Logical OR

Table 1.11: Logic expressions

a	!a
true	false
false	true

They all take boolean operands and produce boolean results. Logical NOT is a unary operator in the sense it has one operand. However logical AND and logical OR are binary operators since they each have two operands. The logical NOT operation is also called logical negation or logical complement. If the Boolean condition a is true, then !a is false; if a is false, then !a is true. Logical expressions can be shown using truth tables in the Table 1.11:

The logical AND expression $a\&\&b$ is true if both a and b are true, and false otherwise. The logical OR expression $a||b$ is true if a or b or both are true, and false otherwise. Example 55 is a program which decides what is the current season from the user input month using the logical operator OR.

Example 55

```
public class Season
{
  public static void main (String[] args)
  {
    String  season;
    int     month;

    System.out.print("Enter the current month: ");
    month = Keyboard.readInt();       // for example 4 for April

    if (month==12 || month ==1 || month ==2)      season = "Winter";
    else if (month==3 || month ==4 || month ==5)  season = "Spring";
    else if (month ==6 || month ==7 || month ==8) season = "Summer";
    else if (month ==9 || month ==10 || month ==11) season = "Autumn";
    else season = "Bogus Month";

    System.out.println(" Now is in " + season + ".");
  }
}
```

A truth table shows the possible true/false combinations of the terms. Since && and || each have two operands, there are four possible combinations of true and false shown in the Table 1.12.

Table 1.12: Truth table

a	b	a&&b	a||b
true	true	true	true
true	false	false	true
false	true	false	true
false	false	false	false

Table 1.13: Truth table of a specific expression

total < MAX	found	!found	total < MAX && !found
false	false	true	false
false	true	false	false
true	false	true	true
true	true	false	false

Table 1.14: Evaluation of increment and decrement operators

Expression	Operation	Value of Expression
count++	add 1	old value
++count	add 1	new value
count-	subtract 1	old value
-count	subtract 1	new value

Conditions in selection statements and loops can use logical operators to form complex expressions, e.g.,

```
if (total < MAX && !found) System.out.println ("Processing...");
```

Logical operators have precedence relationships between themselves and other operators. In ($exp1$ && $exp2$), exp1 is evaluated first. If it is false, the value of the entire expression is immediately determined to be false without evaluating exp2. In ($exp1||exp2$), exp1 is evaluated first. If it is true, the value of the entire expression is immediately determined to be true without evaluating exp2. Specific expressions, e.g. $total < MAX\&\&!found$, can be evaluated using truth tables shown in the Table 1.13.

De Morgan's Law can be used to obtain an expression that checks if it is out of range, e.g.,

$$!(p\&\&q) = !p||!q$$

$$!(p||q) = !p\&\&!q$$

1.3.3.2 Increment and Decrement Operators

The increment and decrement operators add or subtract one from a variable and are very useful in controlling loops. The increment operator $(++)$ adds one to its operand, and the decrement operator $(--)$ subtracts one from its operand.

The increment and decrement operators can be applied in prefix form, namely before the variable, or postfix form, namely, after the variable. When used alone in a statement, the prefix and postfix forms are basically equivalent. However, when such a form is written as a statement by itself, it is usually written in postfix form. When used in a larger expression, the prefix and postfix forms have different effect. In both cases the variable is incremented or decremented, but the value used in the larger expression depends on the form shown in the table 1.14.

The detailed explanation is as follows:

- $x++$ post-increment: add 1 to the value, and the value is returned before the increment is made, e.g.

```
x = 1;
y = x++;
```

Then y will hold 1 and x will hold 2.

- $x - -$ post-decrement: subtract 1 from the value, and the value is returned before the decrement is made, e.g.

```
x = 1;
y = x--;
```

Then y will hold 1 and x will hold 0.

- $+ + x$ pre-increment: add 1 to the value, and the value is returned after the increment is made, e.g.

```
x = 1;
y = ++x ;
```

Then y will hold 2 and x will hold 2.

- $- - x$ pre-decrement: subtract 1 from the value, and the value is returned after the decrement is made, e.g.

```
x = 1;
y = -- x ;
```

Then y will hold 0 and x will hold 0.

Example 56 shows the application of these operators.

Example 56

what do you expect for the output from?

```
int i = 3, j = 3;
System.out.println( "i++ produces " + i++);
System.out.println( "++j produces " + ++j);
```

The output of the program is :

```
3
4
```

NOTE: it is not clear whether the increment will take effect before or after the value is printed, because expressions like these tend to be confusing. Therefore it is suggested to restrain yourself from using them.

1.3.3.3   Assignment Operators

Often we perform an operation on a variable, then store the result back into that variable. Java provides assignment operators to simplify that process. For example,

$num+ = count$; is equivalent to

$num = num + count$;

There are many assignment operators as shown in the Table 1.15.

The right side of an assignment operator can be a complete expression. The entire right side expression is evaluated first, then the result is combined with the original variable. Below, the left side program is equivalent to the right side program.

Table 1.15: Assignment operators

Operator	Example	Equivalent To
$=$	x $+=$ y	x = x + y
$-=$	x $-=$ y	x = x - y
$*=$	x $*=$ y	x = x * y
$/=$	x $/=$ y	x = x / y
$\%=$	x $\%=$ y	x = x % y

```
total  + = (sum-12) / count;
```
```
total = total + ( (sum-12) /count );
```
```
result /= (total-MIN) % num;
```
```
result = result / ((total-MIN) % num);
```

1.3.3.4   Boolean Expression

Boolean expressions are often used to control branch and loop statements, they can exist independently as well. A boolean variable can be given the value of a boolean expression by using an assignment statement. A boolean expression can be evaluated in the same way that an arithmetic expression is evaluated. The only difference is that arithmetic expressions produce a number as a result, while boolean expressions produce either true or false as their result.

Boolean and arithmetic expressions need not be fully parenthesized. If some or all of the parentheses are omitted, Java will follow **precedence and associativity rules** (summarized in the Figure 1.21) to determine the order of operations. If one operator has higher precedence, it is grouped with its operands earlier than the operator of lower precedence during compiling phase. If two operators have the same precedence, associativity rules determine which is grouped first.

Short-Circuit and Complete Evaluation Java can take a shortcut when the evaluation of the first part of a boolean expression produces a result that evaluation of the second part cannot change. This is called short-circuit evaluation. For example, when evaluating two boolean subexpressions joined by &&, if the first subexpression evaluates to false, then the entire expression will evaluate to false, no matter the value of the second subexpression is true or false. Likewise, when evaluating two boolean subexpressions joined by ||, if the first subexpression evaluates to true, then the entire expression will evaluate to true. Sometimes using short-circuit evaluation can prevent a runtime error. For example, for the piece of code:

```
if (x>=0 && Math.sqrt(x)<15.0)
```

it won't get to sqrt(x) if $x < 0$. Similarly, for the piece of code :

```
if ((kids !=0) && ((toys/kids) >=2))
```

if the number of kids is equal to zero, then the second subexpression will not be evaluated, thus preventing a divide by zero error.

1.3.4   Branching Statements

The Java programming language supports three branching statements: 1) the break statement, 2) the continue statement and 3) the return statement.

1.3.4.1   The Break Statement

The break and continue statements should be combined together. They can be used with or without a label. If they are used without labels, they refer to the most closely enclosing statement such as for, while, do, or switch statements. If they are used with labels, the break statement is

	PRECEDENCE	ASSOCIATIVITY
Highest Precedence (Grouped First)	From highest at top to lowest at bottom. Operators in the same group have equal precedence.	
	Dot operator, array indexing, and method invocation ., [ ], ( )	Left to right
	++ (postfix, as in x++), -- (postfix)	Right to left
	The unary operators: +, -, ++ (prefix, as in ++x), -- (prefix), and !	Right to left
	Type casts (*Type*)	Right to left
	The binary operators *, /, %	Left to right
	The binary operators +, -	Left to right
	The binary operators <, >, <=, >=	Left to right
	The binary operators ==, !=	Left to right
	The binary operator &	Left to right
	The binary operator |	Left to right
	The binary operator &&	Left to right
	The binary operator ||	Left to right
	The ternary operator (conditional operator) ? :	Right to left
Lowest Precedence (Grouped Last)	The assignment operators: =, *=, /=, %=, +=, -=, &=, |=	Right to left

Figure 1.21: precedence and associativity rules

legal in a labeled "for" statement or a labeled { } block. A label is an identifier placed before a statement. The label is followed by a colon (:), for example,

statementName: someJavaStatement;

Break can be used to exit immediately from any loop, namely, while, do-while and for statements. Example 57 reads numbers from input until negative number is encountered, where loop only terminates when break is executed, which only happens when $n < 0$.

Example 57

```
int n;
while (true) {
    n = Keyboard.readInt ();
    if (n < 0) break;
    else System.out.println (" n is " + n);
}
```

A break statement, if executed, jumps out of the innermost enclosing loop of the statement, as Example 58 shows.

Example 58

```
for ( int i = 0 ; i < num ; i++ ) {
  if ( num >= 2 * val )
     break ;
  val = val / 2 ;
```

```
} // break comes here if it runs
```

In general, you can only break out of a single loop (i.e., the innermost enclosing loop of the break statement), as Example 59 shows.

Example 59

```
for ( int i = 0 ; i < num ; i++ ) {
    for ( int j = 0 ; j < num ; j++ ) {
        if ( i + j >= 2 * val )
            break ;
        val = val / 2 ;
    } // break comes here if it runs
}
```

Example 60 shows the loops, generating and printing a random number for each iteration. If the number is less than 0.1, it breaks out before printing it.

Example 60

```
public class BreakTest1 {
    public static void main(String[] args) {
        for ( ; ; ) { //creates an infinite loop
            double x = Math.random();
            if (x < 0.1)
                break;
            System.out.print((int) (x * 10) + " ");
        }
        System.out.println("Done!");
    }
}
```

A sample output of the program is as follows:
    5, 6, 7, Done!

1.3.4.2 Labeled Break Statement

In normal usage, break and continue only affect the current loop. However there is a type of break statement that, when it is used in nested loops, can end all containing loop besides the innermost loop. The break statement can be applied as follows:

1. To label a loop, simply precede it with an Identifier and a colon: someIdentifier:.

2. Label an enclosing loop statement with the Identifier, *breaksomeIdentifier*;. With this labeled break statement, the program will exit the labeled loop, even if it is not the innermost enclosing loop.

Labeled break jumps out of several levels of nested loops inside a pair of curly braces. The label must be placed before a enclosing loop of the break statement as shown in the Example 61.

Example 61

```
OUTER_LOOP: // OUTER_LOOP is a label
for ( int i = 0 ; i < num ; i++ ) {
    for ( int j = 0 ; j < num ; j++ ) {
        if ( i + j >= 2 * val )
            break OUTER_LOOP ;
```

```
        val = val / 2 ;
    }
} // break comes here if it runs
```

The label must be placed before a enclosing loop of the break statement. Example 62 shows illegal use.

Example 62

```
LOOP:
for ( int i = 0 ; i < num ; i++ )
{
    sum += i ;
}

for ( int j = 0 ; j < num ; j++ )
{
    if ( i + j >= 2 * val )
        break LOOP ; // ILLEGAL. LOOP not an enclosing loop
    val = val / 2 ;
}
```

Undisciplined use of break can make loops impossible to understand. Termination of loops without break can be understood purely by looking while or for parts. When break is included, arbitrary termination behavior can be introduced. Therefore it is suggested: (1) use break only when loop condition is always true (i.e. break is the only way to terminate loop); (2) when you use it, make sure it has a good comment explaining what is happening.

1.3.4.3   The Continue Statement

If you need to stop the current iteration of the loop, but continue the looping process, you can use the continue statement. Intuitively, continue says "go to the next iteration of the loop". A continue statement must appear in a loop body, or it would not be compiled. Continue statement is used based on a condition that some execution skips to the end of this pass but continues looping.

If the innermost enclosing loop is a for loop, continue jumps to the update of that loop. Example 63 shows a simple application of the continue statement. The continue statement causes control flow to go to the next iteration of the loop, skipping over the remainder of the loop body. Example 64 shows using the continue statement to restart a loop, and check the condition. Example 65 shows if the innermost enclosing loop of a continue statement is a while or do-while loop, running a continue statement causes control flow to jump to the condition of the innermost enclosing loop.

Example 63

```
for ( int i = 0 ; i < num ; i++ )
{
    if ( i > num / 2 )
        continue ;  // jumps to update, i++
    System.out.println( "Here I am!" ) ;
}
```

Example 64

```
int num=0,sum=0;
for (int k = 0; k < 100; k=k+1)
{
    int r = (int)(Math.random() * 100);
    if (r % 3 == 0) // r is a multiple of 3
    {
        num = num + 1;
        continue; // jumps to update, k=k+1
    }
    sum = sum + r;
}
System.out.println( "num = " + num + "; sum ="+sum ) ;
```

Example 65

```
int num = 4,  int i = 0;
while ( i != 3 ) // continue jumps here
{   i++;
    if ( i > num/2 )
        continue; // jumps to condition, i!=3
    System.out.println( "Here I am!" ) ;
}
```

When you use the continue statement, make sure that it has a good comment explaining what is happening. It is suggested to reverse the logic of the condition, and place the remainder of the loop under control of the if statement. Below are some examples with detailed notes explaining how the programs are running. Example 66 and Example 67 show two solutions that can be used to solve the same problem. However Example 66 is easier to use in nested loops, because you can label the level that will be continued.

Example 66

```
public class Continuer{
  public static void main(String[] args) {
    int count = 0;
    do {
                System.out.print("Enter an integer: ");
        int num = Keyboard.readInt();
        if (num < 0)  continue;
        count++;
        System.out.println("Number " +count+ " is " +num);
    } while (count < 10);
    System.out.println("Thank you");
  }
}
```

Example 67

```
public class Continuer2 {
  public static void main(String[] args)
  {
      int count = 0;
      do {
          System.out.print("Enter an integer: ");
```

```
        int num = Keyboard.readInt();
        if (num >= 0) {
            count++;
            System.out.println("Number "+count+ " is "+num);
    }
    } while (count < 10);
    System.out.println("Thank you");
 }
}
```

1.3.4.4   The Exit Statement

A break statement will end a loop or switch statement, but will not end the program. The exit statement will immediately end the program as soon as it is invoked:

System.exit(0);

The exit statement takes one integer argument. By tradition, a zero argument is used to indicate a normal ending of the program.

There are two most common kinds of loop errors : *unintended infinite loops* and *off-by-one errors*. An off-by-one error is that a loop repeats the loop body one too many or one too few times. This usually results from a carelessly designed boolean test expression. Sometimes use of == in the controlling boolean expression can lead to an infinite loop or an off-by-one error.

Tracing variables involves watching one or more variables changing values while a program is running. This can make discovering errors in a program and debugging them easier to discover errors in a program and debug them. Many IDEs (Integrated Development Environments) have a built-in utility that allows variables to be traced without making any changes to the program. Another way to trace variables is to simply insert temporary output statements in a program as follows:

```
System.out.println("n = " + n); // tracing n
```

When the error is found and corrected, the trace statements can simply be commented out.

1.4   Programming with Methods

1.4.1   Static Methods

In the previous sections, several simplest methods within some classes, which do not require any arguments or return any value, were used, for example: $System.out.println("Using Javamethod");$. When a method executes, it may or may not return a value. Methods are similar to procedures, functions or subroutines in other languages.

There are two types of methods : **Instance methods**, which are associated with an object and use the instance variables of that object; **Static methods**, which use no instance variables of any object of the class where they are defined. Static methods typically take all the data from parameters and compute something from those parameters, with no reference to instance variables. Many utility methods in the predefined Math class are such examples.

A method must include:

1. a declaration (or header/definition);
2. an opening curly bracket;
3. a body;
4. a closing curly bracket, as Figure 1.22 shows.

Access modifiers include : public, private, friendly, protected and static. The method declaration contains:

1. optional access modifiers;

2. the return type for the method;
3. the method name;
4. an opening parenthesis;
5. an optional list of method arguments;
6. a closing parenthesis. Method declaration is shown in Figure 1.23.

Figure 1.22: Method body   Figure 1.23: Method declaration

Static method is placed within the program that will use it. In Example 68, the main() method calls the nameAndAddress() method, simply using the name of nameAndAddress() method as a statement. Any method that can be used from anywhere within the class requires the keyword modifier "static".

Example 68

```
public class First  {
    public static void main (String[]  args) {
        nameAndAddress();
        System.out.println("First Java exercise on using method");
    }

    public static void nameAndAddress() {
        System.out.println("Renai Road 111");
        System.out.println("Dushu Lake Higher Education Town");
        System.out.println("Suzhou Industrial Park");
    }
}
```

As Figure 1.24 which shows a method is easily re-useable. Figure 1.25 illustrates methods can be called multiple times. Figure 1.26 illustrates more than one method can be called.

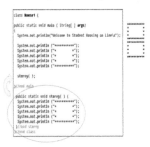

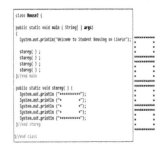

Figure 1.24: A method is easily re-useable   Figure 1.25: Methods can be called multiple times

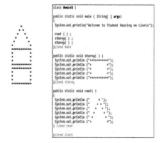

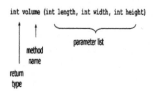

Figure 1.26: More than one method can be   Figure 1.27: More on method declaration
called

As Figure 1.27 illustrates, a method declaration begins with a method header. The parameter list specifies the type and name of each parameter. The name of a parameter in the method declaration is called a formal argument.

The method header is followed by the method body, as shown in Figure 1.28. If a method returns a value, then there must be at least one return statement. A void method does not require a return statement, and will automatically return at the end of the method. When a return statement is executed, control immediately returns to the statement in the calling method, and processing continues. The return type specified in the method header can be a primitive type, or a class name, or the reserved word "void". When a method does not return any value, "void" is used as the returning type. Example 69 shows an application of testing temperature conversion. When a method is called, the flow of control jumps to the method and executes its code. It then returns to the place where the method was called. Example 70 shows testCircle application, where when the method *circleArea* is called, each statement is executed one after another until a return statement is reached, then the specified value is immediately returned to the client. In this example, return type of a method indicates the type of value that the method sends back to the calling location. Method should be relatively small, so that it can be readily understood.

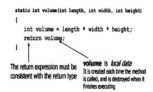

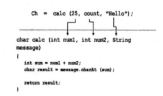

Figure 1.28: more on method body   Figure 1.29: method parameter

Example 69

```
public class testTempConversion {
  public static void main(String[] args) {
    double temp;
    System.out.println("Enter temperature in C:");
    double c = Keyboard.readDouble();
    temp = celsiusToFahrenheit(c);
    System.out.println("The temperature in Fahrenheit
```

```
                    is " + temp);
  }
}

public double celsiusToFahrenheit (double  c) {
    double  f ;
    f = 32 + c * 9 / 5 ;
    return  f ;
}
```

Example 70

```
      public class testCircle {
    public static void main(String[] args) {
          System.out.print("The radius of circle?");
    double radius = Keyboard.readDouble();
    double area = circleArea(radius);
    System.out.print ("\nThe area  is " + area );
    }
}
static double circleArea (double r) {
      return Math.PI*r*r;
}
```

Each time a method is called, the actual arguments (values) in the invocation are copied into the formal arguments (the local variables), as shown in Figure 1.29.

There are two cases of calling methods:

1. Called from within the same class. In this case, you just write the static method name. E.g, $area = circleArea(radius)$;

2. Called from outside the class. In this case, something must be given before the method name to specify the class where the method is defined. For static methods, the class name should be specified, e.g, the method is called from outside the testCircle class as follows: $doublearea = testCircle.circleArea(radius)$;

Example 71 is a program printing the cubes of integers from 1 to 5. Example 72 compares two integers and prints out the minimum. Example 73 implements factorial function. All these examples illustrate how to define and call methods.

Example 71

```
public class TestCube {
   public static void main(String[] args)
   {
    for (int i =0; i<6; i++)
       System.out.println(i+ "\t" + cube(i) );
   }

   static int cube(int n) {
    return n*n*n;
   }
 }
The output of the program is :

0 0
1 1
2 8
3 27
```

```
4 64
5 125
```

Example 72

```java
public class TestMin {
  public static void main(String[] args) {
    for (int i=0; i<3; i++)
    {
      System.out.println("Enter your 1st integer:");
      int m = Keyboard.readInt();
      System.out.println("Enter your 2nd integer:");
      int n = Keyboard.readInt();
      int y = min(m,n);
      System.out.println("min("+ m +", " +n +")="+y);
    }
  static int min( int x, int y)
    {
    if (x<y)  return x;
    else  return y;
    }
  }
}
```

The output of the program is :

```
Enter your 1st integer: 2

Enter your 2nd integer: 7

min(2,7)=2
```

Example 73

```java
public class TestFactorial {
  public static void main( String[] args )
  {
    for (int i=0;i<8;i++)
        System.out.println("f(" + i + ")= " + f(i) );
  }

static long f(int n){
    long f =1;
    while (n>1) f *= n--;
    return f;
    }
}
```

The output of the program is :

```
f(0) = 1
f(1) = 1
f(2) = 2
f(3) = 6
```

```
f(4) = 24
f(5) = 120
f(6) = 720
f(7) = 5040
```

1.4.1.1 Local Variables

A local variable is a variable that is declared in a method. They can be used only within that method, and they cease to exist when the method finishes its execution. Example 74 shows a local variable f.

Example 74

```
static int celsiusToFahrenheit (int   c)
  {
      int  f ;  // f is a local variable
      f = 32 + c * 9 / 5 ;
      return  f ;
  }
```

A same variable name can be used in two or more methods. As Example 75 shows, these variables are independent from each other. You can have local variables with the same name r in different methods. Sometimes it is convenient to have temporary working storage for data in a method. You can declare local variables for this purpose.

Example 75

```
public static double circleArea(double radius)
  {
    double r = Math.PI*radius*radius;
    return r;
  }
```

`.  .  .`

```
r = Keyborard.readDouble();
double area = circleArea(r) ;
```

The scope of a variable is the region of a program in which you can refer to the variable by its name. The scope of a local variable extends from the point of declaration to the end of the block that ends. Variables declared in a for loop are special case:

```
for (int i; i<=years; i++)
  { . . .
  } // scope of i ends here
```

1.4.2 Recursive Methods

A method that invokes itself is called "recursive method" and the resulting process is called recursion. Example 76 computes summation $1 + 2 + 3 + \ldots + n$. If sum(n) represents the value $1 + 2 + 3 + \ldots + n$, then $for(n >= 2), sum(n) = n + sum(n - 1)$. This suggests the recursive method sum(int x).

Example 76

```
public class TestSum {
  public static void main(String[] args) {
    int t;
    System.out.println("Enter n :");
    int z= Keyboard.readInt();
    t = sum(z);
    System.out.println("sum=" + t);
  }
  static int sum(int x)
    {// compute 1 + 2 + 3 + ... + n
        if ((x==1))  // this is called the "base case"
                return(1);
        else return(sum(x-1)+x);
    }
}
```

The reasons why recursion is used are as follows:

- It is easier to code a recursive solution once you are able to identify the solution. The recursive code is usually smaller, more concise, more elegant and possibly easier to understand.

- There are some problems which are very difficult to solve without recursion. Those problems that require backtracking such as searching a maze for a path to an exit are best solved recursively.

- There are also some interesting sorting algorithms that use recursion.

1.4.2.1   Characteristics of Recursion

To implement the recursion, you shall think recursively. That is, you consider the solution to the problem be a smaller version of the same problem. You shall solve recursive programming, imaging that your method does what its name says even before you have actually finished writing it. In another word, you pretend the method to do its job and then use it to solve the more complex cases.

First you shall design a base case which is the simplest possible problem (or case) your method could solve. Moreover the base case returns the correct value. Your recursive method will then be comprised of an if-else statement where the base case returns one value and the non-base case recursively calls the same method with a smaller parameter or set of data. Thus, your problem is decomposed into two parts:

(1) The simplest possible case which you can answer,

(2) All other more complex cases which you will solve by returning the result of a second calling of your method. This second calling of your method (recursion) will pass on the complex problem but reduced by one increment.

Let us consider writing a method to find the factorial of an integer. For example, 7! equals $7 * 6 * 5 * 4 * 3 * 2 * 1$. However, you are also correct if you say 7! equals 7*6!. Generally,

$n! = n * (n - 1)!$

$(n - 1)! = (n - 1) * (n - 2)!$

$(n - 2)! = (n - 2) * (n - 3)!$

The problem is now expressed in terms of a simpler version of it so that you know how to make it progressively more simple. That is, the base case is the simplest factorial, e.g 1!. Also 7! is defined in terms of 6!, which is the essence of recursive problem solving.

Example 77 shows recursive implementation of factorial function.

Example 77

```
public class TestFactorial {
  public static void main(String[] args)
  {
      for (int i=0; i<9; i+=)
      {
       System.out.println("f("+i+")="+f(i));
      }
          static int f(int n)
          {
              if (n<2) return 1;
              return n*f(n-1);
          }
 }
static int f(int n){
      if (n<2) return 1;
      return n*f(n-1);
      }
}
```

Note that the base case (the factorial of 1) is solved and the return value is given.

When you write recursive methods, make sure you write the base case in the method as the first statement, otherwise the program will go to infinite recursion.

Suppose that you need to compute 3 to the power 5, since 3 to the power 4 is 81, so the answer is 3 times 81. In general, if you wish to compute base to the power exponent, where base and exponent are positive integers, you have to multiply base by the result of raising base to the power, i.e. exponent -1. If exponent = 1, then the answer is simply base. Example 78 shows the program that computes base to the power exponent.

Example 78

```
static int power(int base, int exponent)
{
  // raise base to the power exponent
  if (exponent == 0) return 1;
  else return base*power(base, exponent - 1);
}
```

1.4.2.2   Boolean Methods

A Boolean method is simply a method that returns the boolean type. The method is usually invoked when boolean expression is used to control loops and conditions. Suppose you are required to write a method $isPrime()$ for the Example 79. The boolean method $isPrime()$ can judge whether the number is prime or not. Two solutions are shown in Example 80.

Example 79

```
public class TestPrimes {
  public static void main(String[] args)  {
    System.out.println("Enter the integer range n to be checked: ");
    int n = Keyboard.readInt();
    for (int i=0;i<n;i++)
    {         if (isPrime(i))
                  System.out.print(i+ " ");
    }
  }
}
```

Example 80

Solution 1:

```
static boolean  isPrime (int  n) {
        int check =0;
        if (n==1)  return true;
        for (int d=2;d<n; d++) {
          if (n%d==0)  return false;
                else  check = check + 1;
        }
        if (check == n-2)              return true;
        else return false;
}
```

Solution 2:

```
static boolean  isPrime (int  n) {
    boolean answer = true;
    for (int i=2;i<=n/2;i++ )
    {
            if ( n % i == 0)
            {
                answer = false;
                return answer;
            }
    }
    return answer;
}
```

A year is a leap year if it is divisible by 4 except for the century years (divisible by 100). Century years are only leap years if they are divisible by 400. Example 81 shows the method of judging the leap year.

Example 81

```
public class Askleapyear {
    public static void main(String[] args){
    System.out.println("Enter a year : ");
    int year = Keyboard.readInt();
    if isLeapYear(year)
        System.out.print(year+ "is leap year");
}
static boolean  isLeapYear (int  n){
    if (n%4==0 && n%100!=0)          return true;
    else if (n%100==0 && n%400==0) return true;
        else return false;
}
}
```

You can use the same name for different methods as long as they have different parameter type lists. This is called overloading. Example 82 shows the overloading of *max* method.

Example 82

```
public class TestMax {
  public static void main(String[] args) {
    System.out.println("Enter your first number: ");
    int a = Keyboard.readInt();
    System.out.println("Enter your second number: ");
    int b = Keyboard.readInt();
    System.out.println("Enter your third number: ");
    int c = Keyboard.readInt();
    System.out.println("max(" + a + "," +b + "," +c+")="+max(a,b,c));
    static int max(int n1, int n2, int n3){
                return max(max(n1, n2), n3);
  }
  static int max(int m, int n){
            if (m>n)
                return m;
            return n;
  }
 }
}
```

1.5 Class and Object

1.5.1 Introduction to Class and Object

1.5.1.1 Class

A class is a collection of objects with related properties and behaviors. In real-life things are grouped into classes to reduce complexity. For example, as Figure 1.30 shows the set of all dogs forms the class Dog. Each individual dog is an object of the class. Dog Spot, Rover and Rex, ... are all instances of the class Dog. To some extent, you can interact with Spot based on your knowledge of dogs in general, rather than Spot himself. Figure 1.31 shows how you could define classes. A waiter is someone who has the following : **properties** and **behaviors**. Properties of a waiter include full name. Behaviors of a waiter include "bring menus", "take orders", and "bring meals". This collection of properties and behaviors defines the class of waiters. Since these behaviors are standardized, you can deal with any waiter just based on your "general knowledge" of waiters.

Therefore, a class is formally defined as a general description of the properties and behaviors of some group of entities. The class waiter is described by giving the general description of what properties waiters have and what things waiters can do, as the Figure 1.32 shows.

An object is a specific member of a class. An object belonging to the class of waiters is an actual individual waiter. Peter is an object of the class waiter, and so is Mary and Jimmy. They can all bring menus, take orders and bring meals. The difference between class and objects is shown in Figure 1.33.

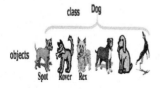

Figure 1.30: Dog example

Figure 1.31: Waiter example

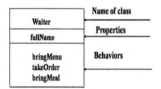

Figure 1.32: Waiter class

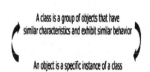

Figure 1.33: Class vs. object

The definitions are daunting, but the concept is easy. Rex, Rover and Spot are all objects in the class Dog. Wenjin, Daniel and Nan are all objects in the class Lecturer. Mel Gibbson, Bruce Wills and Julie Robert are all objects in the class Superstar.

The reasons why classes are used in real-life are as follows : 1. Classes help to deal with complexity. 2. You may expect certain behaviors from all Dogs, Lecturers and Superstars even before you meet any particular individual dog, lecturer or superstar. For example,

Dogs' properties, which are called states in Java, include name, size, color, breed, and hungry. Dogs' behaviors, which are called methods in Java, include barking, fetching, and wagging tail.

1.5.1.2   Software Object

Software objects are conceptually similar to real-world objects. They consist of state and related behavior too. An object stores its state in fields (or variables in some programming languages) and exposes its behavior through methods (or functions in some programming languages). Methods operate on an object's internal state and serve as the primary mechanism for object-to-object communication, as Figure 1.34 shows. Figure 1.35 illustrates the Bank class with properties and behaviors. Every BankAccount has a balance (property) and operations on the account such as depositing or withdrawing money (behaviors).

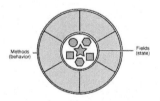

Figure 1.34: The syntax of for statement

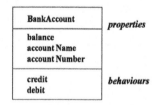

Figure 1.35: Bank class

Benefits of bundling code into software objects are as follows:

- **Modularity:** The source code for an object can be written and maintained independently of the source code for other objects. Once created, an object can be easily passed around inside the system.

- **Information-hiding:** By interacting only with an object's methods, the details of its internal implementation remain hidden from the outside world.

- **Code re-use:** If an object already exists (perhaps written by another software developer), the object can be reused in other program. This allows specialists to implement/test/debug complex, task-specific objects. These objects can run in your own code then.

- **Easy to plug and debug:** If a particular object turns out to be problematic, you can simply remove it from your application and plug in a different object as its replacement. This is analogous to fixing mechanical problems in the real world. If a bolt breaks, you replace it, not replace the entire machine.

Java is an object-oriented programming language, i.e, everything is object. Every object is a member of a more general class. A program you write to use other classes is a class itself. You can use the "is a test" to distinguish an object from a class. It is a convention to capitalize the first letter of each word in a class name when declaring the class. Figure 1.36 shows the relationship of car class and car objects.

A class definition is a precise description/definition of exactly what properties and behavior the objects of that class have. So a class definition is a "blueprint" for the objects of the class.

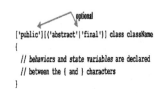

Figure 1.36: Car example

Figure 1.37: The syntax of class

1.5.2 Declaring Classes and Objects

1.5.2.1 Declaring Classes

A class is a source code blueprint (or template) for objects that specifies each object's behaviors and properties (state variables). General syntax is shown in Figure 1.37. Specifying public will make className accessible to all classes in all packages.

As Figure 1.38 shows, to create a class, first you need to assign a name to the class. Secondly you need to determine what data (properties) and methods (behaviors) will be part of the class. Public classes are accessible by all classes, i.e., public classes can be extended, or used as a basis for any other classes. A program usually consists of several classes. Each class has some fields and some methods. A class contains data declarations and method declarations, as Figure 1.39 shows. Example 83 shows typical class declaration.

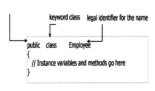

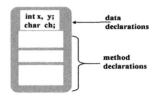

Figure 1.38: Create a class

Figure 1.39: General structure of class

Example 83

```
class ClassName
{
```

```
    field declarations;
    methodA (paras) {
       local variables
          declarations;
             body;
          }
          methodB (paras) {
       local variables
       declarations;
       body;
    }
}
public class GenericClass
{
    int x; // field with a declaration of an integer variable
    public int getX ()
    {
     return x;
    }
    public void setX (int i)
    {
     x=i;
    }
}
```

1.5.2.2   Declaring Objects

Declaring a class does not create any actual objects. A class is just an abstract description of what an object will be like if any objects are actually instantiated. An object is declared as follows

Classname objectname;

Every object name is also a reference, that is, a computer memory location. There is two-step process that creates an object : Firstly you supply a type and an identifier, just as when you declare any variable; Secondly computer memory is allocated for that object.

Each object is created (or instantiated) by a parent class which serves as a template (or blueprint or model or pattern) for the class, e.g., as Figure 1.40 shows,

House myHouse = new House();

Object myHouse is "instantiated" by the "new" operator. The first House declares a storage location for holding a value of a reference.

The process of creating and using an instance (or object) of a class definition is referred to as instantiation. The role of **new** operator:

1. Reads the code for the class being "instantiated".
2. Allocates memory space to the objects data.
3. Calls the constructor to assign default values to object attributes.

Note : Objects are created by a special method in a class called a constructor, which always has the same name as the class to which it belongs. As Figure 1.41 shows, you can create multiple objects from a same class.

Figure 1.42 gives an example of the class declaration. In conclusion, creating an object is known as instantiating a class. An object is an instance of a class. A class does not exist physically, whereas an object is a physical entity.

1.5.2.3   Variables Declaration and Instance Variables

Variable declaration gives the name and the type of the variable, e.g., *int balance*;. You can also provide an access modifier, which indicates whether other objects can access the variable. e.g.

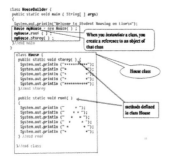

Figure 1.40: House builder

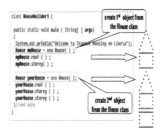

Figure 1.41: House builder1

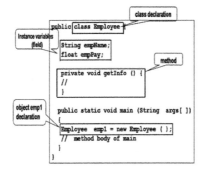

Figure 1.42: Summary of the class declaration

```
public  int balance;
private int balance;
```

When the data field declaration does not assign an explicit value to the data, default values will be used as shown below:

```
int, byte, short, char : default 0
float, double : default  0.0
boolean : default  false
```

A variable is the name of a place used to store some information. It is called variable because the information can be changed as the program runs. For example, a BankAccount needs a variable to store the balance of the bank account. You may think of this as a shoebox in which you store a number, as Figure 1.43 shows. The shoebox can only store one number, but that number can be changed. As Figure 1.44 shows, each instance of the class BankAccount has its own variable called balance, so these types of variables are called instance variables.

Figure 1.43: Shoebox for the balance of the   Figure 1.44: Instance of the class BankAccount
bank account

Each instance variable belongs to a specific instance. To avoid confusion, you can distinguish
them by using the name of the instance:

savings.balance means "the balance variable belonging to the object savings".

cheque.balance means "the balance variable belonging to the object cheque".

1.5.3   Instantiation

1.5.3.1   Static Fields/Data

Java offers static data and methods that are contained in a class definition and can be accessed
without creating an instance of the class. A static variable or method is also called a class variable
or method, because it belongs to the class itself rather than to an instance of that class. When the
Java Virtual Machine (JVM) loads the byte code for the class description of MyClass, it creates a
single memory location for the pi variable and loads it with the 3.14 value. The pi data exists so
you can access it even when no instance of MyClass is created. You can access the data directly
using the name of the class, $double\ x\ =\ 2.0 * MyClass.pi$;

Static data fields may include only one instance of data item for the entire class, but not one
per object. "Static" is a historic keyword from C/C++. "Class data field" is a better term, as
opposed to "instance data fields" (per object). Static methods do not operate on objects and do
not use any specific object. Static method has access only to static data fields of class, cannot
access instance fields in objects either. "Class method" is a better term, as opposed to "instance
method" (that operates on an object).

If a class property is also declared final it is referred to as a constant since it cannot be altered:

```
class MyClass  {
     public final static double PI = 3.14;
     }
```

Note that main method is static, which means you can not call the non-static variable in a
main method. If you try to call the non-static data in the main method then the compiler will
prompt you that:

"non-static variable cannot be referenced from a static context".

Example 84 shows a program *SomeClass*. Note that class methods can only refer to static
data and to the data passed in the argument list. The static methods cannot refer to the non-static
data members of the class because values for those only exist for instances of the class. Example 85
contains a mix of static and non-static data and methods.

Example 84

```
class SomeClass {
    static int i = 5; // a class field
    void print () {
         System.out.println (i); // access i from an instance method
    }
```

```
        public static void main (String [] args){
                System.out.println(i); // access i  from class method
        }
}
```

Example 85

```
public class Test {
        public final static double PI = 3.14; // static variable
        double b = 3; // non-static, "instance" variable
            public double func (double x) {
                return (4.0 * Math.sin (x)**2);
                }
            public static double tfunc (double x) {
                return (3.0 * x * PI);
                }
        public static double wfunc (double x) {
                return (3.0 * x * b);
                // error! cannot use non-static variable b in a class method.
                }
}
```

1.5.3.2   Class Instantiation

The process of creating and using an instance (or object) of a class definition is referred to as instantiation. The declaration of a car class is shown in Example 86. Example 87 instantiates a car object.

Example 86

```
class Car {
  String licensePlate;
  double speed;
  double maxSpeed;
}
```

or

```
class Car {
 String licensePlate=" ";
 double speed =0.0;
 double maxSpeed =80.0;
}
```

Example 87

```
Car c; //Declares the type of variable c
c = new Car( ); // =  is the assignment operator
                // new  is construction operator
                // car( ) is a   constructor
```

An object often needs to access data in other objects. This is done with a reference and "" or dot operator, as Example 88 shows.

Example 88

```
class CarTest {
   public static void main(String args[]) {
      Car c = new Car();
         c.licensePlate = "Su12345";
         c.speed = 80.0;
         c.maxSpeed = 160.5;
         System.out.println(c.licensePlate + " is moving at "
                            + c.speed + "kilometers per hour.");
   }
}
```

In Example 89, when you create the object emp, the memory gets allocated for the name id, age, and salary variables. These variables are specific to the object and are available only to the object. Refer to them as: objectName.variableName

Example 89

```
class Employee {
   String name;
   int id;
   int age;
   double salary;
// the above are instance variables, that is, those variables are created when you
// instantiate a class. They exist within the object only.

   public static void main(String args[]) {
      Employee emp = new Employee();
      emp.name = "fake"; //instance variable  name for object emp
      emp.id = 12345;
      emp.age = 35;
      emp.salary = 2933.78;
         System.out.println("The employee name:" + emp.name);
      System.out.println("The employee ID:" + emp.id);
      System.out.println("The employee age:" + emp.age);
      // statement to print content of an object
      System.out.println("The employee salary:" + emp.salary);
   }
}
```

The above examples illustrate when a number of objects are created from the same class, the same copy of instance variable is provided to all. Each instance variable belongs to a specific instance. You can distinguish them by using the name of the instance:

Zhang.salary means "the salary variable belonging to the object Zhang".

Li.salary means "the salary variable belonging to the object Li".

If you want to print out the contents of the object emp, you have to refer to each data member by using the dot operator with the same object name.

1.5.3.3   Instance Variables

For a class BankAccount, you need something to store the balance, account number and account name. Therefore you may define some variables for this information. Variable names should be chosen so they are meaningful to someone reading your program, for example,

```
    int accountNumber;
    String accountName;
```

Members of a class that are declared with private visibility can be referenced only within that class. For example, in the following class definition, the *balance* can only be accessible to the BankAccount class. String is a built-in Java type that stores a string of characters like "abcde". Therefore, the BankAccount is shown below:

```
public class BankAccount {
    private int balance;
    private int accountNumber;
    private String accountName;
}
```

Example 90 shows the complete BankAccount class.

Example 90

```
class BankAccount {
    private int balance;
    private String accountName;
    private int accountNum;

    public BankAccount(int num, String name){
        accountNum = num;
        accountName = name;
        balance = 0;
    }
    public void credit (int amount) {
        balance = balance + amount;
    }
    public void debit (int amount) {
            balance = balance - amount;
    }
    public int getBalance() {
        return balance;
    }
}
```

1.5.3.4 Instance methods

Instance method is a method of class that is not declared with the static keyword. An object reference is used to access an instance method. Instance methods operate on a particular instance of an object. Those methods describe the behavior of the object, namely, what it can do, as Example 91 shows.

Example 91

```
class SomeClass {
    int i = 5; // an instance field
    void print() { // access instance field from an instance method
        System.out.println (i);
    }
```

```
public static void main(String[] args) {
    // access instance field from a class method
    SomeClass sc = new SomeClass();
    sc.print();
    System.out.println (sc.i);
}
}
```

Below shows the syntax of Method signature:

```
access_modifier return_type method_name(list_of_arguments)
        {
        // statements, including local
        // variable declarations
        }
```

- Access modifier : determines what other classes and subclasses can invoke this method.

- Return type : what primitive or class type value will return from the invocation of the method. If there is no return value, use void for the return type.

- Method name : follows the same identifier rules as for data names. Customarily, a method name begins with a lower case letter.

- List of arguments : the values passed to the method.

Figure 1.45 shows structure for GenericClass.

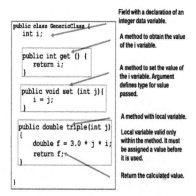

Figure 1.45: The structure of genericlass

Suppose you have created an object of the class BankAccount : *savings or cheque*. Then you must write code for the methods of the class, so that the objects can behave as their interface promises. Consider what the method getBalance does. If a client calls the getBalance method on a BankAccount object, he/she wants to know the balance.

```
public int getBalance() {
    return balance;
}
```

A method is called by specifying the target object, followed by a dot (i.e. full-stop or period), the method name, the method arguments (if there are any), e.g.

```
cheque.getBalance();
```

The target object is the one called cheque. The getBalance method has been called. There are no arguments for this method. The result will be returned to whoever calls the method.

Object oriented programming can be described as creating a community of interacting objects. Instance methods provide some services for an object so that the values of its attributes may be altered and/or displayed. We identify three types of communication: giving information, asking for information, and requesting action. Two objects interact when one object calls a method of another object. In this case, the object that calls the method is called the client; the object that executes the method is called the server. While the program is running, every object may act as a client, as a server or as both.

In the this example, the same method call is being made on two different objects:

```
cheque.getBalance();
savings.getBalance();
```

The difference is as follows: the first call is enquiring about the balance of the object cheque; the second call is enquiring about the balance of savings. The below code shows the method getBalance in action. Client object (target) makes the call with the method *savings.getBalance();*. Figure 1.46 shows the getBalance method.

```
public int getBalance() {
    return balance;
}
```

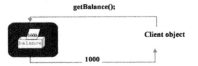

Figure 1.46: Get balance method

The method like getBalance is called a getter. It simply "gets" the value of one of the properties of the object, namely the value of the balance. Why cannot you just "look" at the value? This is due to the word *private* prevents other objects from accessing that field.

```
public class BankAccount {
    private int balance;
    private int accountNumber;
    private String accountName;
}
```

A getter is a method that simply reports on the state of an object, usually just returns the value of some variable. Objects from other classes are prevented from accessing the internal state of an object so that the implementation can be changed without affecting any code using that class, and the external object cannot change the internal state in a way that corrupts the object. It is considered a good practice to only permit access to an object through its methods.

Let us consider what other methods for BankAccount are. For example, what should the method credit do? It should add some money to the balance. The amount of money to be added is a parameter of the method. The method does not return anything so it is declared to be void. Therefore, the method credit is as follows:

```
public void credit(int amount)
{
        balance = balance + amount;
}
```

The amount to be added is stored in a local variable called amount, which is created when the method is called, and destroyed when it is finished. The assignment statement takes the values of balance and amount, adds them together and stores the result in balance. Figure 1.47 shows the method credit in action. Figure 1.48 shows the result after the method call.

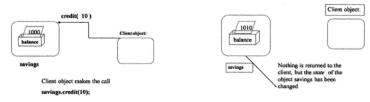

Figure 1.47: Credit in action   Figure 1.48: After credit method

Below summarize access instance field:

- To access an instance field from an instance method in the same class, you only specify the field's name.

- To access an instance field from another class's instance method, you must have an object reference variable that contains the address of an object created from the class that declares the instance field you want to access.

- To access an instance field from a class method in the same class, you create an object from the class, assign its reference to an object reference variable, and prefix that variable to the instance field's name.

- To access an instance field from another class's class method, you complete the same steps as when you access that field from a class method in the same class.

1.5.4   Setting Classes to Work

1.5.4.1   Using Classes

You may use two types of classes to do some real work:

- A class that can create objects with pre-defined attributes (or data types). It provides services (or methods) for the objects. It has no main method so it cannot do anything by itself.

- A "driver" class or a "test class" where the work is initiated. This class has a main method that controls the execution of all the steps in the program.

For example, you could define an account class which can create bank accounts, provide the methods for operating those accounts and display account details. You could then create a test class that would create several accounts, do some operations and display account details. In a simple account class you could define the following data:

accountNr a string that represents the account number;

customerName a string that represents the customer name.

You might also define the following methods:

an *Account* constructor, to set up the object;

a *deposit* method;

a *withdrawl* method;

a *getBalance* method, to return the current balance;

a *toString* method, to return a string description of the object for printing.

Example 92 shows the account class.

Example 92

```
public class Account {
   String name;
   double balance;
   static double interestrate = 0.04;

   public Account (String n, double b) {
   name = n;
   balance = b;
   }

   public String getname() {return name;}

   public double getbalance() {return balance;}

   public void withdraw (double amount) {
      if ((balance - amount) > 0)
      { balance -= amount;
      }
      else { } // later will return exception
             // "insufficient funds"
   }

public void deposit(double amount)    {
      balance += amount;
   }
   // returns monthly interest and
   // updates balance

public double monthactivity() {
      double interest = (balance * interestrate)/12;
      balance += interest;
      return interest;
   }
}
```

The main method is the place where the application is started. It sends messages to the "defining" class asking for the objects to be created and jobs to be done (methods). It may be located within the class you are testing or it may be located in a separate test class.

When you write your own classes, each class will specify the attributes of any objects it creates and the methods available to those objects. For example, you may be asked to write a program that simulates a "Sheep Counter". You could write a counter class to model a sheep counter. It could have a single attribute "count" to represent the number of sheep and methods add( ) and display() to do the counting and display results.

Example 93 shows an example of a car class. Example 94 defines a class whose objects represent point in the cartesian plane. Example 95 shows a coin class that is a model for a coin. The coin class can be used by other programs to instantiate coin objects as show in Example 96.

Example 93

```
class Car2 {
   String licensePlate =" ";
   double speed = 0.0;;
   double maxSpeed = 120.0;

  public floorIt() {
    this.speed = this.maxSpeed;
  }
}
class Car2Test {
   public static void main(String args[])    {
      Car c = new Car();
      c.licensePlate = Su12345";
      c.maxSpeed = 120.45;

      System.out.println(c.licensePlate + "  is moving at " + c.speed +
                " kilometers per hour.");

      c.floorIt();
      System.out.println(c.licensePlate + "  is moving at " + c.speed +
                " kilometers per hour.");
   }
}
```

Example 94

```
public class Point {
  private double x,y;
  // two fields, x and y, whose values are the coordinates of  a point

  public Point(double a, double b){
    x = a;
    y = b;
  }

  public double x() {
    return x;
  }

  public double y() {
    return y;
  }

  public boolean equals(Point p) {
    return (x==p.x && y==p.y);
```

```
    } // determine whether the two objects are equal

    public String toString() {
      return new String("(" + x + "," + y + ")");
    }
    // the method will be invoked whenever a reference to an object
    // of that class is passed    // to the  println() method,
    // as in System.out.println("p="+p)

    // In other words, this statement is equivalent
    // to System.out.println("p ="+p.toString());
}
public static void main(String[] args)
{
    Point p = new Point(2,3);
    // it declares p to be a reference to  Point  objects. it applies the new
    // operator to create a Point  object with values 2 and 3 for the fields
    // x and y. Then it initializes the reference p with this new object

    System.out.println("p.x() = " +p.x()+",p.y() = " + p.y());
    // invokes the methods  x() and  y()  to obtain the values of p's fields

    System.out.println("p = " +p);

    Point q = new Point(7,4);
    System.out.println("q = " +q);
    // repeat the previous steps for the object q representing the point (7,4)

    if (q.equals(p))
        System.out.println("q equals p");
    else
        System.out.println("q does not equal p");
    // invokes the equals()  method to determine whether the two
    // objects are equal. Obviously they are not equal

}
}
```

Example 95

```
public class Coin {
    private char side='H';

    public void flip() {
      int x = (int)(Math.random()* 2);

      if (x==0) side = 'H';
      else side = 'T';
    }

    public boolean isHeads()
    {
      if (side=='H') return true;
      else return false;
    }
}
```

Example 96

```
public class CoinApp {
   public static void main(String[] args) {
      final int NUM_FLIPS = 100;
      int heads = 0, tails = 0;

      Coin myCoin = new Coin();

      for (int count=1; count <= NUM_FLIPS; count++) {
            myCoin.flip();

         if (myCoin.isHeads())
                heads++;
         else
             tails++;
      }
      System.out.println ("There were " + heads+ " heads " );
      System.out.println ("and   " +tails+" tails");
      System.out.println ("in "+NUM_FLIPS+" tosses. " );
   }
}
```

The result is :
There were 43 heads and 57 tails in 100 tosses.

1.5.4.2   Class Constructors

Let us recall: the *new* operator creates an instance of a class, e.g.,

```
int i = 4;
Test test = new Test(i);
```

The statement declares a variable of the Test type and creates an instance of the class with the new operator. The argument of new must correspond to a special method in the class called a **constructor**. The constructor signature looks similar to that of a regular method. It has a name that matches the class name and holds a list of arguments in parenthesis. However, a constructor has no return type (not even void).

Constructors are useful for initializing values and invoking any methods needed for initialization. For example, in the following example, Test(int j) i = j; is a constructor, which is called when an instance of this class is first created.

```
class Test {
        int i;
        Test(int j) {
           i = j; }
        int get(){
           return i;}
        }
```

Below an initial value for the instance variable i is passed as an argument in the constructor to initialize the variable.

```
int i = 4;
Test test = new Test(i);
```

In Example 97, assume that you have a class Car. Each time you instantiate the class, you will have to explicitly initialize all the variables.

Example 97

```
class Car {
    String name;
    int model;
    float horsepower;
    // it is tedious to type this data when you have classes with many variables

    public Car(String nm, int mdl, float hp)
    {
        name = nm;
        model = mdl;
        horsepower = hp;
    }
    // constructor as a special method to initialize objects

    public static void main(String args[ ])
    {
        Car myCar = new  Car("Ford",2000, 150.5f);
    }
}
```

If you write a class with no constructors, the compiler will automatically supply a no-argument constructor for you. In the left side of Example 98, the default constructor is equivalent to the explicit Test() at the right side.

Example 98

```
class Test {
    int i;
    int get()
        {return i;}
    }
```

```
class Test {
    int i;
    Test()
        {i = 0;}
    int get()
        {return i;}
    }
```

Constructor can be overloaded providing that they should have different arguments because JVM differentiates constructors on the basis of arguments passed in the constructor.

This is similar to the overloading methods: you can have several versions of a method in class with different types/numbers of arguments, as Example 99, Example 100 and Example 101 show.

Example 99

```
public class Cube {
        double length;
        double breadth;
        double height;

        Cube () {
                length = 10.0;
                breadth = 10.0;
                height = 10.0;
        }
    // default constructor
```

```
        Cube (double l, double b, double h) {
            length = l;
                breadth = b;
                height = h;
        }
    // constructor

        public double getVolume() {
                return (length*breadth*height);
        }
}

public class CubeTest {
   public static void main(String [] args)
   {
     Cube cubeObj1, cubeObj2;
     cubeObj1 = new Cube();
     cubeObj2 = new Cube(10.0, 20.0, 30.0);

     System.out.println("Volume of cube1 is :" + cubeObj1.getVolume());
     System.out.println("Volume of cube2 is :" + cubeObj2.getVolume());
   }
}
```

The output:
    Volume of cube is : 1000.0
    Volume of cube is : 6000.0

Example 100

```
Class Rectangle {
   int l, b;
   float p, q;

public Rectangle(int x, int y){
                l = x;
                b = y;
                }

public Rectangle(int x){
                l = x;
                b = x;
                }

public Rectangle(float x){
                p = x;
                q = x;
                }

public Rectangle(float x,float y){
                p = x;
                q = y;
                }

public int first(){
                return (l*b);
                }
```

```
public float second(){
                return (p*q);
                }
}

public class ConstructorOverloading {
            public static void main(String args[]){

            Rectangle rectangle1=new Rectangle(2,4);
            int areaInFirstConstructor=rectangle1.first();
            System.out.println("The area of a rectangle in 1st constructor is:"
                            + areaInFirstConstructor);

            Rectangle rectangle2=new Rectangle(3.0f,2.0f);
            float areaInFourthConstructor=rectangle2.second();
            System.out.println("The area of a rectangle in 2nd constructor is:"
                            + areaInFourthConstructor);
    }
}
```

Example 101

```
public class Point {
  public double x,y;
  // fields x and y, whose values are the coordinator of a point

  public Point(double a, double b){
    x = a;
    y = b;
  }
  // constructor

  public double x() {
    return x;
  }
  public double y(){
    return y;
  }
  public String toString() {
    return new String("(" + x + "," + y + ")");
  }
  // Override default toString (string representation of the object)
  // the method will be invoked whenever a reference to an object of
  // that class is passed to the  println() method, as in
  // System.out.println("p="+p);

  public static void main(String[] args)
  {
    Point p = new Point(2,3);
    System.out.println("p.x()=" +p.x() +",p.y() = " + p.y());
    // invokes the methods  x() and  y() to obtain the values of p's fields

    System.out.println("p = " +p);

    Point q = new Point(7,4);
    System.out.println("q = " +q);
    // repeat the previous steps for the object q representing the point (7,4)
```

```
  }
}
The output:

p.x() = 2.0, p.y() = 3.0

P = (2.0, 3.0)

q = (7.0, 4.0)
```

There are two steps involved in creating objects :

- Declaring a variable to refer to an object: for example, *Rectangle rect*. The value of rect will be undetermined until an object is actually created and assigned to it. Simply declaring a reference variable does not create an object. You must assign an object to rect before you use it in your code. Otherwise, you will get a compile error.

- Instantiating a class (creating an object): for example, *new Rectangle*(50, 100);. The new operator instantiates a class by allocating memory for a new object and returning a reference to that memory. The new operator also invokes the object constructor. The new operator returns a reference to the object it created. This reference is usually assigned to a variable of the appropriate type, for example, *rect = new Rectangle*(50, 100);.

In another example, *Student s = new Student*("*Joe*", 20);, s is a reference variable (or object type variable), which may reference a Student object (or an object of a subclass of Student). Objects do not have names, instead they only have just types and locations in memory. The above statement can be understood as: create a new Student object in memory, initialize it with the data sent as arguments to a constructor, and when created, assign a reference of that object to the Student variable s.

In another example, *int x = s.getValue*();. The statement can be understood as : Go to the object referenced by variable s, execute its getValue() method and assign the return from that method to the int variable x. The reference returned by the new operator does not have to be assigned to a variable. It can also be used directly in an expression, for example,

int height = new Rectangle().*height*;.

In summary, an object is a piece of memory with space for all the instance variables. A class is instantiated (or object is created) using the "new" operator. The "new" operator creates an object and invokes a constructor. An object reference variable stores the address of an object even though the address never is disclosed. The procedure of creating an object involves two steps: firstly declare a variable to hold the object reference; secondly apply the "new" operator to an appropriate class to specify a constructor, and store object reference in a variable.

1.5.5   Some Important Classes

1.5.5.1   NumberFormat Class

NumberFormat class provides generic formatting capabilities for numbers. You do not instantiate a NumberFormat object using new operator, instead you can request an object from one of the methods such as getCurrencyInstance and getPercentInstance you can invoke through the class itself. You can set the format for currency and include a dollar sign in the print out using the pattern , "$0.00", e.g., Example 102 shows the application of the NumberFormat class.

Example 102

```
import java.text.NumberFormat;

public class Price {
```

```
public static void main (String[] args)    {
    final double TAX_RATE = 0.06;  // 6% sales tax
    int quantity;
    double subtotal, tax, totalCost, unitPrice;

    System.out.print ("Enter the quantity: ");
    quantity = Keyboard.readInt();
    System.out.print ("Enter the unit price: ");
    unitPrice = Keyboard.readDouble();
    subtotal = quantity * unitPrice;
    tax = subtotal * TAX_RATE;
    totalCost = subtotal + tax;
}
}
NumberFormat fmt1 = NumberFormat.getCurrencyInstance();
NumberFormat fmt2 = NumberFormat.getPercentInstance();

System.out.println("Subtotal: " + fmt1.format(subtotal) );
System.out.println("Tax: " + fmt1.format(tax) + " at " + fmt2.format(TAX_RATE) );
System.out.println("Total: " + fmt1.format(totalCost));
```

The output of the program is :
   Enter the quantity: 1000
   Enter the unit price: 10
   Subtotal: $1000.00
   Tax: $60.00 at 6%
   Total: $1060.00

1.5.5.2   DecimalFormat Class

DecimalFormat class is a public class derived from NumberFormat. DecimalFormat class needs
an import statement *import java.text.DecimalFormat;*.

You may create a formatting object whose only attribute is a string specifying a formatting
pattern. The format is controlled with "zeros" and "hashes". The formatting pattern can specify
the number of digits before or after the decimal point.

The format is usually set by the constructor when a DecimalFormat object is created, e.g.,
DecimalFormat fmt = new DecimalFormat(0.##);. However the format may be altered at a
later stage by calling methods from the DecimalFormat class, e.g., *fmt.applyPattern("0.##");*.
Below the syntax is shown:

```
DecimalFormat fmt;
fmt = new DecimalFormat("0.##");
System.out.println("The value is " + fmt.format(value));
```

You shall set the format of DecimalFormat both on the left and right side.

- On the left side of the decimal point: zero is set to the minimum number of digits, e.g.,
  the pattern "00.00" turns 3.14 into 03.14. Extra space is automatically added to allow for
  larger numbers, e.g., the pattern "0.00" turns 23.14 into 23.14. Note: hashes do nothing on
  the left of the decimal point.

- On the right of the decimal point: zero defines the exact number of digits and round up the
  decimal number or zero is added where necessary. e.g., the pattern "0.00" turns 3.348 into
  3.35. The pattern "0.00" turns 6.3 into 6.30. Hashes set the maximum number of digits and
  round up the decimal number, e.g, the pattern "0.##" turns 3.348 into 3.35. You can set

the format for currency and include a dollar sign in the print out using the pattern "$0.00",
e.g, *DecimalFormat fmt = new DecimalFormat("$0.00")*;

System.out.println("Thecostis" + fmt.format(cost));

Example 103 shows the application of the DecimalFormat class. In this example "import" is a
feature introduced in Java that allows members (fields and methods) defined in a class as public
static to be used in Java code without specifying the class in which the field is defined.

Example 103

```
import java.text.DecimalFormat;
Public class simple {
            public static void main(String[ ]  args){
                    DecimalFormat   fmt = new
                    DecimalFormat(0.\hash\hash);
                    double PI = 3.14159; // prints formatted value of PI
                    System.out.println("PI is:"+ fmt.format(PI) );
                    }
                }// end class simple

import java.text.DecimalFormat;

public class CircleStats {
    public static void main (String[] args) {
        int radius;
        double area, circumference;
        screen.print ("Enter the circle's radius: ");
        radius = Keyboard.readDouble();
        area = Math.PI * Math.pow(radius, 2);
        circumference = 2 * Math.PI * radius;
        DecimalFormat fmt = new DecimalFormat ("0.###");
        screen.println ("The circle's area: " + fmt.format(area) );
        screen.println ("The circle's circumference: " + fmt.format(circumference) );
    }
}
```

1.5.5.3   The Strings Class

Strings are objects rather than primitive data types. Each string object is a member of the string
class. Since strings are so common, Java has a simple way to create them:
   String title = "Java is fun"; Here the string object is the variable "title" and its contents
is the string literal "Java is fun". The string class is available as part of the normal Java package.
   String s1 = new String("today");.
   The first character of a string is always at position 0, e.g,:
      Indexes   0   1   2   3   4
                 t   o   d   a   y
   String OBJECT includes set of instance variables and set of methods for manipulating strings.
The methods provide information about the contents of a string object or perform actions on
it. String concatenation operator (+) appends one string to the end of another, e.g. "Java
programming is" + "lots of fun". It can also be used to append a number to a string, e.g. "Java
programming is" + 2 + "much fun". A string literal cannot be broken across two lines in a
program.
   The plus operator (+) can be used both for string concatenation and arithmetic addition. The
function performed by the + operator performs depending on the context : if both operands are
strings, or if one is a string and one is a number, it performs string concatenation. If both operands

are numeric, it adds them. The + operator is evaluated from left to right but parentheses can be used to change the operation order.

```
public class DemoPlus {
    public static void main(String[] args) {

        System.out.println("24 and 45 concatenated: " + 24 + 45);
            System.out.println("24 and 45 added: " + (24 + 45));
    }
}
```

A reference variable does not currently point to an object which is called **a** null reference. When a reference variable is initially declared as an instance variable, it is a null reference. You can not follow a null reference as there is no object to reference. For example,

```
public class NameIsNull {
    String name; // not initialised, thus null
    void printName() {
        System.out.println( name.length() );
    }
    public static void main(String[] args) {
        NameIsNull test = new NameIsNull();
        test.printName();
    }
}
```

This allows an object to refer to itself. Inside a method, the this reference can be used to refer to the currently executing object. The this reference can be used to distinguish the parameters of a constructor from their corresponding instance variables with the same name. Example 104 shows the first program can be rewritten to the second program.

Example 104

First program :

```
public Account (String name, long acctNumber, double balance){
        this.name = name;
        this.acctNumber = acctNumber;
        this.balance = balance;
}
```

Second program:

```
public Account (String owner, long account, double initials){
        name = owner;
        acctNumber = account;
        balance = initial;
}
```

String constructors and methods include:

- String( ) constructs a new empty String " ".

- String(String s) constructs a new copy of String s.

- String(char[ ] charArray) constructs a new String from character array. Once a string object has been created, you can use the dot operator to invoke its methods, e.g. title.length().

- Common methods : length( ), charAt(int x), indexOf(char ch) and equals(String s).

Example 105 shows an Alphabet class.

Example 105

```
public class Alphabet {
   public static void main(String[] args)  {
      String alphabet = "ABCDEFGHIJKLMNOPQRSTUVWXYZ";
      System.out.println(alphabet);
      System.out.println("This string contains " + alphabet.length() + " characters.");
      System.out.println("The character at index 4 is " + alphabet.charAt(4) );
      System.out.println("The index of the character Z is " + alphabet.indexOf('Z') );
   }
}
```

To search a particular word in a given string $indexOf$ method is used. indexOf returns a position index of a word within the string if found. Otherwise it returns -1. To search a word after particular position $indexOf(String word, int position)$ is used. You may use lastIndexOf method to search a last occurrence of a word within a string, as Example 106 shows.

Example 106

```
String strOrig = "Hello world Hello World";

int intIndex = strOrig.indexOf("Hello") ;
System.out.println("Found Hello at index " + intIndex);

int positionIndex= strOrig.indexOf("Hello",11) ;
System.out.println("Index of Hello after 11 is " + positionIndex);

int lastIndex = strOrig.lastIndexOf("Hello") ;
System.out.println("Last occurrence of Hello is at index " + lastIndex);
```

The output of the program is :
   Found Hello at index 0
   Index of Hello after 11 is 12
   Last occurrence of Hello is at index 12
   You may use the following methods to replace character or substring from the given String object:
   1) String replace(int oldChar, int newChar) replaces a specified character with new character and returns a new string object.
   2) String replaceFirst(String regularExpression, String newString) replaces the first substring of this string that matches the given regular expression with the given new string.
   3) String replaceAll(String regex, String replacement) replaces the each substring of this string that matches the given regular expression with the given new string. Example 107 shows the application of the above methods.

Example 107

```
String str = "Replace Region";
String str1 = str.replace( 'R','A' );
// replaces all occurrences of given character with new one and returns new String object

The result : Aeplace  Aegion

String str2 = str.replaceFirst("Re","Ra") ;
// replaces only first occurrences of given String with new one and returns new
// String object.

The result : Raplace  Region

String str3 = str.replaceAll("Re", "Ra") );
// replaces all occurrences of given string with new one and returns new String object
```

The result of the program : Aaplace Ragion

You may use the following methods to get substring from a given String object:

1) String substring(int startIndex) returns new String object containing the substring of the given string from the specified startIndex (inclusive). IndexOutOfBoundException is thrown if startIndex is negative or grater than length of the string.

2) String substring(int startIndex, int endIndex) returns new String object containing the substring of the given string from the specified startIndex to endIndex. Here, startIndex is inclusive while endIndex is exclusive. Example 108 shows the application of these string methods.

Example 108

```
String name = "Hello World";

System.out.println(name.substring(6));

System.out.println(name.substring(0,5));
```

The output of the program is :

WorldHello

The contents of a string object can be altered and assigned to a new object variable. For example, *String str2 = str1.toUpper();*. Alternatively the contents of a string object can be altered and re-assigned to the same object variable, e.g., *str1 = str1.toUpper();*. Example 109 prints a string and various mutations of it.

Example 109

```
public class StringMutation {
    public static void main (String[] args) {
        String phrase = new String ("Change is  inevitable");
        String mutation1, mutation2, mutation3, mutation4;
        System.out.println ("Original string: \"" + phrase + "\"");
        System.out.println ("Length of string: " + phrase.length());

        mutation1 = phrase.concat(", except from vending machines.");
        mutation2 = mutation1.toUpper();
        mutation3 = mutation2.replace('E', 'X');
        mutation4 = mutation3.substring (3, 30);

        // Print each mutated string
```

```
    System.out.println ("Mutation #1: " + mutation1);
    System.out.println ("Mutation #2: " + mutation2);
    System.out.println ("Mutation #3: " + mutation3);
    System.out.println ("Mutation #4: " + mutation4);
    System.out.println ("Mutated length: " + mutation4.length());
  }
}
```

Example 110 tests strings to see if they are palindromes. A palindrome is a word that is spelled the same forwards as backwards, e.g., shown in Figure 1.49 and the Figure 1.50.

Figure 1.49: Rotator   Figure 1.50: A palindrome of rotator

Example 110

```
String str = "madam";
if(isPalindrome(str))
    System.out.println(str + " is a palindrome" );
else
    System.out.println(str + " is not a palindrome");

public static boolean isPalindrome (String s) {
    int left = 0;
    int right = s.length() - 1;
    while ( left < right )    {
        if (s.charAt(left)!=s.charAt(right))
            return   false;

        left++ ;
        right-- ;
    }
    return   true;
}
```

String Comparisons : == can be used to check if two strings string1 and string2 refer to the same object. You should use String method equals() for equality comparison of the contents of a string object. For example,

```
String s0 = "Java!";
String s1 = "Welcome to" + s0;
String s2 = "Welcome to Java!";
System.out.println("s1=s2 is" + ( s1==s2 ));
System.out.println("s1.equals(s2)is" + (s1.equals(s2)));
```

Two String references are the same if they are created with the same literal value using the shorthand notation. However strings with same content do not always share the same object. You may use the equals() method to test whether two strings have the same content.

Extracting numbers from Strings: sometimes you may want to convert a number stored as a string into an integer to enable arithmetic operations. The Integer class and the Double class available in the standard Java class library have static methods that to do this. For example,

```
String numTxt1 = "124";
int numInt = Integer.parseInt(numTxt1);
String numTxt2= "124.56";
double num = Double.parseDouble(numTxt2);
```

The toString Method: toString is the method of wrapper classes for converting a number into a string. It is customary to provide a toString method for your class. toString converts an object into a String (for printing it out or for debugging). In any class, if toString definition conforms to: *public String toString()*, then the method will be invoked whenever a reference to an object of that class is passed to println() method. *System.out.print (obj);* is the same as *System.out.print (obj.toString());.* Example 111 and Example 112 show the application of these methods.

Example 111

```
class MyPoint {
        private final int x, y;
        public MyPoint(int x, int y) {
            this.x = x;
            this.y = y;
        }
        public String toString() {
            return "X=" + x + " " + "Y=" + y;
        }
        public int getX() {
            return x;
        }
        public int getY() {
            return y;
        }
}
public class TSDemo {
        public static void main(String args[]) {
            MyPoint mp = new MyPoint(37, 47);
            // call MyPoint.toString()
            System.out.println(mp);
            // get X,Y values via accessor methods
            int x = mp.getX();
            int y = mp.getY();
            System.out.println(x);
            System.out.println(y);
        }
    }
```

The output of the program is :
   X=37 Y=47
   37
   47

Example 112

```
public class Date {
    int year, month, day;

    public Date() { }
```

```
    public Date(int month,int day,int year) {
        this.year = year;
        this.month = month;
        this.day = day;
    }
    public int getYear() {
        return year;
    }
    public int getMonth(){
        return month;
    }
    public int getDay() {
        return day;
    }
public void setYear(int newYear)
{

        year = newYear;
}
public void setMonth(int newMonth)
{

        month = newMonth;
}
    public void setDay(int newDay) {
        day = newDay;
}
public String toString() {
    return new String(month + "/" + day + "/" + year);
}
}
public class TestDate{
    public static void main (String args[]) {
        Date today = new Date(11,29,2001);
        Date empty = new Date();
        System.out.println("today is " + today.getMonth() + "/"
                        + today.getDay() + "/" + today.getYear());
        today.setDay(30);
        System.out.println("tomorrow will be " + today.getMonth()
                + "/" + today.getDay() + "/" + today.getYear());
        System.out.println("An empty date is " + empty.getMonth()
                + "/" + empty.getDay() + "/" + empty.getYear());
        empty.setMonth(9);
        empty.setDay(26);
        empty.setYear(87);
        System.out.println("Another date is " + empty.getMonth()
                + "/" + empty.getDay() + "/" + empty.getYear());

        Date2 improvedDate = new Date2(5,12,2003);
        System.out.println("New improved date output :
                        + improvedDate.toString() );
}
}
```

The output of the program is :
    today is 11/29/2001
    tomorrow will be 11/30/2001
    An empty data is 0/0/0
    Another data is 9/26/87
    New improved date output : 5/12/2003

The StringTokenizer Class : you may use StringTokenizer class to break a string into its component tokens, as determined by a set of delimiters. The delimiters can be the 4 default delimiters (space, newline, tab, and carriage return) or other delimiters can be specified for the StringTokenizer. A StringTokenizer object is a kind of foreman who organizes the tasks (calls the methods) to break up a string into pieces. It can be accessed with the following import statement: *importjava.util.StringTokenizer.*

StringTokenizer(Strings) creates a StringTokenizer for String s that will use default delimiter string "\n\t\r" for tokenization. *StringTokenizer(Strings, Stringdelims)* creates a StringTokenizer for String s that will use the characters in String delims for tokenization. StringTokenizer methods include the following :

- int countTokens( ) returns number of individual tokens in the String.

- Boolean hasMoreTokens( ) returns true if there are more tokens in the String and returns false if there are no more tokens left.

- String nextToken( ) returns a String with the next token in the String being tokenized.

In the Example 113, the first call to tz.nextToken returns "The" and the second call to tz.nextToken returns "rain" and so on.

Example 113

```
str = "The rain in Spain falls mainly on the plain"
StringTokenizer  tz = new StringTokenizer(str);
```

Example 114 finds palindrome words in a sentence.

Example 114

```
public class Stringpalindrom {
public void main (String args[]) {
StringTokenizer words;
String word;
String line = Keyboard.readString();
while ( !line.equals("DONE")) {
    words = new StringTokenizer(line);
    while (words.hasMoreTokens() )   {
            word = words.nextToken() ;
            if ( isPalindrome(word) )
            System.out.println(word);
    }
    line  = Keyboard.readString();
}
}
}
```

The result of the program is :
  A deed worth doing
  deed
Example 115 shows an example of counting words.

Example 115

Table 1.16: Wrapper class

Primitive Type	Wrapper Class
byte	Byte
short	Short
int	Integer
long	Long
float	Float
double	Double
char	Char
boolean	Boolean
void	Void

```
public class Wordcount {
    public void main (String args[]) {
    int wordCount = 0,
    String line, word;
    StringTokenizer tokenizer;
    System.out.println("Please enter text (DONE to quit):");

    line = Keyboard.readString();

    while (!line.equals("DONE"))   {
     tokenizer = new StringTokenizer(line);
     while(tokenizer.hasMoreTokens()) {
         word = tokenizer.nextToken() ;
         wordCount++;
     }
     line = Keyboard.readString();
}
System.out.println ("Number of words: " + wordCount);
}
}
```

The output of the program is :
   To be or not to be.
   That is the question.
   DONE.
   Number of words: 10

Wrapper Classes : the java.lang package contains wrapper classes that correspond to each primitive type as shown in Table below. Except for int and char, the wrapper class name is exactly the same as the primitive type name EXCEPT that it starts with a capital letter. double is a primitive Double is a class. Wrappers allow for situations where numerical values are needed but objects instead of primitives are required, as Table 1.16 shows.

Except for int and char, the wrapper class name is exactly the same as the primitive type name except that it starts with a capital letter. For example, double is a primitive type while Double is a class; boolean is a primitive type while Boolean is a class; long is a primitive type while Long is a class. However the wrapper classes for int and char are different. That is, int is a primitive type while Integer is a class and char is a primitive type while Character is a class.

An object of a wrapper class can be used in any situation where a primitive value will not suffice. For example, some objects serve as containers of other objects. Primitive values could not be stored in such containers, but wrapper objects could be. Another example is that some methods take an object as a parameter. So a primitive cannot be used, but an object of any class can be used.

All wrapper classes except character can be instantiated using a String argument as shown below.

```
Integer age = new Integer("40");
Double num = new Double("8.2");
Boolean isDone = new Boolean("true");
```

Wrapper classes contain various methods that help convert from the associated type to another type.

```
Integer num = new Integer(4);
float flt = num.floatValue(); // stores 4.0 in flt
Double dbl = new Double(8.2);
int val = dbl.intValue(); // stores 8 in val
```

For example,

```
int x =25;
    Integer y = new Integer (33);
    int z = x + y; // wrong!
    int z = x + y.intValue();
// ok!, intValue is a method obtaining the integer value of current variable
```

Some Wrapper classes also contain methods that will compare the value of two objects of that class.

```
Integer num1 = new Integer(4);
Integer num2 = new Integer(11);
if(num1.compareTo(num2)< 0)          // executes if num1 < num2
```

The wrapper classes often contain useful constants as well. The Integer class contains MIN-VALUE and MAX_VALUE which hold the smallest and largest int values. Other numeric classes will also have MIN_VALUE and MAX_VALUE which hold the smallest and largest value for their corresponding types.

Wrapper classes also contain static methods that help managing the associated type. Each numeric class contains a method to convert a representation in a String to the associated primitive:

```
int n = Integer.parseInt(s);
double x = Double.parseDouble(s);
```

The conversion from numeric to string can be implemented by the toString method.

```
String s1 = Integer.toString (i);
String s2 = Double.toString (d);
```

There are three ways to convert a number into a string as shown below:
1. String s = " " + num;
2. String s = Integer.toString(i);
String s = Double.toString(d);
3. String s = String.valueOf(num);
In Example 116, the code at the left side is same as the right side.

Example 116

```
String s = String.valueOf(i);          String s = new Integer(i).toString();
String s = String.valueOf(f);          String s = new Float(f).toString();
String s = String.valueOf(d);          String s = new Double(d).toString();
String s = String.valueOf(l);          String s = new Long(l).toString();
```
Example 117 converts any data type value in to String type.

Example 117

```
public class Stringconversion {
    public static void main(String[] args){
        boolean result = true;
        int in = 234;
        char ch = 'u';
        double dou = 34.86;
        float flt = 54.889f;

        System.out.println("String represented boolean value:  "
            +String.valueOf(result)
            +"\nString represented integer value: " +
                                String.valueOf(in)
            +"\nString represented char value: " +
                        "'"+ String.valueOf(ch) + "'"
            + "\nString represented double value:  " + String.valueOf(dou)
            + "\nString represented float value:  " + String.valueOf(flt));
    }
}
```

1.6 Array

1.6.1 Basic Concepts of Array

An array is a fixed-length sequence of values of the same type used to group and organize data. These values can be primitive type or objects. Simple example is shown in Figure 1.51, where single variable height can hold many values. Individual items in an array are called **elements** of the array. The position of an element in an array is called its **index**. Like most programming languages, Java's array indexes start from 0. For example, an array with three elements indexes those elements with 0, 1 and 2. Array variable declarations indicate a dimension by using []. The standard convention for declaring arrays is:

```
int[] counts;            // one-dimensional array
double[] scores;         // one-dimensional array
String[] studentNames;   // one-dimensional array
String s[];              // one-dimensional array
String[][] s;            // two-dimensional array
```

You can not declare the size of the array like

```
String[5] s; // illegal declaration
```

An array implicitly extends java.lang.Object. An array is an instance of Object class. Hence, arrays in Java are objects. Declaring an array does not create an array object or allocate space in memory. It only creates a variable with a reference to an array. Since arrays are Objects they can be initialized using the "new" operator. The syntax is: *new type[size]*;. When arrays are created, they are automatically initialized with the default value of their type. For example,

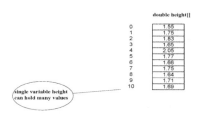

Figure 1.51: A simple example of array

```
String[] s = new String[100];    // default values: null
boolean[] b = new boolean[4];    // default values: false
int[] i = new int[10];           // default values: 0
```

As arrays are allocated at run-time, you can use a variable to set their dimension. For example,

```
int arrSize = 100;
String[] myArray = new String[arrSize];
```

Arrays can contain any one type of value (either primitive values or references). All elements of the array must be of the same type. You can create an array containing integers or an array holding strings, but not array holding both integers and strings. Subscripts are used to access specific array values. Example 118 shows an array of 10-dimension.

Example 118

For an array counts of 10-dimension:

```
counts[0]     // first variable in counts
counts[1]     // second variable in counts
counts[9]     // last variable in counts
counts[10]    // error, trying to access variable outside counts
```

In Figure 1.51, the array consists of 11 elements, indexed from 0 to 10. A value is accessed by reference to the index, for example,

```
double i, average; int j = 3;
i = height[6];          // i = 1.66
average = (height[0] + height[1] + height[2])/3
i = height(j + 1)       // i = 2.05
```

Example 119 illustrates initialization of array values.

Example 119

```
public class Multiplelimit {
   public static void main( ){
   final int LIMIT =15, MULTIPLE =10;
   int[] list = new int[LIMIT];
```

```
for (int i = 0; i < LIMIT; i++)
    list[i] = i*MULTIPLE; // initialize array values
    list[5] = 999;// change one array value
for (int i = 0; i < LIMIT; i++) System.out.print(list[i] + "  ");
}
}
```

Expressions as Subscripts : array subscripts do not have to be constants. Array subscripts do need to be integer expressions that evaluate to valid subscript values for the current array allocation either. For example, the below are valid array subscripts.

```
counts[i]
counts[2*i]
counts[I/2]
```

The size of an array is held in a constant called length in the array object and it is accessed in the usual way. For example,

```
i = a.length              // i = 3
```

Shorthand for Initializing Arrays :   arrays can be initialized by giving a list of their elements. If a list contains n elements the subscripts will range from 0 to $n-1$. You can use curly braces { } as part of an array declaration to initialize an array. For example,

```
int[] arr = new int[] {1,2,3};
int [] primes = {2, 3, 5, 7, 11, 13, 17};
String[] oneDimArray = {"abc", "def", "xyz"};
```

You cannot create an empty array by using a blank index though as shown below.

```
int[] array = new int[]; // illegal
```

For example, $int[]\ ageList\ =\ \{23, 17, 42, 5\};$ is shorthand for the array shown in Example 120.

Example 120

```
public class Arrayshorthand {
    public static void main(){
int[] ageList = new int[4];
ageList[0] = 23;
ageList[1] = 17;
ageList[2] = 42;
ageList[3] = 5;
}
}
```

The type of each value must match the type of array, e.g. $char[]\ letter\ =\ \{A, B, C, D, E, f, g\};$. Example 121 shows a string array.

Example 121

```
public class Stringarray{
    public void main() {
    String arr[] = {"Zero", "One", "Two"};
    for (int i = 0; i < arr.length; i++) {
            System.out.println(arr[i]);
    }
    String arr1[] = new String[]{"Zero", "One", "Two"};
    for (int i = 0; i < arr1.length; i++) {
            System.out.println(arr1[i]);
}
    String arr2[] = new String[3]; // allocates the array but they are all null
    arr2[0] = "Zero";
    arr2[1] = "One";
    arr2[2] = "Two";
    for (int i = 0; i < arr2.length; i++) {
        System.out.println(arr2[i]);
}
}
}
```

Loops for Array Processing : a convenient way to traverse an array is to use the for loop operator. You may use the length attribute to get the number of elements in an array. For example,

```
// initializes counts to 0, 10, 20, ..., 90
for (int i=0; i < 10; i++) {
    counts[i] = i * 10;
}
// prints the contents of counts using length
for (int i=0; i < counts.length; i++) {
  System.out.println(counts[i]);
}
```

Arrays and Methods :

- An array can be passed as a parameter to a method. For example,

```
int a[] = { 1, 2, 3, 4, 5};
...
modifyArray (a );
...
public void modifyArray (int b[]) { ...}
```

- An element of an array can be passed to the method. For example,

```
int a[] ={1, 2, 3, 4, 5};
...
modifyElement(a[4]);
...
public void modifyElement(int elem) {...}
```

- A method may return an array as its result. For example,

```
public static double [] readArray()  // declare return type
{
    . . . // ask for now many, n
    double result[] = new double[n]; // declare local array for receiving input
    for (i = 0; i < n; i++)
    { System.out.print("Enter ");
      result[i] = Keyboard.readDouble();
    }
    return result;  // local array is returned
}
```

More on Array Initializing and Constructors : Note that the instruction

```
int[ ] number = {21, 83, 7, 1, 64, 17, 34, 8, 12,10};
```

cannot be split into

```
int[ ] number ;
number = {21, 83, 7, 1, 64, 17, 34, 8, 12,10};
```

Thus the following class is not syntactically correct:

```
class ArrayContainer {
    private int[] number;
    public ArrayContainer () {  // a syntax error
        number = {21, 83, 7, 1, 64, 17, 34, 8, 12,10};
    }
    public void print () {
        for ( int i = 0 ; i < number.length ; i++ )
        System.out.print(number[i] + " ");
    }
}
```

The correct definition is as follows:

```
class ArrayContainer {
 private int[] number = {21, 83, 7, 1, 64, 17, 34, 8, 12};
 public void print () {
    for ( int i = 0 ; i < number.length ; i++ )
       System.out.print(number[i] + " ");
 }
}
```

Note that the constructor disappears as there is no need for it here. You may want to add
a different constructor, as shown below, to test number to an array of numbers defined in an
external program. However this is a different issue.

```
public ArrayContainer (int [] input_data) {
    number = new int[input_data.length];
    for ( int i = 0 ; i < number.length ; i++ )
       number[i] = input_data[i];
}
```

1.6.2 Advanced Topic of Array

1.6.2.1 Array Method arraycopy

A copy of an array can be made with the System static method:

```
arraycopy(Object src, int src_position, Object dst, int dst_position, int length)
```

where src is the array to be copied, dst is the destination array (of same type). The copy begins from src_position and starts in destination at dst_position for length number of elements. Example 122 copies the array a into the middle of array b. Example 123 shows array copy demo. In the example, the copy begins at element no.2 in the source array (element 'c'). The arraycopy method puts the copied elements into the destination array beginning at the first element (element 0) in the destination array copyTo. The arraycopy copies 7 elements: 'c', 'a', 'f', 'f', 'e', 'i', and 'n'.

Example 122

```
class ArrayCopy {
    public static void main(String[] args) {
        int[] a = {1,2,3};
        int[] b = new int[5];
        System.arraycopy(a, 0, b, 1, a.length);
        for (int i = 0; i < b.length; ++i)
            System.out.print(b[i] + " ");
    }
}
```

Output:
    0 1 2 3 0

Example 123

```
public class ArrayCopyDemo {
    public static void main(String[] args) {
        char[] copyFrom = { 'd', 'e', 'c', 'a', 'f', 'f', 'e',
                            'i', 'n', 'a', 't', 'e', 'd' };
        char[] copyTo = new char[7];
        System.arraycopy(copyFrom, 2, copyTo, 0, 7);
        System.out.println(new String(copyTo));
    }
}
```

Effectively, the arraycopy method takes the "caffein" out of "decaffeinated", shown in Figure 1.52. Note that the destination array must be allocated before you call arraycopy and must be large enough to contain the data being copied.

Extra Capacity Array : arrays cannot grow after they have been allocated. You can allocate more space than you believe your application will need. If your estimation is too low, you will still run out of space. You do not need to use all the elements in an array.

1.6.2.2 Array of Objects

Let us recall : *String[] words = new String*[25];. The array words references to String objects. Memory space is reserved for 25 String references. Note declaration does not create actual strings and it only declares that the array can store 25 Strings. For example,

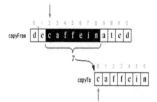

Figure 1.52: Array copy example

```
words[0] = "Xian";
words[1]= "Jiaotong"
words[2] = "Liverpool"
words[3] = "University"
```

In the example above there are 21 slots that are not initialized yet. The default value of an uninitialized object is null. Since a String is an object in Java it will have this default value of null.

Array elements can be generally referenced to objects, e.g., suppose that a Date object has fields y,m,d, you can create an array of Date objects: *Date[] hols = new Date[3];*.

Arrays of objects are declared in the same manner as arrays of primitive variables. In the above example, you can update the array of Date objects:

```
hols [ 0 ] = new Date(2002, 1, 1);
hols [ 1 ] = new Date(2001, 5, 1);
hols [ 2 ] = new Date(2001, 12, 25);
```

Example 124 shows an application of testing date.

Example 124

```
public class Date {
    int year;
    int month;
    int day;

    public Date() {
        year = 1970; month = 1; day = 1;
    }
    public Date(int m, int d, int y) {
        year = y;
        month = m;
        day = d;
    }
    public int getYear() {return year;}
    public int getMonth() {return month;}
    public int getDay() {return day;}

    public void setYear(int newYear) {year = newYear;}
    public void setMonth(int newMonth) {month = newMonth;}
    public void setDay(int newDay) {day = newDay;}
```

```
    public String toString() {
            return new String(month + "/" + day + "/" + year);
    }
}

public class TestDate{
  public static void main (String args[]) {
      Date2 [ ] hols = new Date2 [3];
          hols [ 0 ] = new Date2(2002, 1, 1);
      hols [ 1 ] = new Date2(2001, 5, 1);
      hols [ 2 ] = new Date2(2001, 12, 25);

      System.out.println("The 1st holiday: " + hols[0].toString());
      System.out.println("The 2nd holiday: " + hols[1].toString());
      System.out.println("The 3rd holiday: " + hols[2].toString());

  }
}
```

Example 125 shows a class student was declared elsewhere, a client application could declare and allocate an array of 10 students.

```
                Student[ ] students;
                students = new Student[10];
```

Example 125

```
class Student {
        int regno,total;
        int mark[];
        String name;
    public student(int r, String n, int m[]){
                regno=r;
                name=n;
                mark =new int[3];
                for(int i=0;i<3;i++) {
                        mark[i] = m[i];
                total+=mark[i];
        }
}
public void displaystudent() {
        System.out.println("NAME:"+name);
        System.out.println("REGNO:"+regno);
        System.out.println("TOTAL:"+total);
    }
}
class teststudent {
  public static void main(String args[]) {
    int mk1[]={73,85,95};
    int mk2[]={71,85,95};
    Student st[] = new Student[2];
    st[0]=new Student(1,"Ganguly",mk1);
    st[1]=new Student(2,"Sachin",mk2);
    for(int i=0;i<2;i++)  st[i].displaystudent();
  }
}
```

Table 1.17: An example of a 2-dimensional array

a[0][0]	a[0][1]	a[0][2]	a[0][3]
a[1][0]	a[1][1]	a[1][2]	a[1][3]
a[2][0]	a[2][1]	a[2][2]	a[2][3]

Table 1.18: Rows of a 2-dimensional array

a[0][0]	a[0][1]	a[0][2]	a[0][3]	row 0
a[1][0]	a[1][1]	a[1][2]	a[1][3]	row 1
a[2][0]	a[2][1]	a[2][2]	a[2][3]	row 2

1.6.2.3   2-Dimensional Array

To declare a 2D array, you add another pair of brackets, e,g,
   $double[][]\ a\ =\ new\ double[M][N];$.
   To refer to the element in row i and column j of a 2D array a[][], you use the notation a[i][j];
In a 2D array, you can use the code a[i] to refer to the ith row (which is a one-dimensional array).
To create the array, you specify the #rows followed by the # columns after the type name (both
within brackets). A 2-dimensional array may be shown as a table, e.g., $int[][]\ a\ =\ new\ int[3][4]$;
as shown in the Table 1.17.
   Rows of the 2-dimensional array is shown in the Table 1.18 below.
   In a 2D array, you need to allocate memory for only the first dimension. You can allocate
the remaining dimensions separately. When you allocate memory to the second dimension, you
can also allocate different number to each dimension. For example, the length of the columns can
vary:

```
int[][] myArray = new int[3][];
myArray[0] = new int[3]; // initialize number of columns
myArray[1] = new int[4];
myArray[2] = new int[5];
```

You can initialize the row dimension without initializing the columns but not vice versa.

```
int[][] myArray = new int[5][]; // legal
int[][] myArray = new int[][5]; // illegal
```

As with one-dimensional arrays, Java initializes all entries in arrays of numbers to 0 and in arrays
of Boolean to false. To access each of the elements in a 2D array, you may use nested loops shown
below :

```
double[][] a;
a = new double[M][N];
for (int i = 0; i < M; i++)
        for (int j = 0; j < N; j++)
                a[i][j] = 0;
```

Initializing Two-Dimensional Arrays :   curly braces {} may be used to initialize two
dimensional arrays. They are only valid in array declaration statements:
   $int[]\ twoDimArray\ =\ \{\{1,2,3\},\{4,5,6\},\{7,8,9\}\};$,
   one for each row in the array.
   Java represents a 2D array as an array of arrays. A matrix with M rows and N columns is
actually an array of length M, each entry of which is an array of length N. Example 126 shows

Table 1.19: The array that stores the test

	0	1	2	3	4	5	6	7	8	9
student0	A	B	A	C	C	D	E	E	A	D
student1	D	B	A	B	C	A	E	E	A	D
student2	E	D	D	A	C	B	E	E	A	D
student3	C	B	A	E	D	C	E	E	A	D
student4	A	B	D	C	C	D	E	E	A	D
student5	B	B	E	C	C	D	E	E	A	D
student6	B	B	A	C	C	D	E	E	A	D
student7	E	B	E	C	C	D	E	E	A	D

grades of multiple-choice tests. Suppose there are eight students and ten questions, the answers are stored in a 2D array. Each row records a student's answer to the questions. For example, the following array shown in Table 1.19 stores the test.

Example 126

```
// students' answers to the questions
    char[][] answers = {
     {'A', 'B', 'A', 'C', 'C', 'D', 'E', 'E', 'A', 'D'},
     {'D', 'B', 'A', 'B', 'C', 'A', 'E', 'E', 'A', 'D'},
     {'E', 'D', 'D', 'A', 'C', 'B', 'E', 'E', 'A', 'D'},
     {'C', 'B', 'A', 'E', 'D', 'C', 'E', 'E', 'A', 'D'},
     {'A', 'B', 'D', 'C', 'C', 'D', 'E', 'E', 'A', 'D'},
     {'B', 'B', 'E', 'C', 'C', 'D', 'E', 'E', 'A', 'D'},
     {'B', 'B', 'A', 'C', 'C', 'D', 'E', 'E', 'A', 'D'},
     {'E', 'B', 'E', 'C', 'C', 'D', 'E', 'E', 'A', 'D'}};
```

Note: an array of characters is not a string

Processing Command-Line Arguments :   recall the heading for the method main() *public static void main(String[] args)*..., args is a handle for an array of String values. These string values can be used in the program.

In UNIX and MS-DOS the user types in commands at the prompt, for example,

$C: mkdir\ mydocs$, where mkdir is a program, and mydocs is the argument sent to the program. This is where you can use args.

At the command line enter: *java ClassName*. The java interpreter is called. It would also be possible to enter, *java ClassName argmt$_1$ argmt$_2$ ... argmt$_n$*. The interpreter builds a String array of n elements for ClassName, arg[i] is the handle for *argmt$_i$*. Example 127 lists the command line arguments received by a program:

Example 127

```
public class Arraycommandline {
    public static void main(String[] args){
    System.out.println("There are "+args.length+" arguments");
    for (int i =0; i < args.length; i++)
        System.out.println(args[i]);
    // a Java application to list the command line arguments
    class CommandLine {
        public static void main(String [] args) {
        if (args.length > 0) {
            for (int i = 0; i < args.length; i++) {
            System.out.println("Argument " + i + " = " + args[i]);
```

```
            }
        }
        else {
            System.out.println( "You did not provide any arguments" );
        }
    }
    }
}
}
```

Given a real value (or values), Example 128 will print the square root for all values received as command-line arguments.

Example 128

```
double y;
for (int i=0; i<args.length ; i++)
{
        String str = args[i];
        int n = Integer.parseInt(str);
        y = Math.sqrt(n);
        System.out.println("y= "+y);
}
```

The output of the program is : java Sqrt 4 25 2

   2

   5

   1.414

Example 129 shows a program that accepts two numbers in the range from 1 to 40 from the command line. It then compares these numbers against a single dimension array of five integer elements ranging in value from 1 to 40. The program displays the message BINGO if the two input values are found in the array element.

Example 129

```
>java prob 3 29
>Your first number was 3
 Your second number was 29
 Its Bingo! // this message if 3 and 29 is found
           // in the array
 Bokya!   // this message if 3 and 29 is not found
           // in the array The array was 7 25 5 19 30

 public class prob {
    public static void main(String args[])
    {
      int matches, num1, num2, rnd, spot;
      int bingos[] = {17,6,36, 1, 2}; // default winner array
      // check for right number of parameters
      if (args.length!=2) // must have two numbers
      {
          System.out.println("Syntax: java prob integer1 integer2");
              System.exit(1); // exit program now!
      }
      // get data on the command line and make into integers
          num1 = Integer.parseInt(args[0]);
```

```
        num2 = Integer.parseInt(args[1]);
    // echo the values to the screen
        System.out.print("Your first number was ");
            System.out.println(num1);
        System.out.print("Your second number was ");
            System.out.println(num2);
    }
    // check for winning numbers here
        matches = 0; // set the number of correct numbers
        for (int i=0;i<=4;i++)
        {
            if (num1==bingos[i]) {matches++;}
            if (num2==bingos[i]) {matches++;}
    }
        if (matches==2)
                    {System.out.println("Its BINGO!");} // winner!
        else        {System.out.println("Bokya");} // loser!
        System.out.print("Array was ");
        for (int i=0;i<=4;i++) System.out.print(bingos[i]);
        System.out.println(" ");
}
```

1.7 Some Advanced OOP Topics

1.7.1 Encapsulation

From the internal point of view, objects provide the details of the variables and methods of the class that defines it. From the external point of view, objects provide the services and describe how the object interacts with the rest of the system. From the outside, an object is an encapsulated entity providing a set of specific services. These services define the interface to the object. One object (called the client) may use another object for the services it provides. The client of an object may request its services, but it should not have to be aware of how those services are accomplished. Any changes to the object's state should be made by that object's methods.

It is suggested a client should not access an objects variables directly. That is, an object should be self-governing. An object can be thought of as a black box. The inner parts of the object are encapsulated or hidden from the client. The client invokes the interface methods of the object, which manage the instance data. Figure 1.53 shows the class encapsulation.

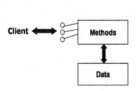

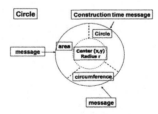

Figure 1.53: Class encapsulation   Figure 1.54: Modifier example

1.7.2 Java Access Modifiers

In Java, encapsulation is accomplished through the appropriate use of visibility modifiers. A modifier is a Java reserved word that specifies particular characteristics of a method or data. The "final" modifier has been introduced to define constants. Java has three visibility modifiers: public, protected, and private. The protected modifier involves inheritance, which will be discussed later. Members of a class that are declared with public visibility can be referenced anywhere. Members of a class that are declared with private visibility can be referenced only within that class. Members declared without a visibility modifier have default visibility and can be referenced by any class in the same package. Example 130 shows visibility declaration. Figure 1.54 illustrates the visibility example.

Example 130

```
public class Box {
private double x,y,z;

// constructor
public Box (double x, double y, double z)
{
        this.x = x;
        this.y = y;
        this.r = r;
 }
// methods to return volume
   public double volume() {
        return x*y*z;
   }
}
```

Members declared without a visibility modifier have default visibility and can be referenced by any class in the same package. Package is used to organize classes. It resolves the name conflicts between class names. To use package, you should add the following line as the first noncomment and nonblank statement in the program: *package packagename;*. If a class is declared without the package statement, the class is said to be placed in the default package. Java recommends that you place classes into packages rather using a default package. For simplicity, however, we mainly use default package in this book. Example 131 illustrates the right use of class within a package.

Example 131

```
package s.t;
public class A {
   private int pv;
   int d;
   public int pb;

   m(...) {
        pv = 0; // OK
        d = 0; // OK
        pb = 0; // OK
   }
}

package s.t;
public class B {
   ...
   m(...) {
        A a = new A(..);
        a.pv = 0; // error
```

Table 1.20: the visibility modifiers

	public	private
Variables	violate encapsulation	enforce encapsulation
Methods	provide services to clients	support other methods in the class

```
        a.d = 0;  // ok
        a.pb = 0; // ok
}
}

package s.u;
public class C {
   ...
   m(...) {
        A a = new A(..);
        a.pv = 0; // error
        a.d = 0;  // error
        a.pb = 0; // ok
}
}
```

If a class is not declared public, it can be accessed only within the same package, as shown in Example 132.

Example 132

```
package p1
class C1
{
   ...
}
public class C2
{
 // can access C1
 ...
}
package p2
public class C3 {
// can not access C1
// can access C2
   ...
}
```

Public variables violate the spirit of encapsulation because they allow the client to "reach in" and modify the object's internal values directly. Therefore, instance variables should not be declared with public visibility. It is acceptable to give a constant public visibility, allowing the constant to be used outside of the class. Public constants do not violate encapsulation because, although the client can access it, its value cannot be changed. Methods that provide the object's services are declared with public visibility so that they can be invoked by clients. Public methods are also called service methods. A method created simply to assist a service method is called a support method. Since a support method is not intended to be called by a client, it should be declared with private visibility. Table 1.20 summarizes the visibility modifiers.

Accessors and Mutators : since instance data is private, a class usually provides services to access and modify data values. An accessor method returns the current value of a variable. A

mutator method changes the value of a variable. The names of accessor and mutator methods take
the form getX and setX, respectively, where X is the name of the value. They are sometimes called
"getters" and "setters". The use of mutators gives the class designer the ability to restrict a client's
options to modify an object's state. A mutator is often designed so that the values of variables
can be set only within particular limits. Example 133 shows the accessors, or "getters/setters".

Example 133

```
public class Box {
    private  double width;
    private  double  height;
    private  double length;

    // methods to return circumference and area
    public double getWidth() { return width;}
    public double getHeight() { return height;}
    public double getLength() { return length;}
    public double setWidth(double x){width= x;}
    public double setHeight(double y){height= y;}
    public double setLength(double z){length= z;}
}
```

1.7.3   Passing Object to Methods

The differences between variables of primitive data types and object types are shown in Figure 1.55.
Figure 1.56 illustrates copying variables of primitive data types and object types. The memory
associated with each object contains just a reference (a memory address) for the actual data.

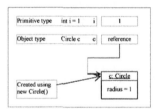

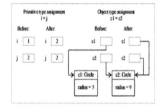

Figure 1.55: Differences between variables of   Figure 1.56: Copying variables of primitive
primitive data types and object types   data types and object types

Sometimes an object has to interact with other objects of the same type; You can pass objects
to methods. For example, you might compare two string objects to arrange alphabetically as
follows: *str1.compare(str2);*. One object (str1) is executing the method and another object (str2)
is passed as a parameter. Like passing an array, passing an object is actually passing the reference
of the object. The following code passes the myCircle object as an argument to the printCircle
method.

```
public class TestPassObject {
    public static void main(String [ ] args) {
        Circle myCircle = new Circle (5.0);
        printCircle(myCircle);
    }

    public static void printCircle(Circle c) {
```

```
System.out.println("The area of the circle of radius"
            + c.getRadius() + "is" + c.getArea());
}
}
```

Java uses "pass-by-value" to pass arguments. In the preceding code, the value of myCircle is passed to the printCircle method. This value is a reference to a Circle object. A method can change an object passed to it as an argument because the method gets a reference to the original object, as the code shows below:

```
// swap the first two elements in the array
public static void swapFirstTwoInArray( int[] array )
{
        int temp = array[0];
        array[0] = array[1];
        array[1] = temp;
}
```

1.7.4 The This Reference

The this keyword can be used either allowing an object to refer itself or refering to a constructor defined in current class. *this*(...) calls another constructor in same class. Often a constructor with few parameters will call a constructor with more parameters, giving default values for the missing parameters. Example 134 and Example 135 illustrate the application of this reference.

Example 134

```
public class Point {
   int m_x; int m_y;

       // constructor
       public Point(int x, int y) {
               m_x = x;
               m_y = y;
       }

       // parameterless default constructor
       public Point() {
         this(0, 0); // calls other constructor
       }
       . . .
}
```

Example 135

```
class Employee {
    private int id, salary;
    private String name;
    public Employee(String newE, int idE) {
        this.name = newE;
        this.id = idE;
    }
    public Employee(String newE, int idE, int salaryE)
    {
        this(newE, idE);  // initialize using the constructor above
```

```
                this.salary = salaryE;
        }
}
```

1.7.5   Class Composition

A class can have references to objects of other classes as members, sometimes referred to as a
"has a" relationship, as the code shown below . Composition is one form of software reuse, in
which a class has as members references to objects of other classes. Example 136 shows the class
composition.

```
class Fruit {
        //...
}
        class Apple {
           private Fruit fruit = new Fruit();
           // Apple has an instance variable that holds a reference to a Fruit object
           //...
}
```

Example 136

```
Public class Date {
   private int month;
   private int day;
   private int year;

   public Date (int theMonth, int theYear, int theMonth)
   {
           month = checkMonth(theMonth);
           year = theYear;
            day = checkDay(theDay);
   }

   public int checkMonth(int aMonth) {...}
   public int checkDay(int aDay) {...}

}
public class Employee {
// employee contains references to two Date objects
   private String firstName;
   private String lastName;
   private Date birthDate;
   private Date hireDate;
   public Employee (String first, String last, Date dateofBirth, Date dateofHire)
   {
           firstName = first;
           lastName = last;
           birthDate = dateofBirth;
           hireDate = dateofHire;
   }

// toString method here:

}
public class EmployeeTest
```

```
{
  public static void main(string  args[ ])
  {
    Date birth = new Date 724 1990
    Date hire  = new Date (3, 12,  2009);
    Employee em = new Employee("Bob", "Blue", birth, hire);
    System.out.println(em);
  }
}
```

1.7.6   Inheritance: Extend Class

Inheritance is a key feature of OOP that offers the ability of a class to inherit an existing class and increase its capabilities. It allows for the implicit definition of variables or methods for a class through an existing class. In short, inheritance allows you to reuse code. Figure 1.57 shows the relationship between the base class and the extend class.

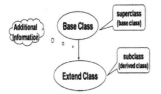

Figure 1.57: base class and extend class   Figure 1.58: Person example

In Figure 1.58, given a class Person, a new class Student is defined as a subclass of Person. This new class Student then inherits all the attributes and methods of the class Person. The Student class has new attributes and new methods and redefines some methods of class Person. Therefore class Student extends class Person. Student poses all the attributes of person as well as additional features. Class Person is the superclass of class Student, while Student is a subclass of person. Thus, inheritance relationships form a hierarchy. Form of Extend Class Definition is shown below :

```
class SubClassB extends SuperClassA {
        // Field Declaration
        // Method Definition
}
```

This means objects of subclass B implicitly have the fields and methods defined in superclass A. As Figure 1.59 shows object class is the super class of all classes. If the super class is not referenced explicitly, the default super class is the object class.

Example 137 is an example of inheritance. Class B inherits, or extends, class A, as shown in Figure 1.60. By convention, the base class is on top and sub-classes are below and point towards the base class.

Example 137

```
public class A {
        int i=0;
        void doSomething(){i=5;}
        }
```

```
class B extends A {
      int j=0;
      void doSomethingMore(){
            j=10;
            i+=j;
      }
}
```

The instances of class B can access to methods and fields in both class B and class A (since they are public). For example:

```
...
B b = new B();// create an instance of class B
b.doSomething(); // access class A methods
b.doSomethingMore();// and class B methods
```

Another class C can in turn inherit class B. The code is shown in Example 138. An instance of class C has its properties and methods to those of both class B and C.

Example 138

```
class C extends B {
int k;
void doEvenMore(){
     doSomething();
     doSomethingMore();
     k=i+j;
     }
}
```

Figure 1.59: Object class

Figure 1.60: Simple inheritance

Example 139 illustrates the application of inheritance.

Example 139

```
class A {    // create a class
   int i, j;

   void showij() {
       System.out.println("i and j: " + i +"   " + j);
   }
 }
class B extends A {  // create a subclass by extending class A
     int k;
     void showk() {
         System.out.println("k:   " + k );
     }
     void sum() {
```

```
        System.out.println("i+j+k: " +(i+j+k));
    }
}
class SimpleInheritance {
    public static void main(String args[]) {
        A superObj = new A();
            B subObj = new B();
            superObj.i = 10;  // the superclass is used by itself
            superObj.j = 20;
            System.out.println("Contents of superObj:  ");
            superObj.showij();
            subObj.i = 7;
        // the subclass has access to all public members of its superclass
            subObj.j = 8;
            subObj.k = 9;
            System.out.println("Contents of subObj:  ");
            subObj.showij();
            subObj.showk();
            System.out.println();
            System.out.println("Sum of i,j,and k in subObj: ");
            subObj.sum();
    }
}
```

Similar to the keyword "this" which is a reference to the "self" class, the keyword "super" is a reference to the superclass. Example 140 shows another simple example of a super class. Here, the use of super acts as somewhat like this: *super.member*, mostly applicable when member names of a subclass hide members by the same name in the superclass. A subclass can call a constructor or any public (or protected) methods of its superclass using the "super". If the subclass constructor uses the superclass constructor, the call to "super" must precede all other statements in the subclass constructor. In another word, the first line of a constructor must either be a call on another constructor in the same class (using "this"), or a call on the superclass constructor (using "super"). A method in the subclass that wants to call an inherited method from the superclass does not need to use the keyword "super" if the two methods do not have the same name, as Example 141 shows.

The super reference can refer the hidden field in the super class, as the code below shows:

```
class SuperClass {
    int a = 1;
    int b = 1;
}
class SubClass extends SuperClass {
    int a = 2;
    int b = super.a;
    // . . .
}
```

Example 140

```
class A {
    int i;
}
class B extends A {
    int i;    // this i hides the i in A

    B(int a, int b) {
```

```
    super.i = a;    // i in A
    i = b;          // i in B
    }
}
```

Example 141

```
class Animal{
        String name;
        public Animal(String name) {
                    this.name = name;
        }
}
class Dog extends Animal{
    // inheritance implements the is-a relationship: a dog  is-a  animal
    int fleas;
    public Dog(String name, int fleas){
    super(name);
    // subclass constructor uses superclass constructor, the call to super must
    // precede all other
    this.fleas = fleas;
    }
}
class Cat extends Animal{
    int hairBalls;
    public Cat(String name, int hairBalls){
        super(name);
        this.hairBalls = hairBalls;
    }
}
```

If the first line is neither of these, the compiler automatically inserts a call to the parameterless super class constructor, as Example 142 shows.

Example 142

```
class Art {
        Art() {System.out.println("Art");}
}
class Drawing extends Art {
        Drawing() {System.out.println("Drawing");}
}
public class Cartoon extends Drawing {
        Cartoon() {System.out.println("Cartoon");}
        public static void main(String[] args) {
                    Cartoon x = new Cartoon();
        }
}
```

The output is :
    Art
    Drawing
    Cartoon
Before you can initialize an object in a constructor, the object's parent constructor must be called first. If you do not write an explicit call to the super() constructor, Java automatically inserts one in your constructor. The default constructor of the superclass will be called before the

subclass constructor is executed, if no superclass constructor is explicitly invoked in the subclass constructor. Example 143 shows a class with a parameterless constructor.

Example 143

```
class Parent {
    int _x;
    Parent(int x) {
        _x = x;
    }
}
```

The above class is compiled without a problem, but this subclass would not be compiled successfully.

```
class Child extends Parent {
        int _y;
        Child(int y) { // this line mysteriously generates an error!
            _y = y;
    }
}
```

The error message from the compiler is:

```
Child.java:5: cannot find symbol : constructor Parent()
```

The problem is : the compiler automatically inserts superclass constructor calls in both constructors, as shown in the code below:

```
Parent(int x) {
    super(); // compiler inserts this statement to call Object().
             // fine, there is a parameterless constructor for Object
    _x = x;
}
```

However, when the Child class constructor is modified to call its superclass constructor, there is a problem, as the code below shows:

```
Child(int y) {
    super();  // Compiler inserts this statement to call Parent()
              // Trouble: the Parent class has no parameterless constructor
    _y = y;
}
```

Therefore, when any constructor is explicitly defined (as in Parent), the compiler no longer produces a default parameterless constructor. The possible solutions are as follows:
Solution 1 Explicit constructor call : usually the best solution is for the subclass constructor to explicitly call the superclass constructor so that its fields are correctly initialized, as the code below shows:

```
Child(int y) {
    super(-666); // Make explicit call to superclass constructor
    _y = y;
}
```

Solution 2 Define a parameterless constructor : You can always define a parameterless constructor to avoid the problem. A constructor should insure that the initial value of an object is valid. Many objects can not give a valid value with a default constructor. In Example 144, the Parent class might be changed to have a parameterless constructor as follows.

Example 144

```
class Parent {
   int _x;
   Parent() { // Parameterless constructor
      this(-666); // call other constructor with default value
   }
   Parent(int x) {  // constructor with a parameter
      _x = x;
   }
}
```

Supposing that a value of -666 makes sense for this class.

Using Inheritance to Achieve Good Software Design: features of good software design include correctness, reliability, robustness, reusability, efficiency and ease of maintenance. Inheritance is a part of good software design. With inheritance, development time can be reduced by building code on ancestors; debugging time can be reduced by testing ancestors; learning time can be reduced because superclass basis is already known and integrity can be maintained since superclass is separately compiled.

1.7.7   Controlling Inheritance Through Visibility Modifier

Visibility modifiers determine which class members get inherited and which do not. Variables and methods declared with public visibility are inherited and those with private visibility are NOT. However, public variables violate the goal of encapsulation. There is a third visibility modifier that helps in inheritance situations: protected.

The protected visibility modifier allows a member of a base class to be inherited into the child. Protected visibility provides more encapsulation than public does. However, protected visibility is not as tightly encapsulated as private visibility.

Private members of the superclass are not inherited by the subclass. A subclass can only access the public and protected members of its superclass. Although a subclass cannot directly access the private members of its superclass, it may call the public (or protected) methods of its superclass, which may access the private members of the superclass.

In summary, the execution order for the constructor of extend class is as follows:

1) Call the constructor of the super class.

2) Execute the part of initializing the field.

3) Execute the body of the constructor.

You may use super() to explicit call the constructor of the super class, as Example 145 shows.

Example 145

```
class SuperClass {
   int a, b;
   SuperClass( ) {
      a = 1;
      b = 1;
   }
   SuperClass(int a, int b){
      this.a = a;
      this.b = b;
```

```
    }
}

class SubClass extends SuperClass {
    int c;
    SubClass( ) {
        c = 1;
    }
    SubClass(int a, int b, int c) {
        super(a, b);
        this.c = c;
    }
}
```

1.7.8   Overriding Methods

A child class can override the definition of an inherited method in favor of its own. That is, a child can redefine a method that it inherits from its parent. The new method must have the same signature as the parent's method, but can have different code in the body. The type of the object executing the method determines which version of the method is invoked. Access to the overridden methods and properties can be obtained with the *super* keyword, as Example 146 shows.

Example 146

```
public class A {
    int i=0;
    int j=3;
    void doSomething(){i=5;}
}
class B extends A {
    int j=0;
    void doSomething(){
        j=10;
        // call the overridden method
        super.doSomething();
        // can use the shadowed property
        j=j+super.j;
    }
}
```

The concepts of overloading and overriding are different. Overloading deals with multiple methods in the same class with the same name but different signatures. Overriding deals with two methods, which have the same signature. However one method is in a parent class and another one is in a child class. Overloading lets you define a similar operation in different ways for different data and object types.

Overloading method differs regarding the number and type of parameters. Overriding method equals regarding the number and type of parameter. Overriding method is replaced with the method of subclass, where the meaning of the method on the super class is changed in subclass. Example 147 illustrates the difference between overloading method and overriding method.

Example 147

```
class SuperClass {
    void methodA ( ) {
        System.out.println(" In SuperClass . . . ");
```

```
        }
}

class SubClass extends SuperClass {
    void methodA ( ) {
        System.out.println(" In SubClass . . . Overriding!");
    }

    void methodA (int i) {
      System.out.println(" In SubClass . . . Overloading!");
    }
}
public class OverridingAndOverloading {
    public static void main(String[ ] args) {
        SuperClass obj1 = new SuperClass( );
        SubClass obj2 = new SubClass( );
        obj1.methodA( );
        obj2.methodA( );
        obj2.methodA(1);
    }
}
```

Final Classes and Methods :   final classes methods and variables can not be extended. Methods that are final can not be overridden by subclasses. Methods called from constructors should generally be declared final. If a constructor calls a non-final method, a subclass may redefine that method to behave in surprising or undesirable ways. Note that you can also declare an entire class final, which prevents the class from being subclass.

Static method or final method cannot be overridden, as Example 148 shows. All methods in final class are final method implicitly, as shown below:

```
final class ClassA {
        void methodA()   /* ... */
        void methodB()   /* ... */
    }
```

Example 148

```
// methods with differing type signatures are overloaded - not overridden.
class A {
  int i, j;
  A(int a, int b) {
    i = a;
    j = b;
  }
  // display i and j
   void show() {
     System.out.println("i and j: " + i + " " + j);
  }
}
// create a subclass by extending class A
class B extends A {
  int k;
  B(int a, int b, int c) {
    super(a,b);
    k = c;
  }
```

```
// overload show()
void show(String msg) {
  System.out.println(msg + k);
  }
}
class Override {
  public static void main(String args[]) {
    B subOb = new B(1, 2, 3);

    subOb.show("This is k: "); // this calls show() in B
    subOb.show(); // this calls show() in A
    }
}
```

1.7.9   Abstract Class

Abstract classes permit declaration of classes that define only part of an implementation, leaving the subclasses to provide the details. A class is considered abstract if at least one method in the class has no implementation. Any class with an abstract method must be declared abstract. An abstract class can contain instance variables and methods that are fully implemented. Non-abstract classes from which objects can be instantiated are called concrete classes. Abstract classes are only used as super classes. The use of abstract classes is a design decision. It helps you to establish common elements in a class that is too general to instantiate. In another word, abstract classes and methods force prototype standards to be followed (i.e., they provide templates). In Example 149, all animals have some common fields and methods, but each can add more fields and methods.

Example 149

```
public abstract class Animal { // class with an abstract method
    private String name;
    public Animal (String nm) {
        name = nm;
    }
    public String getAnimalName() {
        return name;
    }
    public void setAnimalName(String name) {
        this.name = name;
    }
    public abstract void speak();
}
```

Abstract classes are like regular classes with data fields and methods, but you cannot create instances of abstract classes using the new operator. If the subclass overrides all the abstract methods in the superclass, an object of the subclass can be instantiated.

Abstract method does not have real implementation but has only method declaration. To create an abstract method, you need to provide the keyword "abstract", the intended method type, name, and arguments, but you do not provide any statements within the method. The child of an abstract class must override the abstract methods of the parent, otherwise it will be considered abstract too. In another word, an abstract method cannot be contained in a non-abstract class. An abstract method cannot be defined as final (because it must be overridden) or static (because it has no definition yet). In Example 150, the speak() method within the Dog class and Cow class is required because the abstract parent Animal class contains an abstract speak() method.

Example 150

```
public class Dog extends Animal {
    public void speak() {
        System.out.println("Woof!");
    }
}
public class Cow extends Animal {
    public void speak() {
        System.out.println("Moo!");
    }
}
public class UseAnimals{
    public static void main(String[] args){
        Dog myDog = new Dog();
        Cow myCow = new Cow();
        myDog.setAnimalName("My dog Murphy");
        myCow.setAnimalName("My cow Elsie");
        System.out.print(myDog.getName() + " says ");
        myDog.speak();
        System.out.print(myCow.getName() + " says ");
        myCow.speak();
    }
}
```

There are some notes which relates to an abstract class. An abstract class cannot be instantiated using the new operator, but you can still define its constructors, which are invoked in the constructors of its subclasses. A class that contains abstract method must be abstract. However, it is possible to declare an abstract class that contains no abstract methods. In this case, you cannot create instances of the class. It is used as a base class for defining a new subclass. A subclass can be abstract even if its superclass is concrete. A subclass can override a method from its superclass to declare it abstract. This is unusual but may be useful when the implementation in the superclass becomes invalid in the subclass. You cannot create an instance from an abstract class using new operator, but an abstract class can be used as a data type.

1.7.10 Dynamic Method Binding

Even though you cannot instantiate any objects of an abstract class, you can indirectly create a reference to a superclass abstract object. A reference is not an object, but it points to a memory address. When you create a reference, you do not use the keyword new; instead, you create a variable name in which you can hold the memory address of a concrete object. Even though a reference to an abstract superclass object is not concrete, you can store a reference to a concrete subclass object there.

An instantiation of a subclass "is a" superclass object. For instance, every faculty "is an" employee; every dog "is an" animal. That is why you can reference a subclass object with a superclass variable. For example: $Animal mydog = newDog()$;

The opposite is not true, that is, an animal is not a dog. In another word, because every subclass object "is a" superclass member, you can convert subclass objects to superclass objects. Dynamic method binding means correct method bounded to object based on the current (dynamic) context. Example 151 illustrates the dynamic method binding. Example 152 shows super class reference variable can point to subclass object.

Example 151

```
public class AnimalReference {
    public static void main(String[] args) {
        Animal ref;
        Cow aCow = new Cow("Mabel");
        Dog aDog = new Dog("Rover");
        ref = aCow;
        ref.speak();
        ref = aDog;
        ref.speak();
    }
}
```

Example 152

```
class A
{
 void show(){
  System.out.println("This is show() in A");
  }
}
class B extends A
{
 void show() {
  System.out.println("This is show() in B");
  }
}
class subclassref {
    public static void main(
            String args[])
  {

                A a1 = new A();
                a1.show();
                a1 = new B();
                a1.show();
  }
}
```

Dynamic method binding refers to the ability of the program to select the correct subclass method. Dynamic method binding is the most useful when you want to create a method that has one or more parameters that might be one of several types. In Example 153, the header for the talkingAnimal() method accepts any type of Animal argument.

Example 153

```
public class TalkingAnimalDemo
{
    public static void main(String[] args)
    {
      Dog dog = new Dog();
      Cow cow = new Cow();
      dog.setAnimalName("Ginger");
      cow.setAnimalName("Molly");
      talkingAnimal(dog);
      talkingAnimal(cow);
    }
```

```
public static void talkingAnimal(Animal animal)
{ // the method can be used in programs that contain Dog objects,
  // cow objects or objects of any class that descends from Animal
  System.out.println("Come one come all");
  System.out.println("See the amazing talking animal!");
  System.out.println( animal.getAnimalName() + " says");
  animal.speak();
  System.out.println("***************");
}
}
```

It can be convenient to create an array of generic animal references. An animal array might contain individual elements that are Dog, Cow, or Snake objects. The following statement creates an array of three Animal references: *Animal[] ref = new Animal[3]*; This statement reserves enough computer memory for three Animal objects named ref[0], ref[1], and ref[2]. The statement does not actually instantiate Animals as Animals are abstract, as shown in Example 154.

Example 154

```
public class AnimalArrayDemo
{
   public static void main(String[] args)
   {
     Animal[] ref = new Animal[3];
     ref[0] = new Dog();
     ref[1] = new Cow();
     ref[2] = new Snake();
     for(int x = 0; x < 3; ++x)
        ref[x].speak();
   }
}
```

1.7.11   Interface

Java supports single inheritance, meaning that a derived class can have only one parent class. Multiple inheritance means class derives from more than one superclass. Java does not allow multiple inheritance though. Rationale for banning multiple inheritance is as follows :

1.It may produce confused inheritance lines.

2.There may be possible name conflict.

3.Ambiguity may get involved in binding super( ).

4.Interface is an alternative to multiple inheritance.

Interface looks much like a class, except all of its methods. Interface must be abstract and all of its data (if any) must be static final. You may use the keyword "implements" and the interface name in the class header. Interface implements exposes elements of the program to the user without exposing the source code. You may use interfaces to ensure that certain classes have particular methods defined. Example 155 illustrates a worker interface.

Example 155

```
public abstract class animal {
        private String nameOfAnimal;
        public abstract void speak();
        public String getAnimalName() {
                return nameOfanimal;
        }
```

```
        public void setAnimalName(String name) {
                nameOfanimal = name;
        }
}
public class Dog extends Animal {
        public void speak() {
                System.out.println("woof!");
        }
}
public interface Worker {
        public void work();
    // body not defined, an abstract method
}
```

In the below example, both are correct. The abstract and public keywords are implied, so the shorthand is recommended.

```
interface FooInterface{
  void foo1();
    int foo2(double x);
}
abstract interface FooInterface{
  public abstract void foo1();
  public abstract int foo2(double x);
}
```

Interface describes what a class does, not how it does. Features are specific to an interface. All methods are implicitly abstract and final. All data are implicitly public, static and final. Interface methods have full headers, but empty bodies. User subclass must define each interface method.

In Example 156, WorkingDog extends Dog implements Working. WorkingDog is tested in DemoWorkingDogs. The WorkingDog object uses the following methods:
setName(), getName() inherited from Animal, as shown in Example 155.
speak( ) inherited from the Dog (which extends Animal), as shown in Example 155.
setHoursOfTraining( ), getHoursOfTraining( ) in WorkingDog;
work( ) implemented through Worker interface.

Example 156

```
public class WorkingDog extends Dog implements Working {
    private int hoursOfTraining;
    public WorkingDog(String nm) {
                super(nm);
    }
    public void setHoursOfTraining(int hrs){
            hoursOfTraining = hrs;
    }
    public int getHoursOfTraining(){
            return hoursOfTraining;
    }
    public void work() { // this method specific to WorkingDog
     speak();
     System.out.println("I can herd sheep and cows");
     System.out.println("I have " + hoursOfTraining + " hours of professional training!");
    }
}
public class DemoWorkingDog {
```

```
public static void main(String[ ] args) {
  WorkingDog aSheepHerder = new WorkingDog();
  aSheepHerder.setName("Sarkozy the Collie");
  System.out.println(aSheepHerder.getName()+ " says");
  aSheepHerder.speak();
  aSheepHerder.work();
}
}
```

Comparing Abstract Classes and Interfaces :   inheritance relation ia also applied to interfaces. There are "superinterface" and "subinterface". Multiple inheritance is allowed, that is, an interface may extend multiple interfaces, and a class may implement multiple interfaces. The difference between abstract classes and interfaces is shown below:

- Abstract Class: you cant instantiate concrete objects. Abstract classes can contain non-abstract methods. Class can inherit from only one abstract superclass.

- Interface: you cant instantiate concrete objects. All methods within an interface must be abstract. Class can implement multiple interfaces

The application of these classes is shown as follows:

- Abstract Class: you can create an abstract class when you want to provide data or methods that subclasses can inherit AND the subclasses will need to override some specific methods.

- Interface: you can create an interface when you know what actions you want to include, but you want every user to define behavior separately

Example 157 consists of classes implementing the area and volume interface shown in Figure 1.61.

Example 157

```
class circle implements Area{
 ...
 public double area(){...}
}
class Rectangle implements Area{
 ...
 public double area(){...}
}
class BOX implements Area,Volume {
 ...
 public double area()  {...}
 public double volume() {...}
}
```

Interfaces contain data that is public, static and final. You may use constants in interface in order to provide data that can be reused without re-declaration. Example 158 provides a number of constants for a pizzeria Class implementing interface that can use permanent values.

Example 158

```
public interface PizzaConstants {
  public static final int SMALL_DIAMETER = 12;
  public static final int LARGE_DIAMETER = 16;
  public static final double TAX_RATE = 0.07;
```

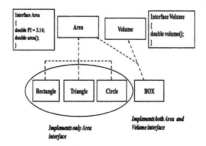

Figure 1.61: Implementing the area and volume Interface

```
    public static final String COMPANY = "Antonio's Pizzeria";
}
public class PizzaDemo implements PizzaConstants {
    public static void main(String[] args){
        double specialPrice = 11.25;
        System.out.println("Welcome to "     + COMPANY);
        System.out.println("We are having a special offer: \na"
                        + SMALL_DIAMETER + " inch pizza with four ingredients\nor a "
                        + LARGE_DIAMETER + " inch pizza with one ingredient\nfor only $"
                        + specialPrice);
        System.out.println("With tax, that is only $" +
                                (specialPrice + specialPrice * TAX_RATE));
    }
}
```

1.8 Lab Exercises

1.8.1 Lab 1 - Elementary Programming

1. Get you familiar with the process of entering, compiling and executing a Java program. We use a text editor to create a file containing a program and save the file. To save time we will use the the the simple program Welcome.java.

   OpenWelcome.java(saved on your memory stick) in EditPlus (or notepad) and have a look at it; Now open the command window, compile and run the program.

   ```
   Compile: F:\ javac Welcome.java
   Run: F:\java Welcome.java
   ```

2. Use a text editor to create a file containing the following program and save the file as *ConversionEx1.java*, then compile and execute your program.

   ```
   public class ConversionEx1 {
       public static void main(String args[])
       {
        int x,y;
        x=(int)22.5+(int)34.7;
   ```

```
        y=(int)'A'+(int)'a';
        System.out.println("x="+x);
        System.out.println("y="+y);
    }
}
```

3. Use a text editor to create a file containing the following program and save the file as *ConversionEx2.java*, then compile and execute your program.

```
class ConversionEx2 {
    public static void main( String args[]) {
        byte b;
        int i = 257;
        double d = 323.142;
        System.out.println("\n Conversion of int to byte.");
        b = (byte) i;
        System.out.println("i and b " + i + " " +b);
        System.out.println("Conversion of double to int.");
        i = (int) d;
        System.out.println("d ad i " + d + " " + i);
        System.out.println("\n Conversion of double to byte.");
        b = (byte) d;
        System.out.println("d and b " + d + " " + b);
    }
}
```

4. Write a program that accepts a time duration in hours , minutes and seconds (one at a time) and then prints the equivalent number of seconds.

5. Write a program that accepts a time duration in minutes. It then converts to hours and minutes and outputs the result.

Solutions for Lab1 Exercises

Q4. Write a program that accepts a time duration in hours, minutes and seconds (one at a time) and then prints the equivalent number of seconds.

```
public class Lab1Q4
{
public static void main(String args[])
    {
        int timeHour, timeMinute, timeSecond,totalDurationSecond;
        System.out.println("Enter hours in the time duration:");
        timeHour= Keyboard.readInt();
        System.out.println("Enter minutes in the time duration:");
        timeMinute= Keyboard.readInt();
        System.out.println("Enter seconds in the time duration:");
        timeSecond= Keyboard.readInt();
        totalDurationSecond = timeHour*3600 +timeMinute*60+timeSecond;
        System.out.println("Total time duration in second is " + totalDurationSecond);
    }
}
```

Q5. Write a program that accepts a time duration in minutes. It then converts to hours and minutes and outputs the result.

```
public class Lab1Q5 {
public static void main(String args[])
{
    int timeHour, timeMinute, DurationMinutes;
    System.out.println("Enter the time duration in minutes:");
    DurationMinutes= Keyboard.readInt();
    timeHour = (int)DurationMinutes/60;
    timeMinute = DurationMinutes%60;
    System.out.println("There are " + timeHour + " hours and "+ timeMinute + "minutes.");
```

1.8.2   Lab 2 - Input/output, Programming Statement

1. Find at least five syntax errors in the following program

```
public class Ex10
{
    Public static void main ( String args)
        { system.out.print( this program adds two numbers );
    x = 5 ;
    int y = 3.5 ;
    System.out.print("The total of " + x + "and" + y is ) ;
    System.out.printline( total );
}
]
```

After correcting the program, compile and execute it.

2. Write a program that prompts the user for two integers, reads and stores them. The program then prints out both integers, each on a separate line. The program prints the product of the two integers on the third line.

3. Write a program that prompts for two integers and stores them as firstNum and secondNum. The program then swaps the contents of these variables and outputs the new values of firstNum and secondNum.

4. Write a program that prompts the user for three integers and reads them. It then finds the average of the three numbers and prints the result to the screen.

5. An absolute value function is one that accepts a positive or negative number and outputs a positive number of the same magnitude. Write a program that asks for a number to be entered and prints the absolute value of that number.

6. Write a program that accepts a number, checks whether it is greater than or equal to zero and then computes the square root of that number (use the sqrt() method from the Math class). If the number is negative an error message is generated.

Solutions for Lab2 Exercises

```
1. public class Lab2Q1
   {
       public static void main ( String args[])
       {
           System.out.print( "this program adds two numbers\n");
           int x = 5 ;
           double y = 3.5 ;
           double total = x+y;
           System.out.print("The total of " + x + " and " + y + " is " ) ;
```

```
            System.out.println( total );
        }
    }
```

```
2. public class Lab2Q2
   {
       public static void main ( String args[])
       {
           int num1, num2, result;
           System.out.print( "Please enter two integers\n");
           num1 = Keyboard.readInt();
           num2 = Keyboard.readInt();
           System.out.println( "The first integer you entered is " + num1 );
           System.out.println( "The second integer you entered is " + num2 );
           result = num1*num2;
           System.out.println( "The product of the two integers is " + result );
       }
   }
```

```
3. public class Lab2Q3
   {
       public static void main ( String args[])
       {
           int firstNum, secondNum, temporary;
           System.out.print( "Please enter two integers\n");
           firstNum = Keyboard.readInt();
           secondNum = Keyboard.readInt();
           temporary = firstNum;
           firstNum = secondNum;
           secondNum = temporary;
           System.out.println( "The new value of first integer from swapping is "
                              + firstNum );
           System.out.println( "The new value of second integer from swapping is "
                              + secondNum );
       }
   }
```

```
4. public class Lab2Q4
   {
       public static void main ( String args[])
       {
           int num1, num2, num3;
           double average;
           System.out.print( "Please enter three integers\n");
           num1 = Keyboard.readInt();
           num2 = Keyboard.readInt();
           num3 = Keyboard.readInt();
           average = (num1+num2+num3)/3;
           System.out.println( "The average of the three integers is " + average );
       }
   }
```

```
5. public class Lab2Q5
   {
```

```
    public static void main ( String args[])
    {
        double num, absNum;
        System.out.print( "Enter a number: \n");
        num = Keyboard.readDouble();
        absNum = Math.abs(num);
        System.out.println( "The absolute value of your number is " + absNum );
    }
}
```

6. public class Lab2Q6
```
   {
       public static void main ( String args[])
       {
           double num, sqrtNum;
           System.out.print( "Enter a number: \n");
           num = Keyboard.readDouble();
           if (num<0)
           System.out.println("There is no real solution for square root
               of a negative number.");
           else
           {
            sqrtNum = Math.sqrt(num);
            System.out.println("The square root of your number is " + sqrtNum );
           }
       }
   }
```

1.8.3 Lab 3 - Control Statements (if , if-else, switch), Repetition Statements (while)

1. The following program declares an integer age, prompts the user to enter a value and classifies their age. There are some errors in the program. Your task is to compile the program, look at the error messages, and then modify it until it works.

```
public class ClassifyAge{
public static void main(String args[]){
    System.out.println("Welcome to Age Classification Program.");
    System.ou.print("Enter age : "|;

    int age = Keyboard.readInt();

    if (age = 0) // for a person born, but not yet having reached first birthday
    {
        System.out.println ("Person aged " + age + " is a baby."):
    }
    else if age <= 12 // for person between 1 and 12
    {
        System.out.println ("Person aged" | age | " is a child.");
    }
    else if (12 < age 13) // for person between 13 and 19
            {
                System.out.println ("Person aged " + age + " is a teenager.");
            }
            else if ( age >19 && age <= 65) // for person between 20 and 65
                {
```

Table 1.21: Leap Year 1800-2400

1804	1904	2004	2104	2204	2304
1808	1908	2008	2108	2208	2308
1812	1912	2012	2112	2212	2312
1816	1916	2016	2116	2216	2316
1820	1920	2020	2120	2220	2320
1824	1924	2024	2124	2224	2324
1828	1928	2028	2128	2228	2328
1832	1932	2032	2132	2232	2332
1836	1936	2036	2136	2236	2336
1840	1940	2040	2140	2240	2340
1844	1944	2044	2144	2244	2344
1848	1948	2048	2148	2248	2348
1852	1952	2052	2152	2252	2352
1856	1956	2056	2156	2256	2356
1860	1960	2060	2160	2260	2360
1864	1964	2064	2164	2264	2364
1868	1968	2068	2168	2268	2368
1872	1972	2072	2172	2272	2372
1876	1976	2076	2176	2276	2376
1880	1980	2080	2180	2280	2380
1884	1984	2084	2184	2284	2384
1888	1988	2088	2188	2288	2388
1892	1992	2092	2192	2292	2392
1896	1996	2096	2196	2296	2396

```
                    System.out.println ("Person aged " + age + " is an adult.");
           }
           else if ( age > 65 && age <= 120) // for person older than 65
           {
            System.out.println ("Person aged " + age + " is a senior citizen.");
           }
                    else // for unknown age
                    {
                    System.out.println ("Unknown age classification.");
                    }
         System.out.println ();
         System.out.println ("Done with Age Classification Program.");
         }
    }
```

2. Write a program that prompts the user for three real numbers and then determines if the three numbers can be the three sides of a triangle. For the three numbers to be the sides of a triangle, none should be bigger than the sum of the other two.

3. Write a program that accepts two characters (assume the same case), arranges them in alphabetical order and prints them to the screen.

4. A leap year is a year with 366 days. A year is a leap year if it is divisible by 4 except for the century years (divisible by 100). Century years are only leap years if they are divisible by 400. Write a program that accepts a year and determines if it is a leap year. Leap Year 1800-2400 is shown in the Table 1.21.

5. Write a program that displays integers from 1 to 10, each on one line.

6. Write a program that sums the digits in an integer. For example, $1729 \rightarrow 1 + 7 + 2 + 9 = 19$

7. Write a program that displays all the even integers between 1 to 20.

8. Write a program that displays all the odd integers between 1 to a user entered integer.

9. Write a program that recommends the number of calories a person should eat each day. Calories are units of energy found in all foods. Base your recommendation on the person's weight and whether the person has an active or sedentary(inactive) lifestyle. If the person is sedentary, that person's activity factor is 13. If the person is active, that person's activity factor is 15. Multiply the activity factor by the person's weight to get the recommended number of calories. Start your program by:

   1) having the user enter their weight;

   2) having the user enter whether they have active or sedentary lifestyle, as a character, 'A' for active or 'S' sedentary;

   3) use a switch selection statement to use the appropriate calculation for the recommended calories for the selected lifestyle;

   4) print out your results on the screen.

10. Write a program that displays all the multiples of 3 between 1 and 100, i.e., 3, 6, 9, 12, 15, 18, 21 . . . 99.

11. Write and run a Java program that generates a random integer and then uses nested if . . . else statements to determine whether it is divisible by 2,3,5,6,10,15 , or 30. HINT: add the import java.util.Random; in the first line in your program.

12. Write a program that allow a user to enter two integer numbers for involving in mathematical operations as his/her choice. Then the program takes a number from the user and checks weather the number lies between 1 to 5. If the user enter the number 1 then the program print addition result, and if the user enter the 2 then the program print subtraction and so on, up to number 4. Otherwise when the user enter after 4 there will a message "Invalid Entry" massage printed out.

Solutions for Lab3 Exercises

```
1. public class ClassifyAgeDebugged{
     public static void main (String args []) {
         System.out.println ("Welcome to Age Classification Program.");
         System.out.print ("Enter age : ");
         int age = Keyboard.readInt();
         if (age == 0)
         // for a person born, but not yet having reached first birthday
         {
             System.out.println ("Person aged " + age + " is a baby.");
         }
         else if (age <= 12) // for person between 1 and 12
             {
             System.out.println ("Person aged " + age + " is a child.");
             }
             else if (age>12 && age <= 19) // for person between 13 and 19
             {
                 System.out.println ("Person aged " + age + " is a teenager.");
             }
                 else if ( age >19 && age <= 65) // for person between 20 and 65
                 {
                     System.out.println ("Person aged " + age + " is an adult.");
```

```
                }
                    else if ( age > 65 && age <= 120) // for person older than 65
                    {
                     System.out.println ("Person aged " + age + " is a senior citizen.");
                    }
                            else // for unknown age
                            {
                            System.out.println ("Unknown age classification.");
                            }
            System.out.println ();
            System.out.println ("Done with Age Classification Program.");
            }
    }
```

2.
```
public class Lab3Q2 {
    public static void main ( String args[]) {
        double l1, l2, l3;
        System.out.print( "Please enter three real numbers\n");
        l1 = Keyboard.readDouble();
        l2 = Keyboard.readDouble();
        l3 = Keyboard.readDouble();
        if (l1+l2>l3&&l1+l3>l2&&l2+l3>l1)
        System.out.println( "A triangle can be formed by the three numbers");
        else
        System.out.println("A triangle can not be formed by the three numbers");
    }
}
```

3.
```
public class Lab3Q3 {
    public static void main ( String args[]) {
        char char1, char2;
        System.out.print( "Please enter three real numbers\n");
        char1 = Keyboard.readChar();
        char2 = Keyboard.readChar();
        if (char1<char2)
            System.out.println( "The two characters in alphabetical
            order are " + char1 + " and " + char2);
        else
            System.out.println( "The two characters in alphabetical
            order are " + char2 + " and " + char1);
    }
}
```

4. Solution1:

```
public class Lab3Q4a {
    public static void main ( String args[]) {
        // declare variables
        int year;
        System.out.print( "Please enter a year\n");
        year = Keyboard.readInt();
        if (year % 400 == 0)
        {
        System.out.print( year + " is a leap year\n");;
        }
```

```
else if (year % 100 == 0)
{
System.out.print( year + " is NOT a leap year\n");;
}
    else if (year % 4 == 0)
    {
    System.out.print(year + " is a leap year\n");;
    }
        else
        System.out.print( year + " is NOT a leap year\n");;
}
}
```

Solution2:

```
public class Lab3Q4b {
public static void main ( String args[]) {
    // declare variable
    int year;
    System.out.print( "Please enter a year\n");
    year = Keyboard.readInt();
    boolean isLeapYear =(((year % 4) == 0) && ((year % 100) != 0))
        || ((year % 400) == 0);
    if (isLeapYear) {
        System.out.println(year + " is a leap year.");
        }
    else {
        System.out.println(year + " is NOT a leap year.");
        }
    }
}
```

```
5. public class Lab3Q5 {
    public static void main ( String args[]) {
        final int LIMIT=10;
        int count=1;
        while( count < LIMIT)
        {
        System.out.print( count +"\n");
        count++;
        }
    }
}
```

```
6. public class Lab3Q6 {
    public static void main ( String args[]) {
        System.out.println("This program sums the digits in
        an integer.\n");
        System.out.println("Enter a positive integer: ");
        int n = Keyboard.readInt();
        int dsum = 0;
        while (n > 0) {
        dsum += (n % 10);
        n = n /10;
        }
```

```
        System.out.println("The sum of the digits is " + dsum + ".");
    }
}
```

7.
```java
public class Lab3Q7 {
    public static void main ( String args[]) {
    final int LIMIT=20;
    int count=1;
    while (count < LIMIT )
        {
        if (count%2==0)
        {
        System.out.print("\t"+count);
        }
        count++;
        }
    }
}
```

8.
```java
public class Lab3Q8{
    public static void main ( String args[])
    {
    int limit;
    System.out.println("Enter an integer :");
    limit = Keyboard.readInt();
    int count=1;
    while (count < limit )
        {
        if (count%2 !=0)
            {
            System.out.print("\t"+count);
            }
        count++;
        }
    }
}
```

9.
```java
public class Lab3Q9 {
    public static void main ( String args[])
    {
    double calories;
    int factor =1;
    System.out.println("Enter your weight:");
    double weight = Keyboard.readDouble();
    System.out.println(" Are you active (A) or sedentary (S) :");
    char style = Keyboard.readChar();
    switch(style)
        {
        case 'A':
        factor = 15;
        break;
        case 'S':
        factor = 13;
        break;
```

```
        }
    calories = factor * weight;
    System.out.println("The recommended calories for you: " + calories );
        }
}
```

10.
```
public class Lab3Q10 {
    public static void main ( String args[])
    {
    System.out.print("Displays all the multiples of 3 btw 1 and 100\n");
    final int LIMIT=100;
    int count=1;
    while( count < LIMIT)
        {
        if (count%3==0)
        {
        System.out.print( count + "\t");
        }
        count++;
        }
    }
}
```

11.
```
import java.util.Random;
public class Lab3Q11
{
    public static void main ( String args[])
    {
    Random randomObj = new Random();
    int n = randomObj.nextInt();
    System.out.println("n = " + n);
    if (n%2==0)
    if (n%3==0)
    if (n%5==0)
        System.out.println(" n is divisible by 30");
    else
        System.out.println(" n is divisible by 6 but not 30");
    else
    if (n%5==0)
        System.out.println(" n is divisible by 10 but not 3");
    else
        System.out.println(" n is divisible by 2 but not 3 or 5");
    else
        if (n%3==0)
        if (n%5==0)
        System.out.println(" n is divisible by 15 but not 2");
        else
        System.out.println(" n is divisible by 3 but not 2 or 5");
        else
        if (n%5==0)
        System.out.println(" n is divisible by 5 but not 6");
        else
        System.out.println(" n is not divisible by 2,3 or 5");
    }
}
```

```
12. public class Lab3Q12
    {
    public static void main ( String args[])
    {
        System.out.println("Enter two integers x and y: ");
        int x = Keyboard.readInt();
        int y = Keyboard.readInt();
        System.out.println("Enter an integer indicating following operation: ");
        System.out.println("1. Add");
        System.out.println("2. Subtract");
        System.out.println("3. Multiply");
        System.out.println("4. Divide");
        System.out.println("enter your choice:");
        int a= Keyboard.readInt();
        switch (a){
        case 1:
            System.out.println("The addition of the two numbers: " + (x+y));
            break;
        case 2:
            System.out.println("The subtraction of the two numbers: " + (x-y));
            break;
        case 3:
            System.out.println("The multiplication of the numbers: "+ (x*y));
            break;
        case 4:
            System.out.println("The division of the numbers: "+ (x/y));
            break;
        default:
            System.out.println("Invalid Entry!");
            }
        }
    }
```

1.8.4   Lab 4 - More on Control Statements (while/do-while/for)

1. Write a program that classifies a given amount of money into its component smaller monetary units. The program will let the user enter a decimal amount representing a total in dollars and cents, and will output a report listing the monetary equivalent in dollars, quarters, dimes, nickels, and pennies.

2. Write a program that uses nested loop to print the following output:

```
              1
           2  1  2
        3  2  1  2  3
     4  3  2  1  2  3  4
  5  4  3  2  1  2  3  4  5
```

3. The factorial function of a positive integer n is the product of all the integers from 1 to n. For example, the factorial of 5 is 1x2x3x4x5 = 120. This is usually expressed as 5!=120. By definition 0!=1. Write a program that calculates the factorial n! . Prompt the user for n which is in the range 0 to 20.

4. Write a program to print the following table to convert temperature from Celsius to Fahrenheit:

Celsius	Fahrenheit
5	41
4	39
...	
-5	23

The conversion formula is $f = c * 9/5 + 32$. The computation must be done in real number mode before converted to the nearest Fahrenheit degrees.

5. Write a program that first reads an integer n in the range 0 to 10 and then tabulates the sin function for n equally spaced values of x in the range 0 to p. Use the constant Math.PI and the Math.sin() method.

6. Predict the output from the following program. Then run it to confirm your prediction:

```
public class Lab4Q6{
    public static void main(String[] args){
    int count =0;
    for (int i =0; i < 3 ; i++ )
    resume:
    for (int j = 0; j < 4; j++ )
    for ( int k =0; k< 5 ; k++ )
    {
        ++count;
        if (i==1 && j==2 && k==3)
        break resume;
    }
    System.out.println("\tcount = " + count);
}
}
```

7. Write and run a program that tests the summation formula:

$$\sum_{i=1}^{n} i = \frac{n(n+1)}{2}$$

Hint: Generate a random integer n in the range 0 to 100, sum the integers from 1 to n, compute the value of the expression on the rightand then print both values to see if they agree. Your output should look like this:

```
x = 0.12363869
n = 14
sum = 105
n*(n+1)/2 = 105
```

8. Suppose you have a scheme to become a millionaire. In the first month, you save $1, in the second month $2, in the third $4, in the fourth $8, and so on. Write a program to find out how long it will take you to become a millionaire.

9. Consider the scheme in the previous question. Write a program to find out how much you would save by the end of the first year.

10. $1000 is deposited in an investment account. At the beginning of each subsequent month a further $100 is deposited. At the end of each month interest is added to the account at a rate of 6% p.a. (i.e., 0.5% per month). Write a program that calculates the balance at the end of five years.

11. Write a program to display the following pattern of * symbols. In each row there has eight starts and the ninth * will automatically change to next row.

```
*   *   *   *   *   *   *   *
*   *   *   *   *   *   *   *
*   *   *   *   *   *   *   *
*   *   *   *   *   *   *   *
*   *   *   *   *   *   *   *
```

12. Using a nested for loop, write a program that will print the following:

```
1
1   2
1   2   3
1   2   3   4
1   2   3   4   5
```

13. Write a program that reads in a series of marks, each in the range 1 to 100. When value .1 is entered the program terminates and outputs the statistics:

   - the mean mark;
   - the maximum mark;
   - the minimum mark;
   - the number of marks 50 or above;
   - the standard deviation. Note: use the formula

$$s = \sqrt{\frac{\sum x^2}{n} - (\bar{x}^2)}$$

14. We can approximate PI by using the following series: $PI = 4 * (1 - 1/3 + 1/5 - 1/7 + 1/9 - 1/11 + 1/13 + \ldots)$ Write a program that approximates PI by taking 10000 terms into calculation.

Solutions for Lab4 Exercises

```
1. public class Lab4Q1 {
       public static void main( String [] args )
       {
       double amount; // Amount entered from the keyboard
       // receive the amount entered from the keyboard
       System.out.println("Enter an amount in double, e.g., 11.67: ");
       amount = Keyboard.readDouble();
       int remainingAmount = (int)(amount * 100);
       // find the number of one dollars
       int numOfOneDollars = remainingAmount / 100;
       remainingAmount = remainingAmount % 100;
       // find the number of quarters in the remaining amount
       int numOfQuarters = remainingAmount / 25;
       remainingAmount = remainingAmount % 25;
       // find the number of dimes in the remaining amount
       int numOfDimes = remainingAmount / 10;
       remainingAmount = remainingAmount % 10;
       // find the number of nickels in the remaining amount
       int numOfNickels = remainingAmount / 5;
       remainingAmount = remainingAmount % 5;
       // find the number of pennies in the remaining amount
       int numOfPennies = remainingAmount;
```

```
        // display results
        System.out.println("Your amount " + amount + "consists of \n" +
            numOfOneDollars + " dollars\n" + numOfQuarters + " quarters\n" +
            numOfDimes + " dimes\n" + numOfNickels + " nickel\n" +
            numOfPennies + " pennies");
    }
}
}
```

```
2. public class Lab4Q2 {
   public static void main(String[] args){
       final int NUM_OF_LINES = 5;
       for(int row = 1; row<= NUM_OF_LINES; row++)
       {
       // print leading spaces
       for(int column =1; column<= NUM_OF_LINES -row; column++ )
       System.out.print(" ");
       // print leading numbers
       for(int num = row; num>=1; num--)
           System.out.print(num);
       // print ending numbers
       for(int num = 2; num<=row; num++)
           System.out.print(num);
       // start a new line
       System.out.println();
   }
   }
}
```

```
3. public class Lab4Q3 {
   public static void main( String [] args )
       {
       System.out.print ("Enter a positive n (0<n<20): ");
       int n = Keyboard.readInt();
       int product =1;
       for(int i = 1; i <= n; i ++)
       {
           product = product*i;
       }
       System.out.println();
       System.out.println ("The factorial function of n = " + product );
   }
}
```

```
4. public class Lab4Q4 {
   public static void main( String [] args ){
       double f;
       System.out.println("Celsius"+"\tFahrenheit");
       for( int c = 5; c >= -5; c-- )
       {
       f = c*9/5 +32;
       System.out.println(c+"\t"+f);
       }
   }
}
```

5.
```java
public class Lab4Q5 {
public static void main( String [] args ){
    double y, x2;
    System.out.print ("Enter an integer n(0<n<=10): ");
    int n= Keyboard.readInt();
    System.out.print ("Enter an angle in degree x(0<x<=180)): ");
    double x= Keyboard.readDouble();
    System.out.println("x"+"\tsin(x)");
    for(int i = 1; i <= n; i ++)
    {
    x2= Math.PI*x/180;
    y = Math.sin(x2*i/n);
    System.out.println(x*i/n+"\t"+y);
    }
}
}
```

6.
```java
public class Lab4Q6{
public static void main(String[] args) {
    int count =0;
    for(int i =0; i < 3; i++)
    resume:
    for (int j = 0; j < 4; j++ )
        for ( int k =0; k< 5 ; k++ )
        {
        ++count;
        if (i==1 && j==2 && k==3)
        break resume;
        }
    System.out.println("\tcount = " + count);
}
}
// result is: count = 54
```

7.
```java
import java.util.Random;
public class Lab4Q7{
public static void main( String [] args ) {
    Random random = new Random();
    float x = random.nextFloat();
    System.out.println(" x = " + x);
    int n = (int) Math.floor(99*x+2);
    System.out.println(" n = " + n);
    int sum =0;
    for(int i = 1; i<= n; i++)
        sum +=i;
    int form = n*(n+1)/2;
    System.out.println(" sum = " + sum);
    System.out.println(" n*(n+1)/2 = " + form);
}
}
```

8.
```java
public class Lab4Q8
{
    public static void main( String [] args )
```

```
        {
        int sum =1;
        int month =1;
        int monthSave=1;
        while(sum<1000000)
        {
            month = month +1;
            monthSave = monthSave*2;
            sum = sum + monthSave;
        }
        System.out.println("The required months " +month);
    }
}
```

9.
```
public class Lab4Q9
{
public static void main( String [] args )
{
    int sum =1;
    int month =1;
    int monthSave=1;
    while(month<=12)
    {
        month = month +1;
        monthSave = monthSave*2;
        sum = sum + monthSave;
    }
    System.out.println("The money you saved at the end of first year: " +sum);
}
}
```

10.
```
public class Lab4Q10
{
public static void main(String[] args)
    {
    int count = 0;
    double interest = 0.5/100;
    double balance = 1000;
    // creat a loop
    while (count <12*5)
    {
        count+= 1;
        balance = balance+(balance*interest);
        balance+=100;
    }
    System.out.println("The balance at the end of five year is " + balance);
    }
}
```

11.
```
public class Lab4Q11 {
public static void main(String args[ ]) {
    int x;
    for(x=1; x<41; x++)
    {
    System.out.print("*");
```

```
    if (x%8 ==0)
        System.out.println();
    }
}
}
```

```
12. public class Lab4Q12 {
    public static void main (String[] args) {
        final int MAX_ROWS = 5;
        for(int row = 1; row <= MAX_ROWS; row++)
        {
            for (int col = 1; col <= row; col++)
                System.out.print (" " +col);
            System.out.println();
        }
    }
}
```

```
13. public class Lab4Q13 {
    public static void main (String[] args) {
        double mark=1;
        double sum=0;
        double sumSquare=0;
        int count=0;
        int count4Fifty=0;
        double minMark=100;
        double maxMark=1;
        while(mark !=-1)
            {
            System.out.print("Enter marks (0 to stop): ");
            mark =Keyboard.readDouble();
            if mark==-1
                break;
            sum = sum + mark;
            sumSquare = sumSquare + Math.pow(mark,2);
            if(mark>maxMark)
            {
            maxMark = mark;
            }
            if(mark <minMark && mark !=-1)
            {
            minMark = mark;
            }
            if(mark>=50)
            {
            count4Fifty = count4Fifty + 1;
            }
            count = count + 1;
            }
        double average = sum / count;
        double std = Math.sqrt( sumSquare/countCMath.pow(average, 2) );
        System.out.println();
        System.out.println("The mean mark is: " + average);
        System.out.println("The minimum mark is: " + minMark);
        System.out.println("The maximum mark is: " + maxMark);
        System.out.println("The number of marks over 50 is: "+count4Fifty);
```

```
            System.out.println("The standard deviation: " + std);
     }
}
```

```
14. public class Lab4Q14 {
    public static void main (String[] args) {
        int terms = 10000;
        double piOverFour = 0.0;
        System.out.println("i"+"\tpi/4");
        for(int i=0; i<terms; i++)
        {
            if(i%2 == 0)
            piOverFour += 1.0/((double)(2*i + 1));
            else
            piOverFour -= 1.0/((double)(2*i + 1));
            System.out.println(i+"\t"+piOverFour);
        }
    }
}
```

1.8.5   Lab 5 - Programming with Static Methods

1. The Math class is automatically provided when we use Java. All of the Math methods are static. We invoke them using the class name, Math, like Math.sqrt( ). The following is an example of a Math method may invoked by a main method. The program computes the hypotenuse of a right triangle given the lengths of its two sides:

```
public class Pythagoras{
public static void main (String[] args){
    double side1, side2, hypotenuse;
    System.out.println("Enter the length of the first side.");
    side1 = Keyboard.readDouble();
    System.out.println("Enter the length of the second side.");
    side2 = Keyboard.readDouble();
    hypotenuse = Math.sqrt(side1*side1 + side2*side2);
    System.out.println("The hypotenuse of a right triangle with sides");
    System.out.println(side1 + " and " + side2 + " is " + hypotenuse + ".");
}
}
```

(A) Enter the above code, compile and execute it;

(B) The length of the diagonal of a rectangular box of dimensions w (width), l (length) and h (height) is the square root of the sum of the squares of w, l and h. Write, and test a program which reads three floating-point numbers (the width, length, and height of a box) and computes (and prints) the length of the diagonal of the box.

2. The following code is a method for taking sum of three floatingpoint numbers:

```
static double sum(double x, double y, double z){
    double result;
    result = x + y +z;
    return result;
}
```

Write a program to test the above method. For example, if the user types three numbers 4, 5.5, 6.7, then the computer will print out that "The sum of 4, 5.5, and 6.7 is 16.2".

3. Implement a method of finding the smallest of three numbers. Then write a program to test it. For example, if the user types three numbers 4, 5.5, 6.7, then the computer will print out that "The smallest of 4, 5.5, and 6.7 is 4".

4. Change the above programming task by implementing a method for picking up the largest of three numbers entered by user.

5. The following code is to implement the conversion from kilometer to mile (1 kilometer = 0.621371192 mile). Write a program to test it. For example, if the user types kilometer value 100, then the computer will print out that "The miles of 100 kilometers is 62.137 miles".

```
static double convertKmToMi(double kilometers) {
    double MILES_PER_KILOMETER = 0.621371192;
    double miles = kilometers * MILES_PER_KILOMETER;
    return miles;
}
```

6. Write and test a method to return a factor of n if n is not a prime, or 0 if n is a prime. For example, if user enters 15, then the computer will print out "The number 15 is not a prime, with factor 3".

7. Write and test a recursive method to compute the sum of the cubes of the first n integers.

8. Write and test a recursive method to computer the sum of the first n odd integers. That is, $1 + 3 + 5 + 7 + \ldots + (2 * n - 1)$.

9. Implementation a method for calculating the permutation function p(n,k) that returns the number of permutation of size k from a set of size n. The number is defined to be:

$$p(n, k) = \prod_{i=n-k+1}^{n} i = (n - k + 1)(n - k + 2) \ldots (n - 2)(n - 1)n$$

For example,

$$p(8, 6) = \prod_{3}^{8} i = (3)(4)(5)(6)(7)(8) = 20160$$

Print out the permutation table, which should look like:

The size of the set in permutation (n=?)

5

```
1
1   1
1   2   2
1   3   6   6
1   4   12  24  24
```

10. Write and test the following Boolean method that determines whether a range of data (from 1 to a given number n) are square numbers:

```
static Boolean isSquare ( long n)
The square numbers are 0, 1, 4, 9, 16, 25, 36, ...
```

Solutions for Lab5 Exercises

1.
```
public class Pythagoras{
public static void main (String[] args){
    double side1, side2, hypotenuse;
    System.out.println("Enter the length of the first side.");
    side1 = Keyboard.readDouble();
    System.out.println("Enter the length of the second side.");
    side2 = Keyboard.readDouble();
    hypotenuse = Math.sqrt(side1*side1 + side2*side2);
    System.out.println("The hypotenuse of a triangle whose sides are ");
    System.out.println(side1 + " and " + side2 + " is " + hypotenuse + ".");
    }
}
```

2.
```
public class Lab5Q2{
public static void main (String[] args){
    double num1, num2, num3, result;
    System.out.println("Enter the length of the first number.");
    num1 = Keyboard.readDouble();
    System.out.println("Enter the length of the second number.");
    num2 = Keyboard.readDouble();
    System.out.println("Enter the length of the third number.");
    num3 = Keyboard.readDouble();
    result = sum(num1, num2, num3);
    System.out.println("The sum of " + num1 + ", " + num2
        + ", and " + num3 + "is " + result);
}
static double sum(double x, double y, double z)
{
    return x+y+z;
}
}
```

3.
```
public class Lab5Q3{
public static void main (String[] args){
    double num1, num2, num3, result;
    System.out.println("Enter the first number");
    num1 = Keyboard.readDouble();
    System.out.println("Enter the second number");
    num2 = Keyboard.readDouble();
    System.out.println("Enter the third number");
    num3 = Keyboard.readDouble();
    result = min(num1, num2, num3);
    System.out.println("The smallest of the three numbers ");
    System.out.println(num1 + "," + num2 + " and " + num3 + " is " +result + ".");
}
static double min(double x, double y, double z) {
    double answer= x;
    if (y < answer)
    answer = y;
    if (z < answer)
    answer = z;
    return answer;
    }
}
```

4.
```java
public class Lab5Q4{
public static void main (String[] args){
    double num1, num2, num3, result;
    System.out.println("Enter the first number");
    num1 = Keyboard.readDouble();
    System.out.println("Enter the second number");
    num2 = Keyboard.readDouble();
    System.out.println("Enter the third number");
    num3 = Keyboard.readDouble();
    result = max(num1, num2, num3);
    System.out.println("The smallest of the three numbers ");
    System.out.println(num1 + "," + num2 + " and " + num3 + " is " +result + ".");
    }
    static double max(double x, double y, double z) {
    double answer= x;
    if (y > answer)
        answer = y;
    if (z > answer)
        answer = z;
    return answer;
}
}
```

5.
```java
public class Lab5Q5 {
public static void main (String[] args) {
    double kilo, miles;
    System.out.println("Enter the kilometer value.");
    kilo = Keyboard.readDouble();
    miles = convertKmToMi(kilo) ;
    System.out.println("The miles of " + kilo + "kilometers" + "is " + miles);
    }
static double convertKmToMi(double kilometers){
    double MILES_PER_KILOMETER = 0.621371192;
    double miles = kilometers * MILES_PER_KILOMETER;
    return miles;
    }
}
```

6.
```java
public class Lab5Q6{
public static void main(String[] args) {
    int factor;
    System.out.println("Enter the range n to be checked: ");
    int n = Keyboard.readInt();
    factor = primeFactor(n);
    if(factor==0)
        System.out.println("number "+ n+ " is a prime.");
    else
        System.out.println("number "+ n+ " is a not prime,
            with factor " + factor);
    }
public static int primeFactor(int n) {
    for (int divisor=2; divisor<n; divisor++ )
    {
    if ( (n%divisor)==0)
        return divisor; //divisible implies not a prime
    }
```

```
        return 0; //must be prime if nothing was able to divide it.
    }
}
```

```
7. public class Lab5Q7 {
   public static void main(String[] args) {
       System.out.println("Enter the integer n : ");
       int n = Keyboard.readInt();
       long result = sum(n);
       System.out.println ("The sum of cubes of the first n integers: " + result);
   }
   public static long sum(int n)
   { //Compute 1^3 + 2^3 + 3^3 + ... + n^3
       if(n==1) //This is called the "base case"
           return 1;
       else
           return n*n*n + sum(n-1);
   }
}
```

```
8. public class Lab5Q8 {
   public static void main(String[] args) {
       System.out.println("How many of the first integers to be added (n =) ");
       int n = Keyboard.readInt();
       long result = oddsum(n);
       System.out.println ("The sum of the first n odd integers: " + result);
   }
   public static long oddsum(int n){ //Compute 1 + 3 + 5 + ... +
       if (n == 1)
       return 1;
       else
       return (2*n-1) + oddsum(n-1);
   }
}
```

```
9. public class Lab5Q9 {
   public static void main(String[] args) {
       System.out.println("The size of the set in permutation(n=?) ");
       int n = Keyboard.readInt();
       for(int i=0; i<n; i++)
       {
       for(int j=0; j<=i; j++)
       System.out.print( p(i,j) + "\t");
       System.out.println();
       }
   }
   static long p(int n, int k){
       long p=1;
       for(int i=0; i<k; i++)
       {
       p*=n--;
       }
       return p;
   }
}
```

10.
```
public class Lab5Q10{
    public static void main(String[] args) {
        System.out.println("How many of the integers to be checked (n =) ");
        int n = Keyboard.readInt();
        for(int i=0; i<n; i++)
        {
        if(isSquare(i))
            System.out.println(i+" is a square.");
        }
    }
    static boolean isSquare(long n) {
        long sum=0;
        long i = 1;
        while(sum<n)
        {
        sum+=i;
        i+=2;
        }
        return (sum==n);
        }
    }
```

1.8.6   Lab 6 - Further Exercises with Static Methods

1. Write a method that converts an uppercase letter to a lowercase letter. Use the following method declaration:

```
public static char upperCaseToLowerCase(char ch)
```

For example, upperCaseToLowerCase('B') returns b.

Hint: In the ASCII table, uppercase letters appear before lowercase letters. The offset between any uppercase letter and its corresponding lowercase letter is the same. So you can find a lowercase letter from its corresponding uppercase letter, as follows:

```
int offset = (int)'a'-(int)'A';
char lowercase = (char)((int)uppercase + offset);
```

2. Write a method that computes the sum of the digits in a positive integer. Use the following method declaration:

```
public static int sumDigits( long n)
```

For example, sumDigits(234) returns 2+3+4=9. Hint: use the % operator to extract digits, and use the / operator to remove the extracted digit. For example, 234%10 = 4 and 234/10 = 23. Use a loop to repeatedly extract and remove the digit until all the digits are extracted.

3. Write a method that computes future investment value at a given interest rate for a specified number of years. The future investment is determined using the following formula:

$$futureInvestmentValue = investmentAmount * (1 + monthlyInterestRate)^{(numOfYears12)}$$

Use the following method declaration:

```
public static double futureInvestmentValue(
double investmentAmount, double monthlyInterestRate, int year)
```

Write a test program that prompt the user to enter investment amount, annual interest rate, and print a table that displays the future investment value for the years from 1 to 30, as shown below:

Enter the amount Invested: 1000

Enter annual interest rate: 9%

Years	Future Values
1	1093.8
2	1196.41
...	...
...	...
...	...
29	13467.25
30	14730.57

4. Create a method, boolean *equiv(double x, double y)*, that returns true if x and y are nearly equal and false otherwise. Then write a main class that verifies that the *equiv* method works correctly.

5. You have used the sqrt method in the Math class before. In this exercise, write your own method to compute square roots. The square root of a number, num, can be approximated by repeatedly performing a calculation using the following formula:

```
nextGuess = (lastGuess + (num/lastGuess) )/2
```

When nextGuess and lastGuess are almost identical, nextGuess is the approximated square root. The initial guess will be the starting value of lastGuess. If the difference between nextGuess and lastGuess is less than a very small number, such as 0.00001, you can claim that nextGuess is the approximated square root of num.

6. In mathematics, the Fibonacci numbers are the numbers in the following sequence:

$0, 1, 1, 2, 3, 5, 8, 13, 21, 34, 55, 89, 144, \ldots$

By definition, the first two Fibonacci numbers are 0 and 1, and each remaining number is the sum of the previous two. Some sources omit the initial 0, instead beginning the sequence with two 1s. In mathematical terms, the sequence Fn of Fibonacci numbers is defined by the recurrence relation

$$F_n = F_{n-1} + F_{n-2}$$

with seed values

$$F_0 = 0 \ and \ F_1 = 1$$

Write a nonrecursive method that computes Fibonacci numbers. Hint: To compute $fib(n)$ without recursion, you need to obtain $fib(n-2)$ and $fib(n-1)$ first. Let $f0$ and $f1$ denote the two previous Fibonacci numbers. The current Fibonacci number would then be $f_0 + f_1$. The algorithm can be described as follows:

```
f0 = 0; // for fib(0)
f1 = 1; // for fib(1)
for (int i=1; i<=n; i++)
currentFib = f0 + f1;
f0 = f1;
```

```
f1 = currentFib;
}
// After the loop, currentFib is fib(n)
```

7. Write and test a method that implements the combination function c(n,k) using the following definition:

$$c(n, k) = \frac{n!}{k!(n-k)!}$$

Here $n!$ means the value of the factorial function $f(n)$. Then have your program print the Pascals Triangle, like this:

```
1
1  1
1  2  1
1  3  3  1
1  4  6  4  1
1  5  10  10  5  1
1  6  15  20  15  6  1
1  7  21  35  35  21  7  1
1  8  28  56  70  56  28  8  1
```

8. Write and test the following method that implements the Fibonacci function recursively: *static long fib(int n)* (see Q6)

9. Implement the power function recursively. Have your test program also invoke the *Math.pow()* method to check your results.

10. Write and test the following recursive method that returns the nth square number:

static long s(int n) The square numbers are 0,1,4, 9, 25, 36,.... Note that $s(n) = s(n-1) + 2n - 1$ for $n > 1$

Solutions for Lab6 Exercises

1.
```
public class Lab6Q1 {
public static void main(String[] args){
    System.out.println("Enter a upper case letter:");
    char upperch = Keyboard.readChar();
    System.out.println("The lower case letter is:");
    System.out.print(toLowerCase(upperch));
    }
public static char toLowerCase(char ch){
    char lowercase;
    int offset = (int) 'a' - (int)'A';
    lowercase = (char) ( (int)ch + offset);
    return lowercase;
    }
}
```

2.
```
public class Lab6Q2 {
public static void main ( String args[]) {
    System.out.println("Sums the digits in an integer.\n");
    System.out.println("Enter a positive integer: ");
    long n = Keyboard.readLong();
    long dsum = sumDigits(n);
    System.out.println("The sum of the digits is " + dsum + ".");
```

```
    }
    public static long sumDigits(long n){
        long result = 0;
        while(n > 0){
        result+= (n % 10);
        n = n /10;
        }
        return result;
    }
}
```

3.
```
public class Lab6Q3 {
    public static void main ( String args[]){
        double value=0;
        System.out.println("This program compute future investment value .");
        System.out.print("Enter amount invested : ");
        double amount = Keyboard.readDouble();
        System.out.print("Enter annual interest rate (%): ");
        double rate = Keyboard.readDouble()/12;
        System.out.println("Years\t" + "Future Value");
        int year =0;
        while(year<30)
        {
        year = year +1;
        value = futureInvestment(rate, year, amount);
        System.out.println(year+ "\t" + value );
        }
    }
    Public static double futureInvestment( double monthlyInterestRate,
    int numberOfYears, double investmentAmount)
    {
        double futureInvestmentValue =
            investmentAmount*Math.pow(1+monthlyInterestRate, (numberOfYears*12));
            return futureInvestmentValue;
        }
    }
```

4.
```
public class Lab6Q4 {
    public static void main ( String args[]){
        System.out.println("This program compares two floating-point numbers.\n");
        System.out.print("Enter the first number: ");
        double x = Keyboard.readDouble();
        System.out.print("Enter the second number: ");
        double y = Keyboard.readDouble();
        boolean cmp = equiv(x, y);
        if (cmp){
            System.out.println("They are essentially the same." );
        }
        else System.out.println("They are not same" );
        }
    public static boolean equiv(double num1, double num2){
        final double smallValue = 1.0E-2 ;
        if (Math.abs(num1 - num2 )< smallValue )
        { return true; }
        else return false;
        }
}
```

5.
```java
public class Lab6Q5 {
public static void main ( String args[]) {
    System.out.println("This program compute square root .\n");
    double N = 3.00;
    double lastGuess = 1.00;
    double value = squareRoot(N,lastGuess);
    System.out.println("The square root of " + N+ " is " + value+ ".");
    }
public static double squareRoot(double n, double guess){
    final double smallValue = 1.0E-8;
    double nextGuess=1+guess, lastGuess=guess;
    while(Math.abs(lastGuess - nextGuess)> smallValue){
    // calculate a new value for the guess
    nextGuess = n/(2*guess) + guess/2 ;
    lastGuess = guess;
    guess = nextGuess;
    }
    return guess;
    }
}
```

6.
```java
public class Lab6Q6 {
public static void main(String[] args) {
    for(int i=0; i<=46; i++)
    System.out.print(fib(i)+", ");
}
public class FibonacciIterative {
public static int fib(int n) {
    int prev1=0, prev2=1;
    for(int i=0; i<n; i++) {
    int savePrev1 = prev1;
    prev1 = prev2;
    prev2 = savePrev1 + prev2;
    }
    return prev1;
    }
}
```

7.
```java
public class Lab6Q7{
public static void main(String[] args){
    for (int i = 0; i < 9; i++)
    {   for (int j = 0; j <= i; j++)
        System.out.print(c(i, j) + "\t");
        System.out.println();
    }
}
static long c(int n, int k)
    {   return f(n)/(f(k)*f(n-k));
    }
static long f(int n)
    {   long f = 1;
        while (n > 1)
        f *= n--;
        return f;
```

```
        }
    }
```

```
8. public class Lab6Q8{
   public static void main(String[] args){
       for(int i = 0; i < 17; i++)
           System.out.print(fib(i) + " ");
       }
   static long fib(int n){
       if (n < 2) return n;
       return fib(n-1) + fib(n-2);
       }
   }
```

```
9. public class Lab6Q9{
   public static void main(String[] args){
       for(int n = -3; n < 7; n++)
           System.out.println("\t" + n + "\t" + pow(2.0, n)
       + "\t" + Math.pow(2.0,n));
       }
   static double pow(double x, int n){
       if (n == 0) return 1.0;
       if (n < 0) return pow(1.0/x, -n);
       return x*pow(x, n-1);
       }
   }
```

```
10. public class Lab6Q10{
    public static void main(String[] args){
        for(int i = 0; i < 10; i++)
            System.out.println(i + "\t" + s(i));
        }
    static long s(int n){
        if (n < 2) return n;
        return s(n-1) + 2*n - 1;
        }
    }
```

1.8.7   Lab 7 - Introduction to Classes and Objects

1. The Sheep Counter: Model a sheep counter, which is a hand-held device that can be used to count sheep. It has two buttons: a click button and a clear button. A press on the click button will increase the counter value by 1. A press on the clear button will set the counter value to 0. The sheep counter can be modeled by a class with one attribute (value) and two operations (click and clear). For ease of testing we let our counter count up to 10 only (a real count can count from 0 to 9999).

   a. Create the above class and save it in a file called Counter.java.

```
class Counter {
    private int value;
    public Counter( ) {
    value = 0; // or clear( );
    }
```

```
public void click( ) {
    if (value < 10 )
    value = value + 1;
    else
    value = 0;
    }
public void clear( ) {
    value = 0;
}
public int getValue( ) {
    return value;
    }
}
```

b. Compile it.

c. Enter the following program, save it in the file TestCounter.java.

```
class TestCounter {
public static void main( String [] args ) {
    Counter counter = new Counter( );
    System.out.println( "value = " + counter.getValue( ) );
    counter.click( );
    System.out.println( counter.getValue( ) );
    counter.click( );
    System.out.println( counter.getValue( ) );
    counter.clear( );
    System.out.println( counter.getValue() );
    }
}
```

d. Compile the program and run it.

e. In the above exercise, we have put the two classes in two different files. In fact, we can put more than one classes in the same file. Enter the two classes in the same file, for example, CounterAndTestCounter.java. Then compile it and run it.

2. Student: Following is a program for creating students objects. It contains the attributes and methods necessary for a student data base.

```
class Student {
    public String name;
    public int studentNumber;
    public void setStudentNo(int number){
    studentNumber = number ;
    }
public int getStudentNo(){
    return studentNumber;
    }
public static void main(String[] args) {
    Student Robert = new Student();
    Robert.setStudentNo(55555);
    System.out.println("Robert's student number is " + Robert.getStudentNo() );
    }
}
```

(a). Enter the code, compile and run it.

(b). Create a newStudent class with the attributes name, studentNumber and two methods (setStudentNo and getStudentNo), save it in a file named newStudent. Then write a Test-NewStudent class to create student objects. The TestNewStudent class should generate the same output as from the above code.

(c). Add other two methods for setting and getting student's age with necessary field declaration. And then test your modified program by printing out student Robert's age.

3. Rectangle: A rectangle is a shape defined by its length and width. Write a class which includes the essential attributes of a rectangle, methods to calculate other properties and a method to display details of a rectangle. It will include a constructor to create instances of the Rectangle class.

(a) Begin by typing the following skeleton of the Rectangle class.

```
class Rectangle
{
    //attributes
    public int length;
    public int width;
}
```

Save it as Rectangle.java and compile it. (b) Type the following main class to test the Rectangle class. Save it as TestRectangle.java. It should be saved in the same directory as Rectangle.java.

```
class TestRectangle {
public static void main(String[] args) {
    Rectangle rect1 = new Rectangle();
    System.out.println( "Length: " + rect1.length
+ " Width: " + rect1.width);
    System.out.println(); // blank line
    System.out.println(rect1.toString());
    }
}
```

Now compile and run the TestRectangle class.

(c). In the above program, we have not yet written a constructor or a toString method but we are able to use the default versions that already exist in Java (This process is called inheritance). Notice what happens when we call these default methods in the TestRectangle class. The default constructor works well but the default toString method does nothing useful. Write your own toString method to override the default version:

```
public String toString(){
    return "Length: " +length + "\nWidth: " + width;
}
```

Add this method at the bottom of the Rectangle class and compile. Now run again the TestRectangle class.

(d). Now add our own constructor to the Rectangle class so that we can set the length and width when we create a rectangle object. Place it below the attributes and above the toString method.

```
//constructor
public Rectangle(int aLength, int aWidth ){
```

```
    length = aLength;
    width = aWidth;
}
```

Modify the corresponding statement in the TestRectangle class to take the input length = 4 and width = 2. Compile and run.

(e) Now add a method to calculate the area of the rectangle and return the answer. Place it below the constructor.

```
//method to calculate area
public int calcArea()
{
    int area = length * width;
    return area;
}
```

(f) Now write a similar method to calculate the perimeter of a rectangle.

(g) Modify the toString method so that we can display these additional properties on the screen.

```
public String toString()
{
    return "Length: " +length + "\nWidth: " + width + "\nArea: "
        + calcArea() + "\nPerimeter: " + calcPerimeter();
}
```

Now compile and run to test the changes. (h) Finally, we may wish to change the length and width attributes after an instance of a rectangle has been created. To enable this we will create methods to set length and width. Use the following headers:

```
public void setLength(int aLength)
public void setWidth(int aWidth)
```

Modify the TestRectangle class to test these two methods. Add the statements:

```
rect1.setLength(10);
rect1.setWidth(20);
```

Re-compile both classes and run the TestRectangle class.

4. Study the Point program discussed in the class. (a). Separate the code into two parts (classes): Point and TestPoint. (b).Then add and test the following method to the Point class:

```
public void translate (double dx, double dy)
// shifts the point dx units to the right and
// dy units up.
```

For example, p.translate(5,1) would change the point p in the example to (7,4).

5. Then add and test the following method to the given Point class:

```
public void rotate (double theta)
// rotates the point theta radians counter-clockwise.
```

For example, p.rotate(Math.PI/2) would change the point p to (-3, 2). Use the following trigonometric transformation equations:

$$x_2 = x_1 cos(\theta) - y_1 sin(\theta)$$
$$y_2 = x_1 sin(\theta) + y_1 cos(\theta)$$

6. Modify the given point class discussed in the class so that it represents 3- dimensional points in space.

Solutions for Lab7 Exercises

```
1. class CounterAndTestCounter {
       private int value;
       public CounterAndTestCounter( ) {
       value = 0; // or clear( );
       }
   public void click( ) {
       if (value < 10 )
       value = value + 1;
       else value = 0;
       }
   public void clear( ) {
       value = 0;
       }
   public int getValue( ) {
       return value;
       }
   public static void main( String [] args ) {
       CounterAndTestCounter counter = new
       CounterAndTestCounter( );
       System.out.println( "value = " + counter.getValue( ) );
       counter.click( );
       System.out.println( counter.getValue( ) );
       counter.click( );
       System.out.println( counter.getValue( ) );
       counter.clear( );
       System.out.println( counter.getValue() );
       }
   }
   Or:

   class Counter {
       public int value;
       public Counter( ) {
       value = 0;
       }
   public void click( ) {
       if (value < 10 )
       value = value + 1;
       else value = 0;
       }
   public void clear( ) {
       value = 0;
```

```
    }
public int getValue( ) {
    return value;
    }
}
public class CounterAndTestCounter {
public static void main( String [] args ) {
    Counter counter = new Counter( );
    System.out.println( "value = " + counter.getValue( ) );
    counter.click( );
    System.out.println( counter.getValue( ) );
    counter.click( );
    System.out.println( counter.getValue( ) );
    counter.clear( );
    System.out.println( counter.getValue() );
    }
}
```

2. (b):
```
class newStudent {
    public String name;
    public int studentNumber;
    public void setStudentNo(int number)
    {
        studentNumber = number ;
    }
    public int getStudentNo()
    {
        return studentNumber;
    }
}
class TestNewStudent {
public static void main(String[] args) {
    newStudent Robert = new newStudent();
    Robert.setStudentNo(55555);
    System.out.println("Robert's student number is " + Robert.getStudentNo() );
    }
}
(c):
class newStudent {
public String name;
public int studentNumber;
public int studentAge;
public void setStudentNo(int number){
        studentNumber = number ;
    }
public void setStudentAge(int age){
    studentAge = age ;
    }
public int getStudentNo(){
    return studentNumber;
    }
public int getStudentAge(){
    return studentAge;
    }
}
class TestNewStudent {
```

```
    public static void main(String[] args) {
        newStudent Robert = new newStudent();
        Robert.setStudentNo(55555);
        Robert.setStudentAge(18);
        System.out.println("Robert's student number is " + Robert.getStudentNo() );
        System.out.println("Robert's age is " + Robert.getStudentAge() );
    }
}
```

3. (b) and (c)

```
class Rectangle {
    public int length;
    public int width;
    public Rectangle(int aLength, int aWidth ) {
    length = aLength;
    width = aWidth;
    }
public String toString(){
    return "Length: " +length + "\nWidth: " + width;
    }
}
class TestRectangle {
public static void main(String[] args) {
    Rectangle rect1 = new Rectangle(4,2);
    System.out.println( "Length: " + rect1.length + " Width: " + rect1.width);
    System.out.println(); // blank line
    System.out.println(rect1.toString());
    }
}
```

(d) (e) (f) (g):

```
class Rectangle1 {
    public int length;
    public int width;
    public Rectangle1(int aLength, int aWidth ){
    length = aLength;
    width = aWidth;
    }
public int Area() {
    int area = length * width;
    return area;
    }
public int Perimeter() {
    int answer;
    answer = length + length + width + width;
    return answer;
    }
public String toString() {
    return "Length: " +length + "\nWidth: " + width
    + "\nArea: " + Area() + "\nPerimeter: " + Perimeter();
    }
}
class TestRectangle1 {
    public static void main(String[] args) {
    Rectangle1 rect1 = new Rectangle1(4,2);
```

```
    System.out.println( "Length: " + rect1.length
    + " Width: " + rect1.width);
    System.out.println(); // blank line
    System.out.println(rect1.toString());
    }
}
(h):
class Rectangle2 {
    public int length;
    public int width;
    public Rectangle2( ){
    length = 0;
    width = 0;
    }
public Rectangle2(int aLength, int aWidth ){
    length = aLength;
    width = aWidth;
    }
public int setWidth(int aWidth ){
    width = aWidth;
    return width;
    }
public int setLength(int aLength ){
    length = aLength;
    return length;
    }
public int Area(){
    int area = length * width;
    return area;
    }
public int Perimeter(){
    int answer;
    answer = length + length + width + width;
    return answer;
    }
public String toString() {
    return "Length: " +length + "\nWidth: " + width
    + "\nArea: " + Area() + "\nPerimeter: " + Perimeter();
    }
}//end class

class TestRectangle2 {
public static void main(String[] args) {
    Rectangle2 rect = new Rectangle2();
    rect.setLength(10);
    rect.setWidth(20);
    System.out.println( "Length: " + rect.length +
        " Width: " + rect.width);
    System.out.println(); // blank line
    System.out.println(rect.toString());
    }
}
```

```
4. public class Point {
public double x, y; // the point's coordinates
public Point(double a, double b) {
    x = a;
```

```
      y = b;
      }
   public double x() {
      return x;
      }
   public double y() {
      return y;
      }
   public String toString() {
      return new String("(" + x + "," + y + ")");
      }
   }
   public class TestPoint {
   public static void main(String[] args) {
      Point p = new Point(2,3);
      System.out.println("p.x() = " +p.x()+",p.y() = " + p.y());
      System.out.println("p = " +p);
      Point q = new Point(7,4);
      System.out.println("q = " +q);
      q = new Point(2,3);
      System.out.println("q = " +q);
      }
   }
```

```
5. public void translate(double a, double b) {
      x = x+a;
      y = y+b;
      }
```

```
6. public class Point {
   private double x, y, z;
   public Point(double a, double b, double c) {
      x = a;
      y = b;
      z = c;
      }
   public double x() {
      return x;
      }
   public double y() {
      return y;
      }
   public double z(){
      return z;
      }
   public String toString() {
      return new String ( "(" +x +", " + y + ", "+ z+")");
      }
   public void translate(double a, double b, double c) {
      x +=a;
      y +=b;
      z +=c;
   }
   public static void main (String [] args) {
      Point p = new Point(2,3,-1);
      System.out.println("p.x() = " + p.x() + ", p.y()= "+ p.y()
```

```
    + ", p.z() ="+p.z() );
    System.out.println("p= " +p);
    p.translate(-3,1,2);
    System.out.println("p= " +p);
    Point q = new Point (7,4,1);
    System.out.println("q= " +q);
    }
}
```

1.8.8 Lab 8 - More on Classes and Objects

1. A class Box is defined as follow:

```
public class Box {
    private int width;
    private int height;
    private int length;
    Box(int w, int h, int l) {
    width = w;
    height = h;
    length = l;
    }
int volume() {
    return width*height*length;
    }
}
```

(1) Write a TestBox class that will use the Box class to generate two box objects: one with width, height and length of 1,2 and 3, and another with width, height and length of 4,5 and 6. Then the volumes of the two boxes will be printed out.

(2) What are the outputs you could expect from running TestBox?

(3) Change the constructor Box's arguments to double width, double height, double length and revise other parts if necessary.

(4) If you define a static variable in the class Box as in the following static int numberOfBoxes = 0; What is the differences between this variable and the three instance variables? How to print out the number of box objects you have created in the TestBox class?

2. Study the following code:

```
// Geometry.java
class Circle {
private int x, y, r;
Circle () {
    // System.out.println ("Before");
    this (0, 0, 1);
    System.out.println ("After");
}
Circle (int x, int y, int r) {
    this.x = x;
    this.y = y;
    this.r = r;
}
int getX () { return x; }
int getY () { return y; }
int getRadius () { return r; }
```

```
}
class Geometry {
public static void main (String [] args){
    Circle c1 = new Circle ();
    System.out.println("Center X = " +c1.getX());
    System.out.println("Center Y = " +c1.getY());
    System.out.println("Center Radius = " +
    c1.getRadius ());
    Circle c2 = new Circle (5, 6, 7);
    System.out.println ("Center X = " +c2.getX());
    System.out.println ("Center Y = " +c2.getY());
    System.out.println ("Center Radius = " +
    c2.getRadius ());
    }
}
```

From the above program:

(1) What is the output from the program?

(2) Add other two methods to the Circle class: area and circumference, which should have one parameter radius .

(3) Add other three setter methods: setX, setY , and setRadius and then test them.

3. Student class Write a class called Student that contains the attributes and methods necessary for a student data base.

(1) The attributes are studentID, name, course, timeFraction (FT for fulltime or PT for part-time). Type in the following skeleton:

```
class Student {
    //attributes
    public int studentID;
    public String name;
    public String course;
    public String timeFraction;
} //end class
```

(2)Write a toString method to display the full details of a students enrolment. Note the method should return a string, it should not use a print statement.

(3)Write a main class called TestStudent to test what we have written so far. It should use the Java default constructor to create (instantiate) an object called student1 and call the toString method to display the initial values of the attributes (instance variables).

(4)Now add a constructor that sets the instance variables. Use the following header:

```
public Student(int anID, String aName,
String aCourse, String tFrac)
```

(5). Modify the main class to test what we have written so far. The main class should instantiate an object called student2 with the instance variables initialised as follows: 3701234, "ZhangSan", "Java", "FT". The toString method is then called to display the details on the screen.

(6). Change the access to the instance variables from public to private so they cannot be accessed directly from outside of the Student class.

(7) Now add methods so that the value of each of the attributes can be accessed individually (get methods). The outside user cannot directly access the variables but the get methods

send out messages carrying the values stored in each of the variables. The methods should use the names:

```
getID()
getName()
getCourse()
getTimeFraction()
```

(8) Now add methods so that selected attributes can be modified (set methods). Once a Student object has been instantiated, then the name or id should not be changed C however the course or time fraction may be altered. The headers are:

```
setCourse (String aCourse)
setTimeFraction (String aFrac)
```

(9) Modify the TestStudent class to test the operation of these methods.

4. Employee class. Create a class called Employee. An employee should have a name (a string) and a salary (a double).

   (1) Write a default constructor (no parameters), a constructor with two parameters (name and salary), and a toString method to display the name and salary. Write a program that tests your class.

   (2) Now add a method raiseSalary(double byPercent) that raises the employee's salary by a certain percentage. Modify your program and again test the Employee class. For example:

```
Employee emp1 = new Employee("Harry Porter", 55000);
emp1.raiseSalary(50);
```

5. Write and a run a Java program that does the following:

   (a) Declare a String object named s containing the String "We are Chinese, and we love China.";

   (b) Print the entire string;

   (c) Use the length() method to print the length of the string;

   (d) Use the charAt() method to print the first character in the string;

   (e) Use the charAt() method to print the last character in the string;

   (f) Use the indexOf() and substring methods to print the first word in the string.

6. Write Java programs to accomplish each of the following tasks.

   (A) Read a string via Keyboard.readString() and print the length of the string.

   (B) Read a sentence (which is really a string) and print whether it represents a declarative sentence (i.e. ending in a "."), interrogatory sentence (ending in "?"), or an exclamation (ending in "!").

   (C) Take a string, either created in your program or read in via Keyboard.readString(), and replace the first occurrence of the word "less" with the word "more". Thus, for example, if sentence = "Try to spend less time debugging and more time thinking."; then the modified string would read "Try to spend more time debugging and more time thinking". (You may assume that "less" occurs in lower-case and that the word is not imbedded in another word, for example, "less" is imbedded in "lesson".)

(D) Read a string and count the number of occurrences of a particular character, for example, the character 'a'. You will need to employ a while loop. Each step of the loop will check a condition like sentence.charAt(i) == 'a'.

(E) Read a string and print the characters in reverse order. For example, if the input string is "Mine is a sad tale, said the mouse.", the output string would be ".esuom eht dias ,elat das a si eniM".

Solutions for Lab8 Exercises

1. (A).
```
public class TestBox0
{
public static void main(String[] args){
    Box b1 = new Box(1,2,3);
    Box b2;
    b2 = new Box(2,2,5);
    System.out.println("b1:" + b1.volume());
    System.out.println("b2:" + b2.volume());
    }
}
(B)
b1:6
b2:20
(C)
public class Box1
{
    private double width;
    private double height;
    private double leng;
    // Constructor
    //Box(double w, double h, double l)
    //{
    // width = w;
    // height = h;
    // leng = l;
    //}
    Box1(double width, double height, double leng){
        this.width = width;
        this.height = height;
        this.leng = leng;
        }
    double volume(){
        return width*height*leng;
        }
}
public class TestBox1{
public static void main(String[] args){
    Box1 b1 = new Box1(1,2,3);
    Box1 b2;
    b2 = new Box1(2,2,5);
    System.out.println("The volume of b1: " + b1.volume());
    System.out.println("The volume b2: " + b2.volume());
    }
}
(D)
public class Box2
{
    private double width;
```

```
    private double height;
    private double leng;
    static int numOfBoxes =0;
    Box2(double width, double height, double leng){
        this.width = width;
        this.height = height;
        this.leng = leng;
    }
double volume(){
    return width*height*leng;
    }
public int countBox(){
    return numOfBoxes++;
    }
}
public class TestBox2{
public static void main(String[] args){
    System.out.println("The number of boxes " + Box2.numOfBoxes);
    Box2 b1 = new Box2(1,2,3);
    b1.countBox();
    Box2 b2;
    b2 = new Box2(2,2,5);
    b2.countBox();
    System.out.println("The volume of b1: " + b1.volume());
    System.out.println("The volume b2: " + b2.volume());
    System.out.println("The number of boxes :" + Box2.numOfBoxes);
    }
}
```

---

2. (A)
```
After
Center X = 0
Center Y = 0
Center Radius = 1
Center X = 5
Center Y = 6
Center Radius = 7
(B), (C)
public class Circle2 {
private int x, y, r;
public Circle2() {
// System.out.println ("Before");
this (0, 0, 1);
System.out.println ("After");
}
public Circle2(int x, int y, int r) {
this.x = x;
this.y = y;
this.r = r;
}
public double area(int radius) {
return Math.PI*radius*radius;
}
public double circumference(int radius) {
return 2*Math.PI*radius;
}
public int getX () { return x; }
```

```
public int getY () { return y; }
public int getRadius () { return r; }
public void setX (int x_value) {
x = x_value;
}
public void setY (int y_value) {
y = y_value;
}
public void setRadius (int r_value) {
    r = r_value;
}
}
public class Geometry2 {
public static void main (String[] args){
    Circle2 c1 = new Circle2 ();
    c1.setX(1);
    c1.setY(1);
    c1.setRadius(2);
    System.out.println ("Center X = " + c1.getX ());
    System.out.println ("Center Y = " + c1.getY ());
    System.out.println ("Center Radius = " + c1.getRadius ());
    System.out.println ("Area = " + c1.area(c1.getRadius ()));
    System.out.println ("Circumference = " +
            c1.circumference(c1.getRadius ()));
    Circle2 c2 = new Circle2 (5, 6, 7);
    System.out.println ("Center X = " + c2.getX ());
    System.out.println ("Center Y = " + c2.getY ());
    System.out.println ("Center Radius = " + c2.getRadius ());
    }
}
```

3. (2), (3)
```
class Student0 {
    public String name;
    public int studentID ;
    public String course;
    public String timeFraction;
    public String toString () {
        return new String ("name " + name + " student ID +
        " + studentID " course + " + course +
        " timeFraction " + timeFraction );
    }
}
public class TestStudent0 {
public static void main(String[] args) {
    Student0 Robert = new Student0();
    System.out.println("Robert's student information is "
    + Robert );
    }
}
(4) (5)
class Student1 {
    public int studentID ;
    public String name;
    public String course;
    public String timeFraction;
    public Student1(int anID, String aName, String aCourse,
```

```
        String aFrac) {
            studentID = anID;
            name = aName;
            course = aCourse;
            timeFraction = aFrac;
        }
    public String toString () {
        return new String ("name " + name + " student ID "
        + studentID + " course + " + course +
        " timeFraction " + timeFraction );
        }
    }
    public class TestStudent1 {
    public static void main(String[] args) {
        Student1 Robert = new Student1(3701234, "ZhangSan","Java", "FT");
        System.out.println("Robert's student information is "
        + Robert );
        }
    }
(6), (7), (8)
class Student2 {
    private int studentID ;
    private String name;
    private String course;
    private String timeFraction;
    public Student2(int anID, String aName, String aCourse,String aFrac){
        studentID = anID;
        name = aName;
        course = aCourse;
        timeFraction = aFrac;
    }
    public int getID() {
        return studentID ;
    }
    public String getName() {
        return name;
    }
    public String getCourse() {
        return course;
    }
    public String getTimeFraction() {
        return timeFraction;
    }
    public void setCourse(String aCourse) {
    course = aCourse ;
    }
    public void setTimeFraction (String aFrac ) {
    timeFraction = aFrac ;
    }
    public String toString () {
        return new String ("name " + name + " student ID " +
        studentID + " course + " + course + " timeFraction
        " + timeFraction );
        }
    }
    public class TestStudent2 {
    public static void main(String[] args) {
        Student2 Robert = new Student2(3701234, "ZhangSan",
```

```
            "Java", "FT");
        Robert.setCourse("Java");
        Robert.setTimeFraction("PT");
        System.out.println("Robert's student information is " + Robert );
        }
    }
```

4. (1)
```
class Employee {
String name;
double salary;
public Employee () {
    name = " ";
    salary = 0.0;
} public Employee (String name, double salary) {
    this.name = name;
    this.salary = salary;
}
public String toString () {
    return new String ("name " + name + " salary " + salary );
    }
}
class TestEmployee
{
public static void main(String args[])
{
    Employee emp1 = new Employee();
    System.out.println("The employee's information: " + mp1);
    System.out.println();
    Employee emp2 = new Employee("Harry Porter", 9999);
    System.out.println("The employee's information: " + mp2);
    }
}
```
(2)
```
class Employee2 {
    String name;
    double salary;
    public Employee2 () {
    name = " ";
    salary = 0.0;
}
public Employee2 (String name, double salary) {
    this.name = name;
    this.salary = salary;
}
public void raiseSalary(double byPercent) {
    salary = salary*(1 + byPercent);
}
public String toString () {
    return new String ("name " + name + " salary " + salary );
}
}
class TestEmployee2 {
public static void main(String args[]) {
    Employee2 emp1 = new Employee2();
    System.out.println("The employee's information: " +emp1);
```

```
        System.out.println();
        Employee2 emp2 = new Employee2("Harry Porter", 9999);
        System.out.println("The employee's information: " +emp2);
        emp2.raiseSalary(0.5);
        System.out.println("The employee's information: " +emp2);
        }
    }
```

5.
```
public class Lab8Q5 {
public static void main(String args[]){
String s = new String("We are Chinese, and we love China.");
// (a)
System.out.println ("Ths string s is: " + s );
// (b)
System.out.println( "The length of the tring is: " + s.length());
//(c)
System.out.println("The character at first index is " + s.charAt(0) );
//(e)
System.out.println("The character at last index is " + s.charAt(34) );
//(e)
int intIndex = s.indexOf("We");
System.out.println("The first word in the string is " +
s.substring(intIndex, intIndex+2) );
//(f)
}
}
```

6.
```
public class Lab8Q6 {
public static void main(String args[]) {
    System.out.println( "Enter a sentence from keyboard: ");
    String str = Keyboard.readString();
    System.out.println( "The length of the tring is: " +
    str.length()); // (A)
    int idxLast = str.length()-1;
    if (str.charAt(idxLast)=='.'){
        System.out.println( "It is a declarative sentence.");
        }
else if (str.charAt(idxLast)=='?'){
        System.out.println( "It is a interrogatory sentence.");
        }
else if (str.charAt(idxLast)=='!'){
        System.out.println( "It is a exclamation");
        }
//(B)
String sentence = "Try to spend less time debugging and more time thinking.";
System.out.println ("The original string is: " + sentence );
String newSentence = sentence.replaceFirst("less", "more");
System.out.println ("The modified string is: " + newSentence );
// (C)
// check how many 't' appeared in the sentence:
int index =-1;
int counter = 0;
int indexLast = sentence.length()-1;
while (index< indexLast ){
    index = index +1;
    if (sentence.charAt(index) == 't' ){
```

```
            counter = counter +1;
        }
    }
    System.out.println ("The number of 't' in the sentence is: " + counter );
    // (D)
    // print the characters in reverse order
    System.out.println ();
    String sen = "Mine is a sad tale, said the mouse.";
    System.out.println ("The original sentence is: " + sen );
    System.out.println ("The senetence in reversed order is: " );
    for (int j=sen.length()-1; j>=0; j-- )
    {
    System.out.print(sen.charAt(j));
    }
    // (E)
    }
}
```

1.8.9 Lab 9 - String and Array

1. Write a program that reads in a string that is a 12 hour version of the time and writes out a 24 hour version of the time.

```
C:\ java Lab9Q1
Input: 12:23AM
0:23
C:\java Lab9Q1
Input:8:30AM
8:30
C:\java Lab9Q1
Input:8:30PM
20:30
C:\java Lab9Q1
Input:8:30 PM
20:30
```

Assume that the user has correctly entered digits separated by a colon and "AM" or "PM" is always given.

2. Design a program that reads integer numbers as string from the user and then count how many are positive and how many are negative. The program uses 0 as sentinel. i.e. it continues to read until 0 value is entered. Then expected printout should be:

```
Enter integers (or 0 to stop):
10
20
-9
50
-89
0
The number of positive numbers is 3
The number of negative numbers is 2
```

3. Design a program that reads ID numbers, names and grades of students contained from user and computes the total of each student by applying the StringTokenizer class. Use the readString() method from the keyboard class. The expected output should look like:

```
Enter id, name, and quiz grades in one line or DONE to stop:
12345, Zhangsan, 50, 40, 10
ID: 12345
Name: Zhangsan
Total: 90
```

4. Complete the following program which attempts to read text from user and then counts the words in the text. Complete the missing lines within the box.

```
import java.util.StringTokenizer;
public class Lab8Q8 {
public static void main (String[] args) {
    int wordCount = 0, characterCount = 0;
    String line, word;
    StringTokenizer tokenizer;
    System.out.println("Enter text (type DONE to quit):");
    line = Keyboard.readString();
    while (!line.equals("DONE")) {




        line = Keyboard.readString();
    }
    System.out.println ("Number of words: " + wordCount);
    System.out.println ("Number of characters:"+ characterCount);
    }
}
```

5. Create a string "Java Application" first, and then copy the characters in the string to a char array by using the getChars method (find the details of the method from

http://java.sun.com/j2se/1.4.2/docs/api/java/lang/String.html).

Then apply the isUpperCase, toLowerCase methods to convert the upper case letters to lower case letters and lower case letters to upper case letters. That is:

```
D:\java Lab9Q5
jAVA aPPLICATIONS
```

6. Write a program to print out the following message by using an array for months and an array for the number of days in different months as in the following output:

```
D:\java Lab9Q6
There are 31 days in January.
There are 28 days in February.
There are 31 days in March.
There are 30 days in April.
There are 31 days in May.
There are 30 days in June.
There are 31 days in July.
There are 31 days in August.
There are 30 days in September.
```

```
There are 31 days in October.
There are 30 days in November.
There are 31 days in December.
```

7. Write a program which reads in 7 temperatures in an array. Then it shows which are above and which are below the average of the 7 temperatures.

8. For each of the following program segments, first predict what the output will be. Then, run each segment (in an myArray class) to see what actually happens.

```
(A)
int[] a = new int[10];
for (int j = 0; j < a.length; j++)
a[j] = 3*j + 1;
for (int i = 0; i < a.length; i++)
System.out.print(a[i] + " ");
System.out.println();
(B)
int[] factorial = new int[8];
factorial[0] = 1;
for (int j = 1; j < factorial.length; j++)
factorial[j] = j*factorial[j-1];
for (int i = 0; i < factorial.length; i++)
System.out.println(i + "! = " + factorial[i]);
(C)
char[] vowel = {'a', 'e', 'i', 'o', 'u'};
System.out.println("length of array = " + vowel.length);
for (int index = 0; index < vowel.length; index++)
System.out.println(vowel[index]);
(D)
String[] director = {"Godard", "Fellini", "Kurosawa", "Antonioni",
"Lang", "Welles"};
for (int index = director.length - 1; index >= 0; index--)
System.out.println(director[index]);
(E)
int[] fibonacci = new int[200];
fibonacci[0] = 1;
fibonacci[1] = 1;
for (int j = 2; j < fibonacci.length; j++)
fibonacci[j] = fibonacci[j-1] + fibonacci[j-2];
for (int i = 0; i < 35; i++)
System.out.println(fibonacci[i]);
```

9. Suppose that we are reading in a sequence of quiz scores (each between 0 and 10), followed by a negative number (sentinel) indicating end of sequence. Instead of storing each quiz score in a separate array compartment, it is more useful (and efficient) to store the "number of 0's", "the number of 1's", ... , "the number of 10's". Toward this end, we need an array, frequency[], of length only 11. The loop which we need will look like:

```
declare the array frequency[];
read first score;
while (score >= 0){
frequency[score]++;
read next score;
}
```

Write and test this program fragment. Add two simple loops that compute (and print):

(1) the average quiz score and

(2) the mode of the distribution (i.e., the index which corresponds to the maximum value stored in the array.)

10. Design a program to read 10 integers, print them out in reverse order, and find their maximum and minimum. The numbers should be represented by an array with the following steps:

(1).Declare a variable values as an array of integers:

```
final int Number = 10;
int[] values = new int [Number];
```

(2). Enter the elements within the array by providing an index through a looping and applying the Keyboard.readInt().

Solutions for Lab9 Exercises

```
1. public class Lab9Q1{
   public static void main(String[] args){
       String str, strHour, strMinute;
       String newStr ="";
       System.out.print("Input:");
       str = Keyboard.readString();
       int idxColon = str.indexOf(':');
       strHour =str.substring(0,idxColon);
       int numHour = Integer.parseInt(strHour);
       int idxLast = str.length()-1;
       strMinute = str.substring(idxColon+1,idxColon+3);
       String substr = str.substring(idxLast-1);
       if (substr.equals("AM")){
           if (numHour>=12){
           numHour = numHour -12;
       }
       newStr=numHour+":"+strMinute;
       }
       if(substr.equals("PM")){
       if(numHour<=12){
           numHour = numHour +12;
       }
       newStr=numHour+":"+strMinute;
       }
       System.out.println(newStr);
       }
   }
```

```
2. import java.util.StringTokenizer;
   public class Lab9Q2{
   public static void main(String[] args){
       String str, numStr;
       int positiveCount=0;
       int negativeCount=0;
       StringTokenizer st;
       System.out.println("Enter an integer (or 0 to stop)");
       str = Keyboard.readString();
```

```
        while( !str.equals("0")){
        st = new StringTokenizer(str);
        numStr = st.nextToken();
        int numInt = Integer.parseInt(numStr);
        if(numInt>0){
            positiveCount = positiveCount + 1;
        }
    if (numInt<0){
        negativeCount = negativeCount + 1;
        }
    str = Keyboard.readString();
        }
        System.out.println("The number of positive numbers is " + positiveCount);
        System.out.println("The number of negative numbers is " + negativeCount);
        }
}
```

3.
```
import java.util.StringTokenizer;
public class Lab9Q3{
public static void main(String[] args){
    String s, name, id;
    StringTokenizer st;
    System.out.println("Enter id name, quiz grades in one line (DONE to stop)");
    s = Keyboard.readString();
    while ( !s.equals("DONE")){
    st = new StringTokenizer(s, "\t ,");
    id = st.nextToken();
    name = st.nextToken();
    int sum = 0;
    while(st.hasMoreTokens()){
    int grade = Integer.parseInt(st.nextToken("\t ,").trim());
    sum += grade;
    }
    System.out.println("ID:" + id);
    System.out.println("Name:" + name);
    System.out.println("Total:" + sum);
    System.out.println("Enter id name, quiz grades in one line (or DONE to stop)");
    s = Keyboard.readString();
    }
}
}
```

4.
```
import java.util.StringTokenizer;
public class Lab9Q4 {
// Reads several lines of text, counting the number of words
// and the number of non-space characters.
public static void main (String[] args){
    int wordCount = 0, characterCount = 0;
    String line, word;
    StringTokenizer tokenizer;
    System.out.println("Please enter text (type DONE to quit):");
    line = Keyboard.readString();
    while (!line.equals("DONE")){
        tokenizer = new StringTokenizer(line);
    while (tokenizer.hasMoreTokens()){
        word = tokenizer.nextToken();
```

```
        wordCount++;
        characterCount += word.length();
      }
      line = Keyboard.readString();
    }
    System.out.println ("Number of words: " + wordCount);
    System.out.println ("Number of characters: " + characterCount);
  }
}
```

5.
```
public class Lab9Q5 {
  public static void main(String args[]) {
    String ko = "Java Applications";
    char ch[] = new char[80];
    int m = ko.length();
    ko.getChars(0,m,ch,0);
    for (int n=0; n<m; n++) {
      if (Character.isUpperCase(ch[n]))
        System.out.print(Character.toLowerCase(ch[n]));
      else System.out.print(Character.toUpperCase(ch[n]));
    }
  }
}
```

6.
```
public class Lab9Q6 {
  public static void main(String args[]) {
    String[] monthes = {"January", "February", "March",
    "April", "May", "June","July","August",
    "September", "October","November","December"};
    int month_days[] = {31, 28, 31, 30, 31, 30, 31, 31,
        30, 31, 30, 31};
    for (int i=0; i<monthes.length ; i++)
    System.out.println("There are " + month_days[i] +
        " days" + " in " + monthes[i]);
  }
}
```

7.
```
public class Lab9Q7 {
/*******************************************************
*Reads in 7 temperatures and shows which are above and
*which are below the average of the 7 temperatures.
*******************************************************/
  public static void main(String[] args) {
    double[] temperature = new double[7];
    int index;
    double sum, average;
    System.out.println("Enter " + temperature.length
    + " temperatures:");
    sum = 0;
    for(index = 0;index < temperature.length;index++){
    temperature[index] = Keyboard.readDouble();
    sum = sum + temperature[index];
    }
    average = sum/temperature.length;
    System.out.println("The average temperature is " + average);
```

```
        System.out.println("The temperatures are");
        for(index = 0; index < temperature.length;index++){
        if(temperature[index] < average)
            System.out.println(temperature[index] + " below average.");
        else if (temperature[index] > average)
            System.out.println(temperature[index] + " above average.");
            else System.out.println(temperature[index] + " the average.");
    }
    }
    }
```

8.
```
public class Lab9Q8 {
public static void main(String args[]) {
    // (A)
    System.out.println("Answer for part (A):");
    int[] a = new int[10];
    for(int j = 0; j < a.length; j++)
        a[j] = 3*j + 1;
    for(int i = 0; i < a.length; i++)
        System.out.print(a[i] + " ");
        System.out.println();
    //(B)
        System.out.println("Answer for part (B):");
    int[] factorial = new int[8];
    factorial[0] = 1;
    for(int j = 1; j < factorial.length; j++)
    factorial[j] = j*factorial[j-1];
    for(int i = 0; i < factorial.length; i++)
        System.out.println(i + "! = " + factorial[i]);
    // (C)
    System.out.println("Answer for part (C):");
    char[] vowel = {'a', 'e', 'i', 'o', 'u'};
    System.out.println("length of array = " + vowel.length);
    for(int index = 0; index < vowel.length;index++)
        System.out.println(vowel[index]);
    //(D)
    System.out.println("Answer for part (D):");
    String[] director = {"Godard", "Fellini",
    "Kurosawa", "Antonioni", "Lang", "Welles"};
    for(int index = director.length - 1; index >=0;index--)
        System.out.println(director[index]);
    //(E)
    System.out.println("Answer for part (E):");
    int[] fibonacci = new int[200];
    fibonacci[0] = 1;
    fibonacci[1] = 1;
    for(int j = 2; j < fibonacci.length; j++)
        fibonacci[j] = fibonacci[j-1] + fibonacci[j-2];
    for(int i = 0; i < 35; i++)
        System.out.println(fibonacci[i]);
    }
}
```

9.
```
public class Lab9Q9{
public static void main (String args []){
    final int Number = 11;
```

```
// declare constant -- number of integers
int[] frequency = new int[Number];
int score, sum;
double average;
// read scores from keyboard
System.out.print("Enter scores:");
System.out.println("\n(Negative value to stop)");
score = Keyboard.readInt();
while(score>=0) {
    frequency[score]++;
    score = Keyboard.readInt();
}
sum = 0;
for(int i = 0 ; i< frequency.length; i ++) {
    System.out.println("The frequency["+i+"] is " + frequency[i]);
    sum = sum + i* frequency[i];
}
average = sum/frequency.length;
System.out.println("The average score is " + average);
// compute maximum and minimum
int maximum = frequency[0];
int mode =0;
for(int i =1; i<frequency.length; i++) {
    if(maximum < frequency[i]){
        maximum = frequency[i];
        mode = i;
    }
}
        System.out.println("The index of maximum score is" + mode);
    }
}
```

```
10. public class Lab9Q10 {
    public static void main (String args []) {
        final int Number = 10;
        int[] values = new int[Number];
        int num=0;
        // read scores from keyboard
        System.out.print("Enter 10 integers:");
        System.out.println("\n(Negative value to stop)");
            for(int i = 0 ; i< values.length; i ++) {
            values[i] = num = Keyboard.readInt();
        }
        // print the array elements in reversed order:
        int N = values.length;
        for(int i = 0; i < N/2; i++){
        int temp = values[N-i-1];
        values[N-i-1] = values[i];
        values[i] = temp;
        }
        System.out.println("Elements in reversed order:");
        for(int i = 0;i<values.length;i ++) {
            System.out.print(" "+values[i]);
        }
        // compute maximum and minimum
        int maximum = values[0];
        int minimum = values[0];
```

```
for(int i =0; i<values.length; i++){
if(maximum < values[i])
    maximum = values[i];
if(minimum > values[i])
    minimum = values[i];
}
System.out.println("\nThe maximum value is " + maximum);
System.out.println("The mimimum value is " + minimum);
}
}
```

1.8.10   Lab 10 - More on Array

1. Implement the following method:

```
static double sum(double[] x)
{ // returns the sum of the elements in the array x
```

which returns the sum of the elements in an array. Then write a program that call the method to display the sum of a double array.

2. Write a program to print the pairs of element from two arrays. The first array is created by multiplying array index by 2, and the second array is created by dividing the array index by 2. The expected printout should be:

   0.   (0, 0.0)
   1.   (2, 0.5)
   2.   (4, 1.0)
   3.   (6, 1.5)
   4.   (8, 2.0)
   5.   (10, 2.5)
   6.   (12, 3.0)
   7.   (14, 3.5)
   8.   (16, 4.0)
   9.   (18, 4.5)

3. Write a method that, given two arrays a and b of integers, returns the array in which b has been attached at the end of a. For example, given $a = \{7, -3, 2\}$ and $b = \{-3, 4, 11, -21\}$, the method returns the array $\{7, -3, 2, -3, 4, 11, -21\}$. Test your method in a complete program.

4. Write an iterative method that, given a string s and an array a of integers, returns an array of characters c such that the element $c[i]$ is the character of s in position $a[i]$. For example, given $s = "abcd"$ and $a = \{2, 1, 0, 1, 3\}$, the method returns $c = \{'c', 'b', 'a', 'b', 'd'\}$. (Assume that $0 \le a[i] \le s.length - 1$ holds for all i). Test your method in a complete program.

5. Write a method that, given an array a of strings and an integer k, returns the array a rotated of k positions towards right.

   For example, given $a = \{"winner", "pump", "rot", "tiger", "kangaroo"\}$ and $k = 3$, the method returns the array $\{"rot", "tiger", "kangaroo", "winner", "pump"\}$. Test your method in a complete program.

6. Write a method that, given an array a of strings and an integer $k(k \ge 2)$, returns true if in a there exist at least k strings of equal length, otherwise the method returns false. For example, given $a = \{"java", "string", "array", "at", "least", "equal", "length"\}$ and $k = 3$, the method returns true. Test your method in a complete program.

7. Write a method that put all the words in a string into an array. For example, given a string s="We are Chinese and we love China", your method will generate a string array { "We", "are", "Chinese", "and", "we", "love", "China"}. Test your method in a complete program. Hint: Apply the StringTokenizer class and its methods countTokens, hasMoreTokens and nextToken.

8. Examine the following program which tries to use assignment operator to copy:

```
public class WhatHappens {
public static void main(String[] args) {
    double [] x = {2.2, 4.4};
    print(x,"x");
    double [] y ={1.1, 3.3, 5.5};
    print (y,"y");
    y =x; // attempts to copy x into y
    print (y,"y");
    x[0] = 8.8;
    print(x,"x");
    print(y,"y");
}
static void print (double[] u, String id){
    for (int i=0; i<u.length; i++ ){
        System.out.println(id+ "[" +i+"] = " +u[i]);
        System.out.println();
    }
}
}
```

Then change the program to copy x into y .

9. Design a Student class with four fields:

```
int regno, total;
int mark[];
String name;
```

Where regno stands for registration number and total for the total marks. A constructor should have three formal parameters:

```
public student(int r,String n,int m[]) {. . .}
```

where r for the passed registration, n for name and m for mark. The constructor will also calculate the total of marks above 50 and any mark below 50 will yield 0 total. Then test the class using array of objects, as in the following:

```
class TestStudent {
public static void main(String args[]) {
    int mk1[]={73,85,95};
    int mk2[]={71,85,55};
    int mk3[]={51,65,45};
    student st[]=new student[3];
    st[0]=new student(1,"Zhang",mk1);
    st[1]=new student(2,"Li",mk2);
    st[2]=new student(3,"Wang",mk3);
    // some display here
}
```

10. Write a program that grades multiple-choice tests. Suppose there are eight students and ten questions, and the answers are stored in a two-dimensional array. Each row records a students answer to the questions. For example, the following array stores the test. The key is stored in a one-dimensional array, as follows:

	0	1	2	3	4	5	6	7	8	9
key	D	B	D	C	C	D	A	E	A	D

Student's Answer to the questions:

	0	1	2	3	4	5	6	7	8	9
student0	A	B	A	C	C	D	E	E	A	D
student1	D	B	A	B	C	A	E	E	A	D
student2	E	D	D	A	C	B	E	E	A	D
student3	C	B	A	E	D	C	E	E	A	D
student4	A	B	D	C	C	D	E	E	A	D
student5	B	B	E	C	C	D	E	E	A	D
student6	B	B	A	C	C	D	E	E	A	D
student7	E	B	E	C	C	D	E	E	A	D

Your program should grade the test and displays the result, as shown in the following:

```
D: java Lab10Q10
Student 0's correct count is 7
Student 1's correct count is 6
Student 2's correct count is 5
Student 3's correct count is 4
Student 4's correct count is 8
Student 5's correct count is 7
Student 6's correct count is 7
Student 7's correct count is 7
Student 8's correct count is 7
```

11. Using a while loop, write a program named SquareRoots.java that prints out a list of square roots from 1 to n where n is a positive integer supplied as a command-line argument. Give a "usage" message if no command-line arguments are given. Note that you can use the Integer.parseInt method to convert a String to an int. For example, the value of the expression Integer.parseInt("15") is the integer 15. Further note that you can use the method Math.sqrt to compute the square root of a number. Here is an example of how your program should work:

```
> java SquareRoots
Usage: java SquareRoots <n>
> java SquareRoots 5
1 1.0
2 1.4142135623730951
3 1.7320508075688772
4 2.0
5 2.23606797749979
```

Make sure your program works for several values of n.

12. Write a program that accepts two numbers from the command line and prints them out. Then use a for loop to print the next 13 numbers in the sequence where each number is the sum of the previous two. For example:

```
> java Lab10Q12 1 3
> 1 3 4 7 11 18 29 47 76 123 322 521 843 1364
```

13. (optional) . Write a program that performs binary arithmetic operations on integers. The
    program receives three arguments: an operator and two integers. To add two integers, use
    this command:

```
java Calculator + 2 3
```

Then the program, will display the following output

```
2 + 3 =5
```

The output of sample runs of your program should be

```
java Lab10Q10 + 63 40
63 + 40 = 103
java Lab10Q10 - 63 40
63 - 40 = 23
java Lab10Q10 "*" 63 40
63 * 40 = 2520
java Lab10Q10 / 63 40
63 / 40 = 1
```

Hint: Use args.length to determine whether three arguments have been provided in the command line. If not, terminate the program using System.exit(0). Perform a binary arithmetic
operation on the operands args[1] and args[2] using the operator specified in args[0].

Solutions for Lab10 Exercises

1.
```
public class Lab10Q1 {
public static void main (String args []){
    final int Number = 10;
    double[] values = new double[Number];
    // read values from keyboard
    System.out.println("Enter " + Number + " numbers on separate lines.");
    for(int i = 0; i < Number; i = i + 1) {
        values[i] = Keyboard.readDouble();
    }
    System.out.println("The sum of the array elements is: "+ arraySum(values));
}
public static double arraySum ( double[] x ){
    // returns the sum of the elements in the array x:
    double s=0.0;
    for(int j=0; j<x.length; j++){
        s +=x[j];
    }
    return s;
}
}
```

2.
```
public class Lab10Q2 {
public static void main (String args []) {
    final int Number = 10;
    // declare int array and double array
    int [] ia = new int[Number];
    double [] fa = new double[Number];
```

```
        // use a for loop to fill it.
        for (int i=0; i < Number; i++) {
            ia[i] = i*2;
            fa[i] = (double)i/2;
        }
    // print out paired values for the two arrays.
    for(int i=0; i <Number ; i++) {
        System.out.println (i + ". (" + ia[i] + ", " + fa[i] + ")");
    }
    }
}
```

```
3. public class Lab10Q3 {
   public static void main(String[] args) {
       int [] a = new int[] {7,-3,2};
       int [] b = new int[] {-3,4,11,-21};
       int[] newarray = append(a,b);
       System.out.println();
       System.out.println("array a:");
       for(int i = 0; i < a.length; i++) {
           System.out.print( a[i]+ " ");
       }
       System.out.println();
       System.out.println("array b:");
       for(int i = 0; i < b.length; i++) {
           System.out.print( b[i] +" ");
       }
       System.out.println();
       System.out.println("the new array:");
       for(int i = 0; i < newarray.length; i++) {
           System.out.print(newarray[i]+" ");
   }
   }
   public static int[] append(int[] a, int[] b) {
       int[] c = new int[a.length+b.length];
       for(int i=0; i<a.length; i++)
           c[i] = a[i];
       for(int j=0; j<b.length; j++)
           c[a.length + j] = b[j];
       return c;
   }
}
```

```
4. public class Lab10Q4 {
   public static void main(String[] args) {
       String s = new String("abcd");
       int [] a = new int[] {2,1,0,1,3};
       char [] newarray = select(s,a);
       System.out.println("String s:" + s);
       System.out.println("array a:");
       for(int i = 0; i < a.length; i++)
           System.out.print( a[i] +" ");
       System.out.println();
       System.out.println("The new char array:");
       for(int i = 0; i < newarray.length; i++)
           System.out.print(newarray[i]+" ");
```

```
    }
    public static char [] select( String s, int[] a ) {
        char [] c = new char[a.length];
        for(int i=0; i<c.length; i++){
        c[i] = s.charAt(a[i]);
        }
        return c;
    }
}
```

5.
```
public class Lab10Q5 {
    public static void main(String[] args) {
        String [] a = {"winner", "pump", "rot","tiger","kangaroo"};
        int k = 3;
        String [] newStr = new String[a.length];
        newStr = rotate(a, k);
        System.out.println("Original string s: " );
        for(int i=0; i<a.length; i++)
            System.out.print(a[i]+" ");
        System.out.println("\nThe new string :");
        for(int i = 0; i < newStr.length; i++)
            System.out.print(newStr[i]+" ");
    }
    public static String [] rotate( String[] a, int k ) {
        int n = a.length;
        String[] b = new String[n];
        for(int i=0; i<n ; i++)
            b[(i+k)%n] = a[i];
        return b;
    }
}
```

6.
```
public class Lab10Q6 {
    public static void main(String[] args) {
        String [] a = {"java", "string","array", "at", "least", "equal", "length" };
        int k = 3;
        boolean check = testing(a, k);
        System.out.println("The strings are: " );
        for(int i=0; i<a.length; i++)
            System.out.print(a[i]+" ");
        if(check)
            System.out.println("\nThere are at least "+ k+
        " strings of equal length.");
    }
    public static boolean testing( String[] a, int k ){
        int i = 0;
        int count =1;
        while(i < a.length) {
        int j = i+1;
        while(j<a.length){
            if((a[i].length() == a[j].length() )){
            count++;
        }
        if(count >=k){
            return true;
        }
```

```
        j++;
        }
        i++;
        count =1;
        }
        return false;
    }
}
```

7.
```
import java.util.*;
public class Lab10Q7 {
public static void main(String[] args){
    String myStr = new String("We are Chinese and we love China");
    String[] words = new String[20];
    words = stringToArray(myStr);
    System.out.println("The original string is: " + myStr);
    System.out.println("The words stored in a string array are: ");
    for(int i=0; i<words.length; i++)
        System.out.print(words[i]+" ");
}
public static String[] stringToArray(String aString){
    String[] result;
    int i = 0; // index into next empty array element
    // declare and create a StringTokenizer
    StringTokenizer st;
    st = new StringTokenizer(aString);
    // create an array which will hold all the tokens.
    result = new String[st.countTokens()];
    // loop, getting each of the tokens
    while(st.hasMoreTokens()) {
        result[i++] = st.nextToken();
    }
    return result;
}
}
```

8.
```
System.arraycopy(x,0,y,0,x.length); //copies x into y
```

9.
```
class student {
    int regno,total;
    int mark[];
    String name;
    public student(int r,String n,int m[]) {
    regno=r;
    name=n;
    mark=new int[3];
    for(int i=0;i<3;i++) {
        mark[i]=m[i];
        if(mark[i]>50)  total+=mark[i];
        else {
        total=0;
        break;
    }
    }
    }
}
```

```java
    public void displaystudent(){
        System.out.println("NAME:"+name);
        System.out.println("REGNO:"+regno);
        System.out.println("TOTAL:"+total);
    }
}
class Lab10Q9 {
public static void main(String args[]) {
    //declare and initialize arrays
    int mk1[]={73,85,95};
    int mk2[]={71,85,55};
    int mk3[]={51,65,45};
    student st[] = new student[3];
    st[0] = new student(1,"Zhang",mk1);
    st[1] = new student(2,"Li",mk2);
    st[2] = new student(3,"Wang",mk3);
    for(int i=0;i<3;i++)
        st[i].displaystudent();
    }
}
```

```java
10. public class Lab10Q10 {
    public static void main(String args[]) {
        // students' answers to the questions
        char[][] answers = {
    {'A', 'B', 'A', 'C', 'C', 'D', 'E', 'E','A', 'D'},
    {'D', 'B', 'A', 'B', 'C', 'A', 'E', 'E', 'A', 'D'},
    {'E', 'D', 'D', 'A', 'C', 'B', 'E', 'E', 'A', 'D'},
    {'C', 'B', 'A', 'E', 'D', 'C', 'E', 'E', 'A', 'D'},
    {'A', 'B', 'D', 'C', 'C', 'D', 'E', 'E', 'A', 'D'},
    {'B', 'B', 'E', 'C', 'C', 'D', 'E', 'E', 'A', 'D'},
    {'B', 'B', 'A', 'C', 'C', 'D', 'E', 'E', 'A', 'D'},
    {'E', 'B', 'E', 'C', 'C', 'D', 'E', 'E', 'A', 'D'}};
        // key to the questions
        char[] keys = {'D', 'B', 'D', 'C', 'C', 'D', 'A', 'E',
        'A', 'D'};
        // grade all answers
        for(int i = 0; i < answers.length; i++) {
        // grade one student
        int correctCount = 0;
        for(int j = 0; j < answers[i].length; j++) {
            if (answers[i][j] == keys[j])
            correctCount++;
        }
        System.out.println("Student " + i + "'s correct count is " + correctCount);
    }
    }
}
```

```java
11. class Lab10Q11 {
    public static void main(String args[ ] ) {
        if (args.length>1)
        System.out.println("Only one argument is required!");
        String str = args[0];
        int n = Integer.parseInt(str);
        double y;
```

```
        for(int x=1; x<=n ; x++){
            y = Math.sqrt(x);
            System.out.println("y= "+y);
        }
    }
}
```

```
12. public class Lab10Q12{
    public static void main(String args[]){
        int num1, num2, sum;
        // check for right number of parameters
        if(args.length!=2) // must have two numbers{
            System.out.println("Syntax: java Lab10Q12 integer1 integer2");
            System.exit(1); // exit program now!
    }
        // get the data on the command line and
        // make into integers
        num1 = Integer.parseInt(args[0]);
        System.out.print(num1); System.out.print(" ");
        num2 = Integer.parseInt(args[1]);
        System.out.print(num2); System.out.print(" ");
        // do the series now
        for(int i=0;i<13;i++) // repeat the calc 13 times
        {
        sum = num1 + num2;
        System.out.print(sum);
        System.out.print(" ");
        num1 = num2;
        num2 = sum;
        // shuffle for next in series
    }
        System.out.println(""); // finish the output line
    }
}
```

```
13. public class Lab10Q13
    {
    /**Main method*/
    public static void main(String[] args){
    // check command-line arguments
        if(args.length != 3){
        System.out.println("Usage: java Calculator operator operand1 operand2");
        System.exit(0);
    }
    // the result of the operation
        int result = 0;
    // determine the operator
        switch (args[0].charAt(0)){
        case '+': result = Integer.parseInt(args[1]) + Integer.parseInt(args[2]);
        break;
        case '-': result = Integer.parseInt(args[1]) - Integer.parseInt(args[2]);
        break;
        case '*': result = Integer.parseInt(args[1]) * Integer.parseInt(args[2]);
        break;
        case '/': result = Integer.parseInt(args[1]) / Integer.parseInt(args[2]);
    }
```

```
// display result
    System.out.println(args[1] + ' ' + args[0] + ' ' +
        args[2] + " = " + result);
}
}
```

1.8.11   Lab 11 - Advanced OOP Topics

1. File Dog.java contains a declaration for a Dog class. Save this file to your directory and
study itnotice what instance variables and methods are provided. Files Labrador.java and
Yorkshire.java contain declarations for classes that extend Dog. Save and study these files
as well.

File DogTest.java contains a simple driver program that creates a dog and makes it speak.
Study DogTest.java, save it to your directory, and compile and run it to see what it does.
Now modify these files as follows:

(1). Add statements in DogTest.java after you create and print the dog to create and print
a Yorkshire and a Labrador. Note that the Labrador constructor takes two parameters: the
name and color of the labrador, both strings. Don't change any files besides DogTest.java.
Now recompile DogTest.java; you should get an error saying something like:

```
./Labrador.java:15: can't find the signal
singal constructor Dogs
location class Dog
^error
```

If you look at line 15 of Labrador.java it's just a {, and the constructor the compiler can't
find (Dog()) isn't called anywhere in this file. a. What's going on? (What call must be
made in the constructor of a subclass?) b. Fix the problem (which really is in Labrador) so
that DogTest.java creates and makes the Dog, Labrador, and Yorkshire all speak.

(2). Add code to DogTest.java to print the average breed weight for both your Labrador
and your Yorkshire. Use the avgBreedWeight() method for both. What error do you get?
Why? Fix the problem by adding the needed code to the Yorkshire class.

2. (1) Add a method called withdraw(long amount) to the BankAcc class to make a withdrawal.
It should be something like:

```
public void withdraw( long amount) {
balance = balance C amount;
}
```

Modify main() to try it out by adding:

```
b2.withdraw(500);
```

Rerun the program BankAcc.java. Does the correct balance come out?

(2). Compile and run the program DepositAcc.java. Override the display( ) method in class
DepositAcc it only displays a message like: Account type is Deposit with the statement:

```
System.out.println("Account type is Deposit");
```

Rerun the program. Which display() method is invoked on acc, the BankAcc one or the DepositAcc one?

(3). The display() method from DepositAcc is not as useful as the one of its superclass or parent class. We can get it the first call display() from BankAcc by adding the following line at its beginning:

```
super.display();
```

Return DepositAcc.java with this addition.

(4). Override the withdraw() method in class DepositAcc so that it first checks to see if the amount to be withdrawn is less than or equal to the balance. If it is, then it calls the withdraw() method of its parent class, otherwise it generates an error message. Modify main() to try this out.

3. Given the following class Box:

```java
class Box {
    double width;
    double height;
    double depth;
    Box() { }
    Box(double w, double h, double d) {
        width = w;
        height = h;
        depth = d;
    }
    void getVolume() {
        System.out.println("Volume is : " + width * height * depth);
    }
}
```

Complete the subclass MatchBox below to make it generate the following output:

```
Volume is: 1000.0
width of MatchBox is 10.0
height of MatchBox is 10.0
depth of MatchBox is 10.0
weight of MatchBox is 10.0
```

The incomplete code of MatchBox is

```java
public class MatchBox extends Box {
double weight;
MatchBox() { }
public static void main(String args[]) {
    MatchBox mb1 = new MatchBox(10, 10, 10, 10);
    mb1.getVolume();
    System.out.println("width of MatchBox 1 is "+ mb1.width);
    System.out.println("height of MatchBox 1 is " + mb1.height);
    System.out.println("depth of MatchBox 1 is "+ mb1.depth);
    System.out.println("weight of MatchBox 1 is " + mb1.weight);
}
}
```

4. Study the provided program Shapes.java carefully. Add a new method in the base class of Shapes.java that prints a message, but dont override it in the derived classes. Explain what happens. Now override it in one of the derived classes but not the others, and see what happens. Finally, override it in all the derived classes.

5. Examine the given program Circle.java first. Then writer a program that creates a new class for Cylinder extended from the Circle. The Cylinder class inherits all the data and methods from the Circle class. In addition, it has a new data field. Length, and a new method, findVolume. Then write a test program to create a Cylinder object and explore the relationship between the Cylinder class and the Circle class by accessing the data and the methods in the Circle class and the data and methods defined in the Cylinder class. A probable output should look like:

```
>java TestCylinder
The length is 2.0
The radius is 5.0
The volume of the cylinder is 157.0795
The area of the cylinder is 78.53975
```

6. Modify the cylinder class defined above to override the findArea method in the Circle class. The findArea method in the Circle class computes the area of a circle, while the findArea method in the new cylinder class computes the surface area of a cylinder.

7. Write LivingThing.java as an abstract class which include a private field name (of String type), method breath() for printing message Living Thing breathing, method eat() for printing message Living Thing eating, setter/getter methods for the name, and an abstract method walk() to be implemented by subclasses of LivingThing

8. Write Human.java as a concrete class that extends the LivingThing abstract class. Provide an implementation of the abstract method, which print a message for a specific human object indicating that he/she is walking. For example, Human Obama walks.

9. Write Monkey.java as a concrete class that extends the LivingThing abstract class. Implement the abstract method walk(), which print a message for a specific monkey object indicating that it walks. For example, Monkey also walks.

10. Fill the details of the following Main program

```
public class Main {
public static void main(String[] args) {
// Create Human object instance
// and assign it to Human type.
// Create Human object instance
// and assign it to LivingThing type.
// Create a Monkey object instance
// and assign it to LivingThing type.
}
}
```

to generate the output as shown below:

```
Human Obama walks...
Human Obama walks...
Monkey also walks...
human1.getName() = Obama
livingthing1.getName() = Obama
```

11. Given the following Java interface:

```
public interface PersonInterface {
// compute person's total wealth
    int computeTotalWealth();
// get person's name
    String getName();
}
```

1) Write program Person.java. The Person class implements PersonInterface interface to Compute person's total wealth. The Person class define the following fields:

```
int cashSaving;
int retirementFund;
String firstName;
String lastName;
```

2) Apply the following program to test your Person class:

```
public class TestPerson {
public static void main(String[] args) {
// create an object instance of Person class.
    Person person1 = new Person(10000, 20000, "George", "Bush");
// display data from person1
    System.out.println("person1.getName() = " + person1.getName()
        + "," + " person1.computeTotalWealth() = " +
        person1.computeTotalWealth());
}
}
```

Solutions for Lab11 Exercises

```
1. public class DogTest {
public static void main(String[] args) {
    Dog dog = new Dog("Spike");
    System.out.println(dog.getName() + " says " +dog.speak());
    Yorkshire yorkshire = new Yorkshire("Tony");
    System.out.println(yorkshire.getName() + " says " + yorkshire.speak());
    Labrador labrador = new Labrador("Mary", "white");
    System.out.println(labrador.getName() + " says " + labrador.speak());
}
}
(1) (a) (b) change the constructor of Labrador to
public Labrador(String name, String color){
    super(name);
    this.color = color;
}
(2)
    System.out.println(labrador.getName() + " has average weight
    " + labrador.avgBreedWeight());
    System.out.println(yorkshire.getName() + " has average
    weight " +yorkshire.avgBreedWeight());
Error:
    Define breedWeight variable and a method in Yorkshire class:
private int breedWeight = 55;
public int avgBreedWeight(){
```

```
        return breedWeight;
}
```

2. (2) The display in DepositAcc:
```
public void display() {
    System.out.println(" Account type is Deposit");
}
```
Then depacc.display(); call the display from DepositAcc
(3) The modified display in DepositAcc:
```
public void display() {
    super.display();
    System.out.println(" Account type is Deposit");
}
```
(4) Overridden method withdraw in DepositAcc
```
public void withdraw(long amount) {
if(amount<balance){
    super.withdraw(amount);
}
else System.out.println("You don't have enough balance to withdraw!");
}
```

3.
```
public class MatchBox extends Box {
    double weight;
    MatchBox() {}
    MatchBox(double w, double h, double d, double m) {
        super(w, h, d);
        weight = m;
    }
public static void main(String args[]) {
    MatchBox mb1 = new MatchBox(10, 10, 10, 10);
    mb1.getVolume();
    System.out.println("width of MatchBox 1 is " + mb1.width);
    System.out.println("height of MatchBox 1 is " + mb1.height);
    System.out.println("depth of MatchBox 1 is " + mb1.depth);
    System.out.println("weight of MatchBox 1 is " + mb1.weight);
}
}
```

4. Change the draw() method in Shape class:
```
void draw() {
    System.out.println("shape.draw()");
}
```
Then without overriding it in the derived classes, there will be the output as:
```
    shape.draw();
    shape.draw();
    shape.draw();
    shape.draw();
    shape.draw();
    shape.draw();
    shape.draw();
    shape.draw();
    shape.draw();
```
If overriding it in one of the derived classes, for example, Circle class, but not the others, you will have the following output:
```
    Circle.draw();
```

```
        shape.draw();
        Circle.draw();
        shape.draw();
        Circle.draw();
        shape.draw();
        Circle.draw();
        shape.draw();
        shape.draw();
```

```
5. public class Cylinder extends Circle {
        private double length;
        public Cylinder() {
            super();
            length = 1.0;
    }
    public Cylinder(double radius, double length) {
        super(radius);
        this.length = length;
    }
    public double getLength() {
        return length;
    }
    public double findVolume () {
        return findArea() * length;
    }
    }
    public class TestCylinder {
    public static void main (String [] args) {
        Cylinder myCylinder = new Cylinder(5.0, 2.0);
        System.out.println ("\nThe length is " +
            myCylinder.getLength() + "\n" );
        System.out.println ("The radius is " +
            myCylinder.getRadius() + "\n");
        System.out.println ("The volume of the cylinder is " +
            myCylinder.findVolume() + "\n" );
        System.out.println("The area of the circle is " +
            myCylinder.findArea() + "\n");
    }
    }
```

```
6. public class Cylinder2 extends Circle {
    private double length;
    public Cylinder2() {
        super();
        length = 1.0;
    }
    public Cylinder2(double radius, double length) {
        super(radius);
        this.length = length;
    }
    public double getLength() {
        return length;
    }
    public double findArea () {
        return 2*super.findArea() + 2*getRadius()*Math.PI*length;
    }
```

```java
        public double findVolume () {
            return findArea() * length;
        }
        public String toString() {
            return "Cylinder length = " + length;
        }
    }
```

7.
```java
    public abstract class LivingThing {
    private String name;
    public LivingThing(String name){
        this.name = name;
    }
    public void breath(){
        System.out.println("Living Thing breathing...");
    }
    public void eat(){
        System.out.println("Living Thing eating...");
    }
    /**
     * Abstract method walk()
     * We want this method to be implemented by subclasses of
     * LivingThing
     */
    public abstract void walk();
    public String getName() {
        return name;
    }
    public void setName(String name) {
        this.name = name;
    }
    }
```

8.
```java
    public class Human extends LivingThing {
    public Human(String name){
        super(name);
    }
    // Provide implementation of the abstract method.
    public void walk(){
        System.out.println("Human " + getName() + " walks...");
    }
    }
```

9.
```java
    public class Monkey extends LivingThing {
    public Monkey(String name){
        super(name);
    }
    // Implement the abstract method
    public void walk(){
        System.out.println("Monkey " + getName() + " also walks...");
    }
    }
```

10.
```java
    public class Main {
    public static void main(String[] args) {
```

```
        // create Human object instance
        // and assign it to Human type.
        Human human1 = new Human("Obama");
        human1.walk();
        // create Human object instance
        // and assign it to LivingThing type.
        LivingThing livingthing1 = human1;
        livingthing1.walk();
        // create a Monkey object instance
        // and assign it to LivingThing type.
        LivingThing livingthing2 = new Monkey(".dE.oi");
        livingthing2.walk();
        // display data from human1 and livingthing1.
        // observe that they refer to the same object instance.
        System.out.println("human1.getName() = " + human1.getName());
        System.out.println("livingthing1.getName() = " + livingthing1.getName());
    }
}
```

```
11. public class Person implements PersonInterface {
        int cashSaving;
        int retirementFund;
        String firstName;
        String lastName;
        // constructor with arguments
        Person(int cashSaving, int retirementFund, String firstName, String lastName){
        this.cashSaving = cashSaving;
        this.retirementFund = retirementFund;
        this.firstName = firstName;
        this.lastName = lastName;
    }
    // compute person's total wealth
        public int computeTotalWealth(){
        System.out.println((cashSaving + retirementFund));
        return (cashSaving + retirementFund);
    }
    // get person's name
        public String getName(){
        return firstName + " " + lastName;
    }
    }
```

Chapter 2

MATLAB Programming

2.1 Introduction

MATLAB is an interactive mathematical modeling and analysis environment and a high-level language. It can be used for algorithms development, data visualization, data analysis and numeric computation. Language supports high-level mathematical objects, therefore many technical computing problems can be solved faster than with traditional programming languages, such as C, C++ or Fortran. MATLAB can be applied to a wide range of tasks, such as signal processing, communications, control design, test and measurement, financial modeling and analysis, image processing and computational biology. Moreover, additional collections of special-purpose MATLAB functions, available separately, so called toolboxes, which extend the environment to solve a particular problem or group of problems.

MATLAB provides a collection of tools for documenting and sharing your code and results. MATLAB code can be integrated with diverse languages and applications, e.g. e.g. C, C++ and Microsoft Excel.

Key features of MATLAB programming are the following [6].

- High-level language for technical computing.

- Development environment for managing code, files and data.

- Interactive tools for iterative exploration, design and problem solving.

- Mathematical functions for linear algebra, statistics, Fourier analysis, filtering, optimization and numerical integration.

- 2-D and 3-D graphics functions for visualizing data.

- Tools for building custom graphical user interfaces.

- Functions for integrating MATLAB based algorithms with external applications and languages, such as C, C++, Fortran, Java, COM and Microsoft Excel.

2.1.1 Main Components of the MATLAB System

The MATLAB system consists of these main parts [6]:

Desktop Tools and Development Environment is the set of tools, mostly with GUI, and facilities that help to use more productively MATLAB functions and files. The following tools are provided: the MATLAB desktop and Command Window, an editor and debugger, a code analyzer, and browsers for viewing help, the workspace and folders.

Mathematical Function Library is a vast collection of computational algorithms ranging from elementary functions, like sum, sine, cosine and complex arithmetic, to more sophisticated functions like matrix inverse and eigenvalues, Bessel functions and fast Fourier transforms.

MATLAB Language is a high-level matrix/array language with control flow statements, functions, data structures, input/output and some object-oriented programming features. It allows both fast and dirty scripting as well as prototyping and developing complex software packages.

MATLAB Graphics has extensive facilities for displaying vectors and matrices as graphs, as well as annotating and printing these graphs. It includes high-level functions for 2D and 3D data visualization, image processing, animation and presentation graphics. Low-level functions allow to fully customize the appearance of graphics as well as to build complete graphical user interfaces on MATLAB applications.

External Interface library allows to write C/C++ and Fortran programs that interact with MATLAB. It includes facilities for calling routines from MATLAB (dynamic linking), for calling MATLAB as a computational engine, and for reading and writing MAT-files (MAT-LAB).

2.1.2   How to Start

Windows users can simply start MATLAB by clicking on icon or choosing it from Start menu: `Start → All Programs → Matlab`.

Linux users can start MATLAB by typing `matlab` at the command prompt. Symbolic links should be set up symbolic links during the installation procedure. Otherwise the full pathname should precede `matlab` command to start MATLAB, e.g. `matlabroot/bin/matlab` (`matlabroot` is MATLAB installation folder).

Apple users can start MATLAB by double-clicking the icon in the applications folder or typing `matlab` or `/Applications/MATLAB_R2010b.app/bin/matlab` at the command prompt.

See `http://www.mathworks.com/help/techdoc/matlab_env/f8-29401.html` for details.

2.1.3   MATLAB Desktop

MATLAB desktop, see Fig. 2.1, which consists of the following components.

Launch Pad/Workspace

Help is one of the most important components of MATLAB desktop, i.e., if you do not know, how to do something with MATLAB, you can always find it in a comprehensive MATLAB help.

Current Directory menu shows current directory.

Command History shows all commands you already run.

Command Window is an area, where you can type commands and see results.

One of the main working areas is `Command Window`. Basically, it is an interactive MATLAB interface, where you can type diverse commands and observe results. For instance, you can use it for different simple tasks.

- As a simple calculator:

```
>> 1 + 2 <Enter>
ans = 3
```

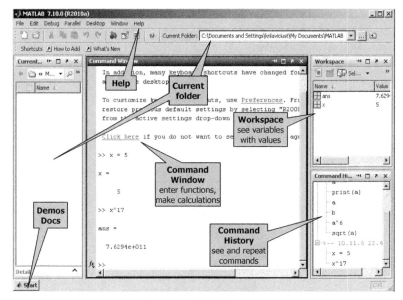

Figure 2.1: MATLAB Desktop

`>>` denotes prompt, i.e., it shows, that MATLAB is waiting for an input. Variable `ans` in MATLAB contains a result of the last operation. We will use `<command>` to denote user commands, e.g. `<Enter>` means "enter" ("return") key on the keyboard. Where it is clear, we will omit such commands.

- To define a variable and assign it a value:

```
>> altitude = 12/4
altitude = 3
```

- Check value of a variable:

```
>> altitude
altitude = 3
```

2.1.4 Help

Help can be accessed via GUI, see fig. 2.1, or from the command line, using command `help`.

```
>> help sin
SIN   Sine of argument in radians.
   SIN(X) is the sine of the elements of X.

   See also asin, sind.
```

```
Overloaded methods:
   codistributed/sin

Reference page in Help browser
   doc sin
```

Help is used when function names is known.

```
>> Help cos
 COS    Cosine of argument in radians.
    COS(X) is the cosine of the elements of X.

    See also acos, cosd.

    Overloaded methods:
       codistributed/cos

    Reference page in Help browser
       doc cos
```

lookfor searches for all functions that contain given keyword.

```
>> lookfor tangent
acot                        - Inverse cotangent, result in radian.
acotd                       - Inverse cotangent, result in degrees.
acoth                       - Inverse hyperbolic cotangent.
atan                        - Inverse tangent, result in radians.
atan2                       - Four quadrant inverse tangent.
atand                       - Inverse tangent, result in degrees.
atanh                       - Inverse hyperbolic tangent.
cot                         - Cotangent of argument in radians.
cotd                        - Cotangent of argument in degrees.
coth                        - Hyperbolic cotangent.
tan                         - Tangent of argument in radians.
tand                        - Tangent of argument in degrees.
tanh                        - Hyperbolic tangent.
...
```

2.1.5   MATLAB Language

MATLAB language is high-level language that supports a wide selection of mathematical functions and operators. It slightly reminds Perl, C and Pascal.

2.1.6   Simple Operators

Order of precedence is usual (ordered from the highest to the lowest precedence level):

- parentheses (,),

- exponential a|^b,

- multiplication, division a*b, a/b,

- addition, substraction a+b, a-b.

See an example of parentheses usage.

Symbol	Operation	MATLAB
+	Addition $a + b$	a+b
/	Division $\frac{a}{b}$	a/b
^	Exponential a^b	a^b
*	Multiplication ab	a*b
$\sqrt{a}$	Square root $\sqrt{a}$	sqrt(a)
-	Substraction $a - b$	a-b

Table 2.1: Basic MATLAB operators

```
>> 4^2-7-2/3*5
ans =
    5.6667

>> 4^2-7-2/(3*5)
ans =
    8.8667

>> 4^2-(7-2)/(3*5)
ans =
   15.6667
```

2.1.7 Variables and Expressions

Variable names in MATLAB start with any letter and then can continue with any letter, number or underscore "_". Variable names are case sensitive. Reserved words, e.g. functions, such as `sin`, can not be used as a variable name. Variable names can be of any length, MATLAB uses only the first N characters of the name, (where N is the number returned by the function `namelengthmax`), and ignores the rest. Therefore, variable name should be unique in the first N characters to enable MATLAB to distinguish them.

Variables can be assigned values directly or via *expressions*.

Expression

$$x = 3$$
$$y = 4$$
$$\frac{x^2 y^3}{(x - y)^2}$$

can be evaluated in MATLAB in the following way

```
>> x=3;
>> y=4;
>> (x^2*y^3)/(x-y)^2
ans =
   576
```

Note, that semicolon ; suppresses results output.

Another example, that shows, how to solve more interesting problems. Given a cylinder of radius `r=0.1`m and length `l=0.5`m. Calculate volume of the cylinder, where volume $V = \pi^2 l$. In MATLAB it can be done in the following manner.

```
>> r=0.1; l=0.5;
>> V=pi*r^2*l
```

```
V =
    0.0157
```

pi is predefined in MATLAB.

Symbols i and j are used to denote imaginary parts of complex numbers, i.e. $i = j = \sqrt{-1}$.

```
>> s=3+7*i,  w=5-9*i
s =
   3.0000 + 7.0000i
w =
   5.0000 - 9.0000i

>> w+s, w-s, w*s, w/s
ans =
   8.0000 - 2.0000i
ans =
   2.0000 -16.0000i
ans =
  78.0000 + 8.0000i
ans =
  -0.8276 - 1.0690i
```

Comma , allows to input several expressions using the same prompt.

2.1.8   MATLAB Workspace

All variables are stored in a *Workspace*. They can be seen in several different ways. Workspace window, see fig. 2.1, shows all variables and their values. It can be done using Command Window using function who.

```
>> who

Your variables are:

V    ans  l    r    s    w
```

Command whos list names and size of variables.

```
>> whos
  Name      Size            Bytes  Class     Attributes

  V         1x1                 8  double
  ans       1x1                16  double    complex
  l         1x1                 8  double
  r         1x1                 8  double
  s         1x1                16  double    complex
  w         1x1                16  double    complex
```

clear removes all variables, and clear V, l would remove only V and l.

2.1.8.1   Saving Workspace Variables

All or selected variables can be saved to a file for future work. Then they can be loaded when required.

```
>> save filename % save all variables to filename
>> save filename g h t v v0 % save selected variables to filename
>> load filename % load saved variables
```

2.1.9 Arrays and Matrices

Arrays are one of the basic data units in MATLAB. Several types of arrays are used in MATLAB.

Scalar is an array with 1 row and 1 column.

Vector is an array with 1 row or 1 column.

Matrix is an array with more than 2 dimensions.

In this section we show how to create and work with diverse arrays.

2.1.9.1 Creation and Addressing

Vectors and matrices can be created using constructor [ ]. Semicolon ; or ENTER are used to separate rows, while spaces or commas , separate columns (elements). % denotes comments, i.e., all the text following % is ignored by MATLAB.

```
>>  a=[1 7 13] % row vector
a =
     1     7    13

>> b=[1; 7; 13] % column vector
b =
     1
     7
    13

>> b=[3
4
5] % column vector
b =
     3
     4
     5
```

Vectors can be created with *range* function `start:step:finish`, or its simplified version `start:finish` with step 1.

```
>> x=3.5:0.25:4.75
x =
    3.5000    3.7500    4.0000    4.2500    4.5000    4.7500

>> x=3:5
x =
     3     4     5
```

Matrices can be created in the similar manner.

```
>> A=[1 7 13; 4 5 6]
A =
     1     7    13
```

```
     4     5     6
>> A=[1 7 13
4 5 6]
A =
     1     7    13
     4     5     6
```

Transpose and complex conjugate transpose (Hermitian) can be created using.

```
>> A
A =
     1     7    13
     4     5     6
>> A'
ans =
     1     4
     7     5
    13     6
>> B=[2+3j 6+j; 1-5j 5-3j], B'
B =
   2.0000 + 3.0000i   6.0000 + 1.0000i
   1.0000 - 5.0000i   5.0000 - 3.0000i
ans =
   2.0000 - 3.0000i   1.0000 + 5.0000i
   6.0000 - 1.0000i   5.0000 + 3.0000i
```

Elements in arrays are indexed from 1. To access an element or sub-array, parentheses are used. Colon : is used to denote interval, e.g. 3:6 denotes 3, 4, 5 and 6.

It is rather simple for vectors.

```
>> vector=[2 3 17 100 -5]
vector =
     2     3    17   100    -5
>> vector(3)
ans =
    17
>> vector(2:4)
ans =
     3    17   100
```

For matrices it gets a bit more complicated, because first rows should be specified, and then column. In case of more dimensions, indices for each dimension should be specified. If instead of indices only colon is given, it means that all elements of this dimension should be selected. Indices can be given as a vector, e.g. for [1 3] only the first and the third elements (row, column) will be selected.

```
>> C
C =
     2     4    10    13    17
     0     1     2     3     9
     3     2     1     0     9
```

```
       1     1     1     1     1
>> C(1,3)
ans =
     10

>> C(:,3)
ans =
     10
      2
      1
      1

>> C(:,2:4)
ans =
      4    10    13
      1     2     3
      2     1     0
      1     1     1

>> C([1 3],2:5)
ans =
      4    10    13    17
      2     1     0     9
```

2.1.9.2 Array Functions and Operations

MATLAB provides a set of convenient functions and operations for handling arrays.

length(vector) returns number of elements in vector vector.

```
>> vector, length(vector)
vector =
    0.8687    0.0844    0.3998    0.2599    0.8001
ans =
      5
```

size(matrix) returns a row vector [m n] containing size $m \times n$ of array A. In case of vector, one of the dimensions is 1.

```
>> matrix, size(matrix)
matrix =
    0.3692    0.2417    0.9421
    0.1112    0.4039    0.9561
    0.7803    0.0965    0.5752
    0.3897    0.1320    0.0598
ans =
      4     3

>> vector, size(vector)
vector =
    0.8687    0.0844    0.3998    0.2599    0.8001
ans =
      1
```

MATLAB provides two types of multiplication and division for matrices, namely array and matrice multiplication and division.

Array operations are element-by-element operations. When a scalar is *added* or *subtracted* to
an array, it is *added* (*subtracted*) to each element of array.
The same holds for *multiplication* and *division*.

```
>> A, A+3, A-2, A*2, A/2
A =
    6.4912      6.4775      5.4701
    7.3172      4.5092      2.9632
ans =
    9.4912      9.4775      8.4701
   10.3172      7.5092      5.9632
ans =
    4.4912      4.4775      3.4701
    5.3172      2.5092      0.9632
ans =
   12.9823     12.9549     10.9402
   14.6344      9.0185      5.9264
ans =
    3.2456      3.2387      2.7350
    3.6586      2.2546      1.4816
```

Array *subtraction* and *addition* are similar, i.e. corresponding elements are *added* (*subtracted*).
Arrays dimensions must agree. Array *multiplication* .* and ./ and *division* are performed element-
wise as well. Dimensions, again, must agree.

```
>> A, B, A+B, A-B, A.*B, A./B
A =
    6.4912      6.4775      5.4701
    7.3172      4.5092      2.9632
B =
    3.6848      7.8023      9.2939
    6.2562      0.8113      7.7571
ans =
   10.1760     14.2797     14.7639
   13.5734      5.3205     10.7203
ans =
    2.8063     -1.3248     -3.8238
    1.0610      3.6980     -4.7939
ans =
   23.9189     50.5389     50.8382
   45.7779      3.6582     22.9860
ans =
    1.7616      0.8302      0.5886
    1.1696      5.5583      0.3820
```

As expected, array exponentiation `matrix.^exp` is also performed element-wise.

```
>> A, A.*A.*A, A.^3
A =
     1      2
    10     20
ans =
        1          8
     1000       8000
ans =
        1          8
     1000       8000
```

	1	**2**	**3**	**4**	**5**
R (Ω)	10^4	2×10^4	3.5×10^4	10^5	2×10^5
v (V)	120	80	110	200	350

Table 2.2: Resistors voltage and resistance

Let current i passing through a resistor R with voltage v across it, is given by $i = \frac{v}{R}$. Let the power dissipated by the resistor is given by $P = \frac{v^2}{R}$. Compute the current and power dissipation for resistors, shown in Table 2.2.

How to solve it using MATLAB? It can be done in several steps. The first step is to create vectors containing resistance and voltage values.

```
>> R=[10e3 20e3 25e3 100e3 200e3]
R =
        10000       20000       25000      100000      200000

>> v=[120 80 110 200 350]
v =
   120    80   110   200   350
```

Then current $i = \frac{v}{R}$ can be easily found by applying array division.

```
>> i=v./R
i =
    0.0120    0.0040    0.0044    0.0020    0.0018
```

Power dissipation $P = \frac{v^2}{R}$ is calculated using array exponentiation and array division.

```
>> P=v.^2./R
P =
    1.4400    0.3200    0.4840    0.4000    0.6125
```

Matrix addition and *subtraction* areperformed element-wise and are the same as for arrays. However, *matrix multiplication* and *division* are completely **different** operations.

Vector-matrix multiplication is defined as follows. Let A be a matrix of size $m \times p$ and x be a vector of length p. Notice, that vector should be of the same length as matrix columns. Result of Ax is a vector of length p. Let $m = 2$ and $p = 2$, then

$$\begin{bmatrix} a_{11} & a_{12} \\ a_{21} & a_{22} \end{bmatrix} \begin{bmatrix} x_1 \\ x_2 \end{bmatrix} = \begin{bmatrix} a_{11}x_1 + a_{12}x_2 \\ a_{21}x_1 + a_{22}x_2 \end{bmatrix}$$

For example

$$\begin{bmatrix} 4 & 9 \\ 9 & 6 \end{bmatrix} \begin{bmatrix} 6 \\ 6 \end{bmatrix} = \begin{bmatrix} 4*6 + 9*6 \\ 9*6 + 6*6 \end{bmatrix} = \begin{bmatrix} 78 \\ 90 \end{bmatrix}$$

In MATLAB it is a lot easier.

```
>> A, x, A*x
A =
     4     9
     9     6

x =
     6
```

```
       6

ans =
      78
      90
```

Matrix-Matrix multiplication is defined as follows. Let A be a matrix of size $m \times p$ and B be a matrix of size $p \times n$. The first matrix has the same number of columns as the second rows. The product of AB is of size of $m \times n$.

$$\begin{bmatrix} a_{11} & a_{12} \\ a_{21} & a_{22} \end{bmatrix} \begin{bmatrix} b_{11} & b_{12} & b_{13} \\ b_{21} & b_{22} & b_{23} \end{bmatrix} = \begin{bmatrix} a_{11}b_{11} + a_{12}b_{21} & a_{11}b_{12} + a_{12}b_{22} & a_{11}b_{13} + a_{12}b_{23} \\ a_{21}b_{11} + a_{22}b_{21} & a_{21}b_{12} + a_{22}b_{22} & a_{21}b_{13} + a_{22}b_{23} \end{bmatrix}$$

In MATLAB it is done in the following manner.

```
>> A, B, C=A*B
A =
      4       9
      9       6
B =
      2       5       8
      3       2       2
C =
     35      38      50
     36      57      84
```

Let

$$A = \begin{bmatrix} 4 & 9 \\ 9 & 6 \end{bmatrix} \quad B = \begin{bmatrix} 2 & 2 \\ 2 & 4 \end{bmatrix} \quad C = \begin{bmatrix} 3 & 4 \\ 9 & 2 \end{bmatrix}$$

Show, that distributivity $A(B + C) = AB + AC$ holds for these matrcies.
In MATLAB it can be shown in the following way.

```
>> A, B, C, A*(B+C)-(A*B+A*C)
A =
      4       9
      9       6
B =
      2       2
      2       4
C =
      3       4
      9       2
ans =
      0       0
      0       0
```

Matrix exponentiation $A^2 = AA$ is a specific case of matrix product, i.e. matrix A should be square.

```
>> A, A^2, A^3, A.^2, A.^3
A =
      4       9
      9       6
ans =
     97      90
     90     117
```

```
ans =
    1198      1413
    1413      1512
ans =
      16    81
      81    36
ans =
      64   729
     729   216
```

Notice, that it differs from arrays multiplication `.^`.

2.1.9.3 Special Matrices

Identity matrix is a square matrix with with diagonal elements ones and other zeros. It is denoted by I, and is generated by function **eye** in MATLAB.

```
>> I=eye(4)
I =
     1     0     0     0
     0     1     0     0
     0     0     1     0
     0     0     0     1
```

Zero matrix is a matrix of zeros, while *One matrix* is a matrix of ones. They are generated by **zeros** and **ones** commands.

```
>> zeros(3), zeros(2,3), ones(3), ones(2,3)
ans =
     0     0     0
     0     0     0
     0     0     0
ans =
     0     0     0
     0     0     0
ans =
     1     1     1
     1     1     1
     1     1     1
ans =
     1     1     1
     1     1     1
```

Of course, there are more different useful operations on matrices, we refer interested reader to MATLAB help

2.1.10 Basic Mathematical Functions

We list some of the main functions in Table 2.3. There are many more diverse functions in MATLAB, and even more can be defined using programming facilities of MATLAB, which will be discussed in Sect. 2.3.

Notice, that trigonometric functions expect and return *radians*, not *degrees*. $\Theta_{\text{radians}} = \frac{\pi}{180}\Theta_{\text{degrees}}$.

Functions are used in a simple way.

Function	Math	MATLAB
Exponential and Logarithmic		
Base-10 logarithm	$\log_{10} x$	log10(x)
Exponential	e^x	exp(x)
Natural logarithm	$\ln x$	log(x)
Square root	$\sqrt{x}$	sqrt(x)
Complex Numbers		
Absolute value	$|x|$	abs(x)
Angle of complex number		angle(x)
Complex conjugate	$\overline{x}$	conj(x)
Imaginary part of complex number	$\Im(x)$	imag(x)
Real part of complex number	$\Re(x)$	real(x)
Numerical Functions		
Round up	$\lceil x \rceil$	ceil(x)
Round down	$\lfloor x \rfloor$	floor(x)
Round		round(x)
Sign	$\mathrm{sgn}(x)$	sign(x)
Truncate (round to 0)		fix(x)
Trigonometric Functions		
Cosine	$\cos(x)$	cos(x)
Sine	$\sin(x)$	sin(x)
Tangent	$\tan(x)$	tan(x)
Inverse cosine	$\arccos(x)$	acos(x)
Inverse sine	$\arcsin(x)$	asin(x)
Inverse tangent	$\arctan(x)$	atan(x)

Table 2.3: Basic Mathematical Functions

```
>> x=9; log10(x), log(x), sqrt(x), exp(x)
ans =
    0.9542
ans =
    2.1972
ans =
    3
ans =
  8.1031e+003

>> s=3+7i; abs(s), angle(s), conj(s), real(s), imag(s)
ans =
    7.6158
ans =
    1.1659
ans =
    3.0000 - 7.0000i
ans =
    3
ans =
    7
```

Mathematical functions can be applied to arrays as well as scalars.

```
>> xa = [9 16 25]; sqrt(xa)
ans =
```

```
        3      4      5
>> z=[4.1 4.6 -2.3 -2.6];
>> ceil(z)
ans =
        5      5     -2     -2

>> fix(z)
ans =
        4      4     -2     -2

>> floor(z)
ans =
        4      4     -3     -3

>> round(z)
ans =
        4      5     -2     -3

>> sign(z)
ans =
        1      1     -1     -1
```

2.2 Plots

Function	Description
grid	Controls grid lines
legend	Adds legend
plot	Creates plot
title	Adds title to plot
xlabel	Adds label to X-axis
ylabel	Adds label to Y-axis

Table 2.4: Plotting functions

MATLAB provides a set of excellent tools for producing diverse plots. We list the main plotting functions in Table 2.4.

2.2.1 Single Plot

Plotting graphs in MATLAB is straightforward. We illustrate it by plotting a simple parabola $y = x^2 - 10x + 15$ in the interval $0 \le x \le 10$.

```
>> x=0:0.5:10; y=x.^2-10*x+15;
>> plot(x,y); xlabel('x'); ylabel('y'); grid on;
>> title('Plot of y=x^2-10x+15')
```

See the generated plot in Fig. 2.2. It can be saved in many different formats via menu commands.

2.2.2 Multiple Plots

Plotting several graphs in one plot window is as easy as plotting single plot. Let us plot $f(x) = \sin 2x$ and its derivative $d/dt \sin 2x = 2 \cos 2x$ in the same window.

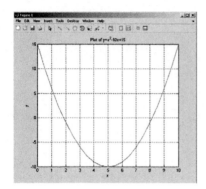

Figure 2.2: Plot of $y = x^2 - 10x + 15$

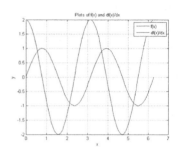

Figure 2.3: Plots of $f(x) = \sin 2x$ and $g(x) = 2\cos 2x$

```
>> x=0:pi/100:2*pi; y1=sin(2*x); y2=2*cos(2*x);
>> plot(x,y1,x,y2); xlabel('x'); ylabel('y'); legend('f(x)','df(x)/dx');
>> title('Plots of f(x) and df(x)/dx'); grid on;
```

Here x=0:pi/100:2*pi creates and array of values from 0 to 2*pi with step pi/100. Each command can be written in a separate line, as well.

See resulting plot in Fig. 2.3

2.2.3 Customizing Plots

Color		Symbol		Line style	
Notation	Color	Notation	Symbol	Notation	Style
b	blue	.	point	–	solid
g	green	o	circle	:	dotted
r	red	x	x-mark	-.	dashdot
c	cyan	+	plus	--	dashed
m	magenta	*	star		
y	yellow	s	square		
k	black	d	diamond		
		v	triangle (down)		
		^	triangle (up)		
		<	triangle (left)		
		>	triangle (right)		
		p	pentagram		
		h	hexagram		

Table 2.5: Plots Customization

MATLAB allows customizing plots. We list most of the characters for configuring plots in Table 2.5. To change color, line style or plot symbols just use a string that defines plot properties, which should be added to plot(x, y, 'cust_string') command.

Some examples:

- `plot(x, y, 'r+)` plots a red dotted line with a plus at each data point.

- `plot(x, y, 'bd)` plots a blue diamond at each data point and does not draw line.

- `plot(x, y1, 'k-', x, y2, 'y--')` plots y1 with a solid black line and y2 with a dashed yellow line.

2.3 Programming in MATLAB

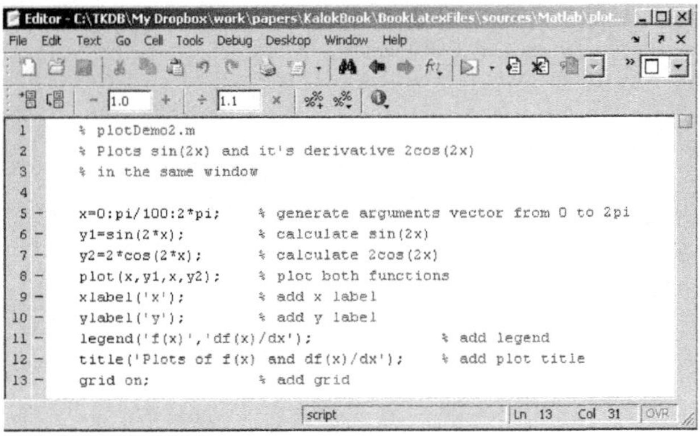

Figure 2.4: MATLAB Edit Window

MATLAB allows placing series of commands in separate *M-files* (files with and extension *.m), that can be reused as many times as necessary, by executing them in the Command Window. It can be just *scripts*, i.e. series of commands, and custom *functions*, that can be used in the same way as usual MATLAB functions.

M-files can be created and edited using **Edit Window**, by choosing `File/New/M-file` or `File/Open`, correspondingly.

We illustrate scripting by a script, see Fig. 2.4, that plots Fig. 2.3. You can get a plot just by typing script name, in this case `plotDemo2` in Command Window.

2.3.1 Function Files

Function files allow defining custom functions, that can be used in the same manner, as regular MATLAB functions. They are especially useful, when the same operation should be repeated several times. Moreover, they hide all internal complexity of the solution, and provide just clear interface.

Function starts from function descriptor

```
Function [output1, output2, ...] = function_name(input1, input2, ...)
```

For instance, let *velocity v* and *distance h* of the falling object are calculated as follows:

$$v = v_0 + gt$$

$$h = v_0 t + \frac{gt^2}{2}$$

Then, let us define MATLAB function `drop.m`, that calculates them.

```
function [ v, h ] = drop( v0, t, g )
% drop computes velocity and traveled distance of a droped object
%    Inputs:
%    v0  - initial velocity
%    t   - (vector) of fall time
%    g   - acceleration
%    Outputs:
%    v   - velocity at time t
%    h   - traveled distance at time t

v = v0 + g*t;           % calculate velocity
h = v0*t + g*t.^2/2;    % calculate distance

end
```

It can be invoked in the following way.

```
>> g=9.8; v0=10; t=0:0.5:2; [v,h]=drop(v0, t, g)
v =
   10.0000    14.9000    19.8000    24.7000    29.6000
h =
        0     6.2250    14.9000    26.0250    39.6000

>> g=9.8; v0=10; t=2; [v,h]=drop(v0, t, g)
v =
   29.6000
h =
   39.6000
```

Notice, that it works with the time given as a single value or a vector, because we use element-wise exponentiation .^.

2.3.2   Control Statements

MATLAB programming language supports standard constructs, that allow controlling work-flow, i.e. branching and loops. We introduce relational and logical operators and then continue with branching and loops.

2.3.2.1   Relational and Logical Operators

MATLAB language includes usual logical and relational operators, we list them in Table 2.6. TRUE in MATLAB is denoted 1 (any non-zero number is treated as TRUE as well), and FALSE is denoted 0. Result of any comparison or logical operation can be assigned to a variable. We illustrate it with simple examples.

```
>> x=2; y=5;

>> z=(x<y)
z =
     1

>> x<=y
ans =
     1

>> x==y, x~=y
```

Operator	Explanation
Relational operators	
==	Equal to
~=	Not equal to
>	Greater than
>=	Greater than or equal to
<	Less than
<=	Less than or equal
Logical operators	
&	pairwise logical AND
|	pairwise logical OR
xor	pairwise logical XOR
~	element-wise negation

Table 2.6: Relational and Logical Operators

```
ans =
     0
ans =
     1

>> x>=y, x>y
ans =
     0
ans =
     0

>> x>=2
ans =
     1
```

Notice, that == is an *equivalence operator*, that is used to compare results, while = is an *assignment operator*, used to assign value to a variable.

Notice, that due numbers with floating point representation in computer and rounding errors, relational operators might produce unexpected results, e.g.:

```
>> a=0, b=sin(pi)
a =
     0
b =
   1.2246e-016

>> a==b, a~=b
ans =
     0
ans =
     1
```

Relational operators can compare arrays (vectors) element-wise as well.

```
>> x, y, z_less = (x<y), z_neq = (x~=y), z_more = (x>8)
x =
     8     9     1
y =
```

```
       9       6       1
z_less =
       1       0       0
z_neq =
       1       1       0
z_more =
       0       1       0
```

Logical operators can be applied to scalars and element-wise to arrays (vectors).

```
>> A, B
A =
       0       1       1
       0       1       0
B =
       1       0       0
       0       0       1

>> ~A, ~B
ans =
       1       0       0
       1       0       1
ans =
       0       1       1
       1       1       0

>> A&B
ans =
       0       0       0
       0       0       0

>> A|B
ans =
       1       1       1
       0       1       1

>> xor(A, B)
ans =
       1       1       1
       0       1       1
```

Function `find` finds indices of non-zero elements and returns their indices in a vector.

```
>> x, y
x =
      -2       0      -3       1      -2
y =
       2       2       2       0      -4

>> find(x>0)
ans =
       4

>> find(y>0)
ans =
       1       2       3
```

```
>> find(x==0 & y==0)
ans =
    Empty matrix: 1-by-0
```

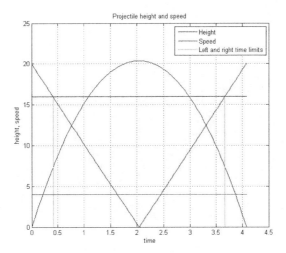

Figure 2.5: Projectile speed and height

Let height h and speed v of a projectile with an initial speed v_0 and angle $90°$ are defined by

$$h(t) = v_0 t - \frac{gt^2}{2}$$
$$v(t) = \sqrt{v_0^2 - 2v_0 gt + g^2 t^2}$$

where $g = 9.81 m/s^2$ is gravity. The projectile will fall down when $h(0) = 0$, i.e. at the time $t_{hit} = \frac{2v_0}{g}$.

Let $v_0 = 20 m/s$. Find the time when the height is $\geq 4m$ and the speed is $\leq 16m/s$. We provide a solution in MATLAB as follows.

```
% projectile.m
% Finds time interval when h>=4m and v<=16m/s

v0 = 20;        % initial speed
g = 9.81;       % acceleration

t_hit = 2*v0/g; % time until the projectile touches the ground

% generate array containing time with step t_hit/100
t = 0:t_hit/100:t_hit;
h = v0*t-0.5*g*t.^2;                        % compute height at each time step
v = sqrt(real(v0^2-2*v0*g*t+g^2*t.^2)); % compute speed at each time step
```

```
u = find(h>=4 & v<=16)                    % find when height>=4 and speed<=16

t_left = t(u(1))    % the first element of vector is the left limit of time
t_right = t(u(end)) % the last element of vector is the right limit of time

% plot system
plot(t, h, 'b', t, v, 'r')                % height and velocity over time
line([t_left t_left],    [0 v(u(1))], 'Color', 'g')  % left limit
line([t_right t_right], [0 v(u(end))], 'Color', 'g')% right limit
line([0 max(t)], [4 4], 'Color', 'b')    % min height
line([0 max(t)], [16 16], 'Color', 'r') % max velocity
xlabel('time');
ylabel('height, speed');
title('Projectile height and speed');
grid on;
legend('Height', 'Speed', 'Left and right time limits');
```

Simulation results and time limits are depicted in Fig. 2.5.

2.3.2.2 Branching Statements

Branching statements allow to choose different executions depending on current execution results. The following constructs are used:

Simple IF if expr, statement end, the statement is executed if expr evaluates to 1.

IF with ELSE if expr, stat1 else stat2 end, expr evaluates to 1 then stat1 is executed, otherwise stat2 is executed.

IF with ELSEIF if expr, stat elseif expr, stat else stat end, allows longer chains of branching.

We demonstrate it on simple examples.

```
% branchingDemo.m
% demonstrates branching statements behavior
x = 5; y = 7;
if (x>0)&(y>0)
    z=log(x)+log(y)
end;

if x>= 0
    disp('x>=0')
elseif y>=0
  disp('y>=0 and x<0')
else
  disp('x,y<0')
end;

>> branchingDemo
z =
    3.5553

x>=0
```

Let

$$y = \begin{cases} \ln x & x \geq 5 \\ \sqrt{x} & 0 \leq x < 5 \\ e^x - 1 & x < 0 \end{cases}$$

We can implement such functions in MATLAB as follows.

```
function [ y ] = BranchingDemo2( x )
% BranchingDemo2 is branching statement demo
% It calculates function y =
%    ln x, if x>=5
%    sqrt(x), if 0<=x<5
%    e^x-1, if x<0

if x>=5
    y = log(x);
elseif x>=0
    y = sqrt(x);
else
    y = exp(x)-1;
end
end

>> BranchingDemo2(-2), exp(-2)-1 % the second parameter is used for testing
ans =
   -0.8647
ans =
   -0.8647

>> BranchingDemo2(3), sqrt(3) % the second parameter is used for testing
ans =
   1.7321
ans =
   1.7321

>> BranchingDemo2(10), log(10) % the second parameter is used for testing
ans =
   2.3026
ans =
   2.3026
```

IF constructs can be nested as well.

Let $ax^2 + bx + c = 0$ and $a = 0$, then

$$x = \begin{cases} \frac{-b \mp \sqrt{b^2 - 4ac}}{2a} & b^2 - 4ac \neq 0 \\ \frac{-b}{2a} & b^2 - 4ac = 0 \end{cases}$$

In MATLAB it can be defined as follows.

```
function [ x1, x2 ] = QuadraticEquation( a, b, c )
% QuadraticEquation solves quadratic equation ax^2+bx+c=0

epsilon = 1e-10; % to solve problems with floating number precision

if a==0
    error('a=0 - it is not a quadratic equation'); % displays (error) message and aborts function
% b^2-4ac==0
elseif abs(b^2-4*a*c)<epsilon
    x1 = -b/(2*a);
    x2 = x1;
else
    x1 = (-b+sqrt(b^2-4*a*c))/(2*a);
```

```
    x2 = (-b-sqrt(b^2-4*a*c))/(2*a);
end
end

>> [x1, x2] = QuadraticEquation(0,1,1) % error at line 7 of function
??? Error using ==> QuadraticEquation at 7
a=0 - it is not a quadratic equation

>> [x1, x2] = QuadraticEquation(1,-4,4)
x1 =
     2
x2 =
     2

>> [x1, x2] = QuadraticEquation(1,0,-4)
x1 =
     2
x2 =
    -2
```

Switch statement allows to choose among several cases based on the provided expression. General form in MATLAB is as follows.

```
switch expression
    case case_expression,
        case_statement
    case case_expression,
        case_statement
    ...
    otherwise
        statement
end
```

We exemplify the usage of `switch` with a function that determines wheteher a number in the interval $[1, 19]$ is odd or even.

```
function OddEven( x )
% OddEven determines whether x is odd or even for 1<x<10

switch (x)
    case {1, 3, 5, 7, 9}
        disp([num2str(x), ' is odd']);
    case {2, 4, 6, 8, 10}
        disp([num2str(x), ' is even']);
    otherwise
        disp([num2str(x), ' is out of range']);
end;
end

>> OddEven(2)
2 is even
>> OddEven(7)
7 is odd
>> OddEven(11)
11 is out of range
```

Function `disp` prints results, and function `num2str` converts numeric value to string for printing purpose.

2.3.2.3 Loops

Loops allow executing statements more than once.

FOR loop executes a block of statements a specified number of times. It has the form

```
for loop_variable =  first : increment : last
        statement 1;
        statement 2;
        ...
        statement n;
end;
```

where loop variable iterates through range `first` to `last` with the step `increment`.

```
% for_demo_1.m - a simple demo of for loop
for i = 5:2:23
    i_square = i^2;
    i_square_double = 2 * i_square;
    disp(['i = ', num2str(i),...
        '  i^2 = ', num2str(i_square),...
        '  2 * i^2 = ', num2str(i_square_double)] );
end;

>> for_demo_1
i = 5   i^2 = 25   2 * i^2 = 50
i = 7   i^2 = 49   2 * i^2 = 98
i = 9   i^2 = 81   2 * i^2 = 162
i = 11  i^2 = 121  2 * i^2 = 242
i = 13  i^2 = 169  2 * i^2 = 338
i = 15  i^2 = 225  2 * i^2 = 450
i = 17  i^2 = 289  2 * i^2 = 578
i = 19  i^2 = 361  2 * i^2 = 722
i = 21  i^2 = 441  2 * i^2 = 882
i = 23  i^2 = 529  2 * i^2 = 1058
```

Dots ... informs MATLAB that statement continues in the following line.

FOR loop can be used to calculate factorial $N!$, where

$$f(N) = N! = \begin{cases} 1, N = 0 \\ N \cdot (N-1) \cdot (N-2) \cdot \cdots \cdot 3 \cdot 2 \cdot 1, N > 0 \end{cases}$$

We use property $N! = N \cdot (N-1)!$.

```
function y = factorial( N )
%factorial returns y=N!

y = 1;

for i = 1 : N
    y = y * i;  % N! = N * (N - 1)!
end;
end

>> factorial(10)
ans =
      3628800
```

```
>> factorial(5)
ans =
   120

>> factorial(0)
ans =
     1
```

Often loops are used to iterate through arrays or vectors and perform required operations on the elements. Let $\mathbf{x}$ is a vector of measurements. Elements $-0.1 \leq x \leq 0.1$ are considered erroneous and removed from the vector, but zero elements are added at the end of $\mathbf{x}$.

```
function xnew = CleanData_Loop( x )
% CleanData_Loop.m  uses a loop to remove x such that -0.1 < x < 0.1
% and replaces them with zeros at the end of array

xnew = zeros(size(x));  % create zero elements vector

ii = 1;                 % index for new vector
for i = 1 : length(x)   % iterate through x
   if abs(x(i)) >= 0.1 % if x<=-0.1 or x >= 0.1
        xnew(ii) = x(i); % then add it to new vector
        ii = ii + 1;     % increment index of the new vector
   end;
end;
end
```

However, many of such operations can be simplified using functions provided by MATLAB. We exemplify them by using function find.

```
function xnew = CleanData_Find( x )
% CleanData_Loop.m  uses find function to locate x such that -0.1 < x < 0.1
% and then replaces them with zeros at the end of array

xnew = zeros(size(x));  % create zero elements vector

i = find( abs(x)>=0.1 );   % get indices of x<=-0.1 or x >= 0.1
xnew(1:length(i)) = x(i);  % put them to the begging of xnew

end
```

We present a short function to test results produced by both functions.

```
% Cleandata_Test.m CleanData_Loop and CleanData_Find functions
x         = [1.92 0.05 -2.43 -0.02 0.85]; % input
xnew_test = [1.92 -2.43 0.85  0 0];        % expected output

xnew_loop = CleanData_Loop(x);  % get results of CleanData_Loop
xnew_find = CleanData_Find(x);  % get results of CleanData_Find

% print results
disp(['x        = ', num2str(x)]);
disp(['xnew_test = ' , num2str(xnew_test)]);
disp(['xnew_loop = ' , num2str(xnew_loop)]);
disp(['xnew_find = ' , num2str(xnew_find)]);
```

```
>> cleanData_test()
x         = 1.92        0.05       -2.43       -0.02        0.85
xnew_test = 1.92       -2.43        0.85        0           0
xnew_loop = 1.92       -2.43        0.85        0           0
xnew_find = 1.92       -2.43        0.85        0           0
```

WHILE loop comes very useful when number of iterations is unknown in advance. General structure of this loop is as follows

```
while expression
        statements
end;
```

Loop is repeated as long as expression remains TRUE. We demonstrate it on simple example.

```
% while_demo_1.m - simple while loop demo
x = 3;                 % initialize loop variable
while x < 27           % loop, if x < 27
    disp(x);           % print x
    x = 2*x - 1;       % evaluate next value of x
end;

>> while_demo_1
    3
    5
    9
   17
```

Notice, that it is very easy to create an *infinite loop*, that never ends. It can be interrupted by pressing ctrl-c.

```
>> while_demo_2
    1
    1
    1
    1
    1
??? Operation terminated by user during ==> while_demo_2 at 6
```

break command can be used to stop for or while loop. However, it is not advisable, because usually the same results can be achieved using proper conditions with while.

Loops can be nested. Usually, it is used to iterate over matrices or higher dimensions arrays.

```
% nestedLoop_demo_1.m  demo of nested loops
n = 3;
A = zeros(n); % generate square zero matrix of size n
for i = 1 : n
    for j = 1 : n
        A(i,j) = i * j;
    end;
end;
disp(A)

>> nestedLoop_demo_1
```

```
1    2    3
2    4    6
3    6    9
```

Some advices on using loops:

- Use **for** when number of iterations is known in advance.

- Use **while** when number of iteratoins is not known in advance.

- **Never** change value of **for** index variable.

- Initialize all the arrays used in the loop in advance - it makes loop faster.

- Use arrays function instead of loops if possible - it is faster.

2.3.2.4 Debugging MATLAB Programs

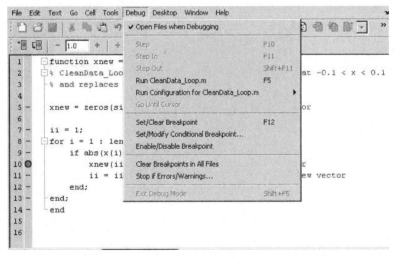

Figure 2.6: MATLAB Editor Window with Breakpoint

It is very easy to introduce errors into programs. In such a case *debugging* techniques come-in handy. Usually it means step-wise execution of program. However, MATLAB provides a set of convenient tools, that makes debugging process easier.

Breakpoints is one of such tools. Basically, it allows to specify a line of the program where MATLAB should execute, and then values of variables can be observed or changed. In Fig. 2.6 the dark circle in line 10 shows the breakpoint. It can be inserted using **F12** or corresponding icon of Editor Window. Debug menu (see Fig. 2.6) allows to choose required operations.

- *Step*: execute the current line of the file.

- *Step In*: execute the current line of the file and, if the line is a call to another function, step into that function.

- *Step Out*: after stepping in, run the rest of the called function or sub-function, leave the called function, and pause.

To exit debugging click **Exit Debug Mode** in **Debug** menu.

2.3.2.5 Polynomials in MATLAB

Given n-th order polynomials of the form

$$f(x) = a_1 x^n + a_2 x^{n-1} + \cdots + a_n x + a_{n+1}$$

Algebraic operations on polynomials are performed using array operations in MATLAB. However, shorter polynomials should be synchronized with longer ones by adding zero coefficients.

The following polynomials

$$f(x) = 9x^3 - 5x^2 + 3x + 7$$
$$g(x) = 6x^2 - x + 2$$

in MATLAB should be represented as

$$f(x) = 9x^3 - 5x^2 + 3x + 7$$
$$g(x) = 0x^3 + 6x^2 - x + 2$$

Thus,

```
>> f=[9 -5 3 7]; g=[0 6 -1 2];
>> h=f+g
h =
     9     1     2     9
```

Polynomial *multiplication* is performed using *convolve* function **conv**.

$$f(x)g(x) = \left(9x^3 - 5x^2 + 3x + 7\right)\left(6x^2 - x + 2\right)$$
$$54x^5 - 39x^4 + 41x^3 + 29x^2 - x + 14$$

in MATLAB

```
>> f=[9 -5 3 7]; g=[0 6 -1 2];
>> product=conv(f, g)
product =
     0    54   -39    41    29    -1    14
```

Polynomial *division* ir performed using *deconvolve* function **deconv**.

$$p(x) = x^4 + 2x^3 - 5x + 6$$
$$s(x) = x^2 + 2x + 3$$

$$q(x) = x^2 - 3$$
$$r(x) = x + 15$$

in MATLAB

```
>> p=[1 2 0 -5 6]; s=[1 2 3];
>> [quotient, remainder]=deconv(p,s)
quotient =
     1     0    -3
remainder =
     0     0     0     1    15
```

`polyval(a, x)` function evaluates polynomial with coefficients `a` at the specified values of its independent variable `x`.

```
>> a=[9 -5 3 7]; x=[0:2:8];
>> f=polyval(a,x)
f =
           7          65         515        1789        4319
```

Roots of the polynomial can be found using function `roots(a)`.

```
>> a=[1 -7 40 -34]; rt=roots(a)

rt =

   3.0000 + 5.0000i
   3.0000 - 5.0000i
   1.0000
```

Polynomial can be constructed from roots using function `poly(rt)`.

```
>> b=poly(rt)
b =
    1.0000   -7.0000   40.0000  -34.0000
```

`roots` solves only polynomials, while `[x, fval] = fzero('function', x0)` can find roots `x` of `function` near `x0`, where `fval` are values of the `function` at `x`.

```
>> [x, fval]=fzero('cos',2)
x =
    1.5708
fval =
  6.1232e-017
```

Explanation of results of the function `[x, fval, exitflag] = fzero('function', x0)` are given in `exitflag`:

- 1 - function converged to a solution x;

- -1 - algorithm was terminated by the output function;

- -3 - NaN or Inf function value was encountered during search for an interval containing a sign change;

- -4 - complex function value was encountered during search for an interval containing a sign change;

- -5 - fzero might have converged to a singular point;

- -6 - fzero can not detect a change in sign of the function.

Let us find the roots of $x + 2e^{-x} = 3$. It is equivalent to finding roots of $f(x) = x + 2e^{-3} - 3$. In MATLAB it can be done in two steps. A function should be defined as follows:

```
function y = Function4RootsDemo(x)
% Function4RootsDemo.m - a function for FunctionRootsDemo
    y = x + 2* exp(-x) - 3;
end
```

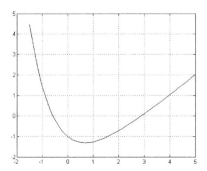

Figure 2.7: Plot of $f(x) = x + 2e^{-3} - 3$

Then it can be explored, e.g. using **plot**, see Fig. 2.7. It shows, that solutions are near -0.5 and 3, and **fzero** can be applied.

```
>> fzero('Function4RootsDemo', -0.5)
ans =
   -0.5831

>> fzero('Function4RootsDemo', 3)
ans =
    2.8887
```

2.3.2.6 Linear Equations in MATLAB

Linear equations of form

$$a_{11}x_1 + a_{12}x_2 + \ldots + a_{1n}x_n = b_1$$
$$a_{21}x_1 + a_{22}x_2 + \ldots + a_{2n}x_n = b_2$$
$$a_{n1}x_1 + a_{n2}x_2 + \ldots + a_{nn}x_n = b_n$$

or, in a matrix form $Ax = b$, where

$$A = \begin{bmatrix} a_{11} & a_{12} & \cdots & a_{1n} \\ a_{21} & a_{22} & \cdots & a_{2n} \\ \vdots & \vdots & \ddots & \vdots \\ a_{n1} & a_{n2} & \cdots & a_{nn} \end{bmatrix} \quad x = \begin{bmatrix} x_1 \\ x_2 \\ \vdots \\ x_n \end{bmatrix} \quad b = \begin{bmatrix} b_1 \\ b_2 \\ \vdots \\ b_n \end{bmatrix}$$

can be easily solved in MATLAB.

```
>> A=[3 1 1; 1 -2 4; 5 7 -1]; b=[1; 0; 2]
b =
     1
     0
     2

>> x=A\b
```

```
x =
     0.3500
     0.0250
    -0.0750

>> A*x
ans =
     1
     0
     2
```

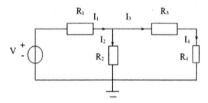

Figure 2.8: Circuit

We show, how it can be used to solve more practical problems. Let us have circuit depicted in Fig. 2.8. Let $V = 10V, R_1 = 15\Omega, R_2 = 10\Omega, R_3 = 5\Omega$ and $R_4 = 20\Omega$. How can we find the values of I_1, I_2, I_3 and I_4? Kirchhoff's voltage law can be applied to write down an equation for each sub-circuit.

$$V = R_1 I_1 + R_2 I_2$$
$$0 = R_2 I_2 - R_3 I_3 - R_4 I_4$$

Kirchhoff's conservation of current law allows to set up two more equationsL

$$I_1 = I_2 + I_3$$
$$I_3 = I_4$$

. They allow to eliminate I_1 and I_4, then we get

$$V = (R_1 + R_2)I_2 + R_1 I_3$$
$$0 = - R_2 I_2 + (R_3 + R_4)I_3$$

In the matrix form it looks as follows.

$$A = \begin{bmatrix} R_1 + R_2 & R_1 \\ -R_2 & R_3 + R_4 \end{bmatrix} \qquad x = \begin{bmatrix} I_2 \\ I_3 \end{bmatrix} \qquad x = \begin{bmatrix} V \\ 0 \end{bmatrix}$$

MATLAB can immediately provide answers after it is given the equations.

```
%resist.m solves for the currents I1, I2, I3, I4
R1=15; R2=10; R3=5; R4=20; V=10;
A=[(R1+R2), R1; -R2, (R3+R4)];
b=[V; 0];
x=A\b;
I2=x(1); I3=x(2);
I1=I2+I3; I4=I3;
[I1 I2 I3 I4]

>> resist
ans =
     0.4516     0.3226     0.1290     0.1290
```

2.3.3 Simulink

SIMULINK is a MATLAB-based environment for simulation and model-based design of dynamic and embedded systems. It consists of and interactive graphical modeling and experimenting environment and a set of customizable block libraries that allow designing, modeling, simulating, testing and implementing diverse systems. These include communication systems, diverse control models, signal, video and image processing and much more.

The idea of SIMULINK is the following. Each dynamic system consists of a set of some standard elements. These elements can be represented as diverse blocks. Therefore, any dynamical systems can be modeled by properly configuring and connecting elements represented by blocks. In SIMULINK it is done using graphical user environment. Basically, elements, called *sources* generate certain signals, that are transfered by lines (connectors) which connect elements, blocks representing elements transform signals, and finally, *sinks* consume signals. Elements can be *discrete* or *continuous*.

2.3.3.1 Using Simulink

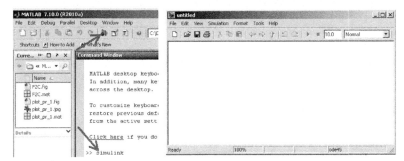

Figure 2.9: SIMULINK Icon   Figure 2.10: SIMULINK: New Model

SIMULINK is started from MATLAB. It can be done from the command window by typing

---

```
>> simulink
```

---

by clicking on the SIMULINK icon, see Fig. 2.9.

Upon execution of the command SIMULINK library is shown, Fig. 2.11. Left frame is referred as the *Tree Pane*, while the right side as the *Contents Part*. Then, by clicking on the *New File*, choosing it from the menu or by shortcut CTRL-N, a *new model* can be started as shown in Fig. 2.10.

Let us model a simple system from [4] depicted in Fig. 2.12 with the initial conditions $i_L(0^-) = 0$ and $v_C(0^-) = 0.5V$. We will compute $v_C(t)$.

By Kirchoff's voltage law

$$Ri_L + L\frac{di_L}{dt} + v_C = u_0(t) \qquad (2.1)$$

Substitution of $i = i_L = i_C = C\frac{dv_C}{dt}$ yields

$$RC\frac{dv_C}{dt} + LC\frac{dv_C^2}{dt^2} + v_C = u_0(t) \qquad (2.2)$$

Figure 2.11: SIMULINK Library

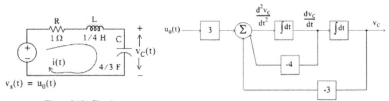

Figure 2.12: Circuit

Figure 2.13: Block Diagram for eq. 2.6

Substituting the values of the circuit constants and rearranging we get:

$$\frac{1}{3}\frac{dv_C^2}{dt^2} + \frac{4}{3}\frac{dv_C}{dt} + v_C = u_0(t) \tag{2.3}$$

$$\frac{dv_C^2}{dt^2} + 4\frac{dv_C}{dt} + 3v_C = 3u_0(t) \tag{2.4}$$

$$\frac{dv_C^2}{dt^2} + 4\frac{dv_C}{dt} + 3v_C = 3 \quad\quad t > 0 \tag{2.5}$$

It can be modeled in a several different ways.

Modeling the Differential Equation with Simulink

Let us model a differential equation 2.4 and depicted by the block diagram in Fig. 2.6 with

Figure 2.14: Eq. 2.6 in SIMULINK (1)

Figure 2.15: Eq. 2.6 in SIMULINK (2)

Figure 2.16: Eq. 2.6 in SIMULINK (3)

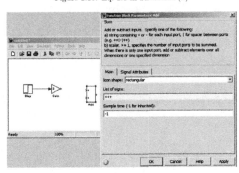

Figure 2.17: Eq. 2.6 in SIMULINK (4)

Figure 2.18: Simulation of Eq. 2.6 in SIMULINK

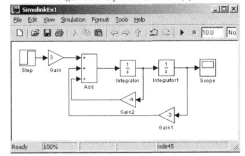

Figure 2.19: Complete Model of Eq. 2.6 in SIMULINK

SIMULINK. We can rewrite it as follows:

$$\frac{d^2 v_C}{dt^2} = -4\frac{dv_C}{dt} - 3v_C + 3u_0(t) \tag{2.6}$$

We model it using SIMULINK. We start from the creating a new model, as explained above, and saving it as usually. Then we continue as follows.

1. Choose source `Step` in the SIMULINK library, then drag and drop it in the model window, see Fig. 2.14

2. We add `Gain` block from the Commonly Used Blocks set, and using mouse right click set gain value to 3, see Fig. 2.15.

Figure 2.20: Block Diagram for Eq. 2.6: Output to Workspace

3. Connect step to gain by clicking by the mouse on the triangle > on the right side of the Step block, then draw a line it to the triangle on the left side of the Gain block, in such a way connecting them, see Fig. 2.16.

4. We add three input adder (Add) by choosing Add from mathematical operations, double-clicking on it and adding + to make it three-input, Fig. 2.17. Then we connect Gain to Add.

5. We add Integrator from the commonly used blocks twice, set initial values by double-clicking on them. Then connect them accordingly. Moreover, we add two more Gain blocks, flip them using Flip Block command from Format menu to point left-wise, configure them and connect them with corresponding integrators and adder.

6. We add Scope from the commonly used blocks for monitoring of the system, Fig. 2.19

7. Simulation can be started by clicking on the start simulation icon (right oriented black rectangle). Simulation results can be seen by double-clicking on the Scope block, see Fig. 2.18.

simout block allows to get output in the workspace for further analysis, see Fig. 2.20.

Modeling Using State Variables with Simulink

Another way to generate model system is to use State-Space block from the Continuous blockset. It allows defining state space models. We illustrate it by continuing model from [4], defined by Eq. 2.6. By substituting given valuses and rearranging equation we obtain

$$\frac{1}{4}\frac{di_L}{dt} = -1 - v_C + 1$$

$$\frac{di_L}{dt} = -4i_L - 4v_c + 4$$

Let $x_1 = i_L$ and $x_2 = v_C$, then

$$\dot{x}_1 = \frac{di_L}{dt}$$

$$\dot{x}_2 = \frac{dv_c}{dt}$$

Because $i_L = C\frac{dv_C}{dt}$, we get

$$x_1 = i_L = C\frac{dv_C}{dt} = C\dot{x}_2 = \frac{4}{3}\dot{x}_2$$

$$\dot{x}_2 = \frac{3}{4}x_1$$

Threfore, we get the state equations

$$\dot{x}_1 = -4x_1 - 4x_2 + 4 \tag{2.7}$$

$$\dot{x}_2 = \frac{3}{4}x_1 \tag{2.8}$$

Then we get

$$\begin{bmatrix} \dot{x}_1 \\ \dot{x}_2 \end{bmatrix} = \begin{bmatrix} -4 & -4 \\ 3/4 & 0 \end{bmatrix} \begin{bmatrix} x_1 \\ x_2 \end{bmatrix} + \begin{bmatrix} 4 \\ 0 \end{bmatrix} u_0(t) \tag{2.9}$$

and output (v_C and i_L)

$$y = \begin{bmatrix} 0 & 1 \end{bmatrix} \begin{bmatrix} x_1 \\ x_2 \end{bmatrix} + \begin{bmatrix} 0 \end{bmatrix} u_0(t) \tag{2.10}$$

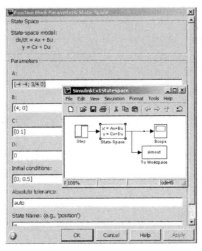

Figure 2.21: State-space Model of Eq. 2.6

These state space equations can be modeled as depicted in Fig. 2.21. Instead of hard-coding variables, they can be taken from MATLAB, i.e. instead of [0; 0.5] variables can be provided [x1; x2] and then assigned in MATLAB.

```
>> x1 = 0; x2 = 0.5;
```

Bouncing Ball Example

We illustrate SIMULINK with one more demo, standard to model hybrid systems. It is a *bouncing ball* example, where ball bounces from the ground and with each bounce loses a fraction of its energy. Dynamics are very simple as follows:

$$\dot{v} = -g \tag{2.11}$$

$$\dot{x} = v \tag{2.12}$$

where g is the acceleration due to gravity, $x(t)$ is altitude and $v(t)$ is the velocity. Loss of energy is defined by the elasticity of the ball c, i.e. at the moment of the collision of the ball and the ground it changes velocity

$$v_{\text{after}} = -cv_{\text{before}} \tag{2.13}$$

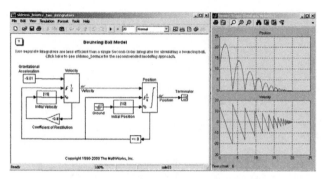

Figure 2.22: Naïve Model and Simulation of the Bouncing Ball

In addition, the model demonstrates the Zeno phenomenon [5], when a finite number of actions occurs in a finite time. In this case, the ball bounces with smaller and smaller jumps. It is quite common in different models and is difficult to simulate.

We use a standard naïve SIMULINK demo to simulate it, the model and simulation results are depicted in Fig. 2.22. For more details we refer readers to SIMULINK help: choose MATLAB Start, then Simulink\Demos.

2.3.3.2 List of Available Blocks

We provide a list of some available blocks in the main SIMULINK library, the main blocksets are listed in Tables 2.7-2.12.

Blockset	Description
Commonly Used	Commonly used blocks
Continuous	Continuous states
Discontinuities	Discontinuous states
Discrete	Discrete states
Logic and Bit Operations	Perform logic and bit operations
Lookup Tables	Lookup tables
Math Operations	Math operations
Model Verification	Model verification
Model-Wide Utilities	Model-wide operations
Ports & Subsystems	Ports and subsystems
Signal Attributes	Signal attributes
Signal Routing	Signal routing
Sinks	Receive output from other blocks
Sources	Input to other blocks
User-Defined Functions	Custom functions
Additional Math & Discrete	Additional math and discrete support

Table 2.7: Main SIMULINK library

See MATLAB and SIMULINK help for description of other blocksets and libraries. A comprehensive and well exemplified description of SIMULINK is available in [4] as well.

Blockset	Description
Derivative	Output time derivative of input
Integrator (Limited)	Integrate signal
PID Controller	Simulate continuous- or discrete-time PID controllers
PID Controller (2 DOF)	the same, but two-degree-of-freedom PID
Second-Order Integrator (Limited)	Integrate input signal twice
State-Space	Implement linear state-space system
Transfer Fcn	Model linear system by transfer function
Transport Delay	Delay input by given amount of time
Variable Time Delay Variable Transport Delay	Delay input by variable amount of time
Zero-Pole	Model system by zero-pole-gain transfer function

Table 2.8: Continuous

Blockset	Description
Display	Show value of input
Outport	Create output port for subsystem or external output
(Floating) Scope	Display signals generated during simulation
Stop	Stop simulation when input is nonzero
Terminator	Terminate unconnected output port
To File	Write data to file
To Workspace	Write data to MATLAB workspace
XY Graph	Display X-Y plot of signals using MATLAB figure window

Table 2.9: Sinks

2.3.3.3 Communication Blockset Library

The Communication Blockset library is one of many SIMULINK libraries. It extends SIMULINK with a library of blocks to design and simulate the physical layer of communication systems. It contains blocksets listed in Table 2.12.

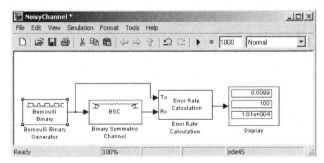

Figure 2.23: Noisy Channel Model and Simulation

Blockset	Description
Band-Limited White Noise	Introduce white noise into continuous system
Chirp Signal	Generate sine wave with increasing frequency
Clock	Display and provide simulation time
Constant	Generate constant value
Counter Free-Running	Count up and overflow back to 0 after reaching maximum value for specified number of bits
Counter Limited	Count and overflow to 0 after specified upper limit
Digital Clock	Output simulation time at specified sampling interval
Enumerated Constant	Generate enumerated constant value
From File	Read data from MAT-file
From Workspace	Read data from workspace
Ground	Ground unconnected input port
Inport	Create input port for subsystem or external input
Pulse Generator	Generate square wave pulses at regular intervals
Ramp	Generate constantly increasing or decreasing signal
Random Number	Generate normally distributed random numbers
Repeating Sequence	Generate arbitrarily shaped periodic signal
Repeating Sequence Interpolated	Output discrete-time sequence and repeat interpolating between data points
Repeating Sequence Stair	Output and repeat discrete time sequence
Signal Builder	Generate interchangeable groups of signals with piecewise linear waveforms
Signal Generator	Generate various waveforms
Sine Wave	Generate sine wave, using simulation time as time source
Step	Generate step function
Uniform Random Number	Generate uniformly distributed random numbers

Table 2.10: Sources

We illustrate usage of the Communication Blockset with an example of Channel-noise model. It consists of the following elements:

- The *source* for the signal. In this model we use the Bernoulli Binary Generator block generating a random binary sequence.

- The *Binary Symmetric Channel* block simulates a noisy channel. It introduces random errors to the signal by changing 0 to 1 and the inverse with a specified probability.

- The *Error Rate Calculation* block calculates the channels error rate. It has two ports:

  - Tx for transmitted signal;
  - Rx for received signal.

  Error Rate Calculator compares these signals and checks for errors. The output is a vector with three entries:

  - bit error rate, which you expect to be similar to the probability of error in the channel;
  - number of errors;

Block	Description
Bus Creator	Signal bus
Bus Selector	Select signals from incoming bus
Constant	Generate constant value
Data Type Conversion	Convert input signal to specified data type
Demux	Extract and output elements of vector signal
Discrete-Time Integrator	Discrete-time integration or accumulation of signal
Gain	Multiply input by constant
Ground	Ground unconnected input port
Inport	Input port for subsystem or external input
Integrator, Integrator Limited	Integrate signal
Logical Operator	Perform specified logical operation on input
Mux	Combine several input signals into vector
Outport	Create output port for subsystem or external output
Product	Multiply & divide (non)scalars Multiply & invert matrices
Relational Operator	Perform specified relational operation on inputs
Saturation	Limit range of signal
Scope, Floating Scope	Display signals generated during simulation
Subsystem Atomic Subsystem Nonvirtual Subsystem CodeReuse Subsystem	Represent system within another system
Sum, Add, Subtract	Add or subtract inputs
Switch	Based on 2nd input switch output to 1st or 3rd
Terminator	Terminate unconnected output port
Unit Delay	Delay signal one sample period

Table 2.11: Commonly used blockset

- total number of transmitted bits.

• The *Display* block displays the output of the Error Rate Calculator.

Creating and simulating the model takes several steps:

1. New model is created in the usual manner.

2. Required blocks are added to the model:

    • The Bernoulli Binary Generator block from the Random Data Sources blockset.

    • The Binary Symmetric Channel from the Channels blockset.

    • The Error Rate Calculation block from the Comm(on) Sinks blockset.

    • The Display from the Simulink library Sinks blockset.

3. Added block should be configured.

    • We do not configure the Bernoulli Binary Generator block in this example, however several parameters maybe set by double-clicking on the block.

Blockset	Description
Communications Sources	Sources of random and nonrandom data
Communications Sinks	Error statistics and plotting
Source Coding	Quantization, companding, and differential coding
Error Detection and Correction	Block, convolutional, and CRC coding
Interleaving	Block and convolutional interleaving
MIMO	Multiple Input Multiple Output blocks
Modulation	Digital baseband and analog passband modulation
Communications Filters	Filtering and pulse shaping
Channels	Modeling channel impairments
RF Impairments	Impairments caused by the radio frequency components
SDR Hardware	Simulate software-defined radio applications
Synchronization	Phase recovery methods and phase-locked loops
Equalizers	Adaptive and MLSE equalizers
Sequence Operations	Scrambling, puncturing, and other operations on sequences
Utility Blocks	Miscellaneous relevant blocks

Table 2.12: Communication Blocksets library

- We set empherror rate to 0.01 and hide error output by removing check mark from the `Output error vector` checkbox for the Binary Symmetric Channel.

- We set `Target number of errors` to 100 and check `Stop simulation` for stopping simulation after 100 errors for the Error Rate Calculator.

- We set simulation time to 100000 to be able to get sufficient number of signals, or we could change frequency of signals generation in the Bernoulli Binary Generator block.

- We resize the Display block to be able to see the bit error rate, the number of errors and the number of transmitted bits.

4. We connect all the corresponding blocks.

5. Then we run the model and obtain results.

Model with simulation results is depicted in Fig. 2.23.

We refer interested reader to the Communication Blockset documentation that can be found in MATLAB and SIMULINK help.

2.4 Problems and Answers

In this section we provide problems and answers to some of the given problems.

2.4.1 Introduction, Sect. 2.1

2.4.1.1 Getting Help

1. Get help on the MATLAB function **exp** using:

   (a) The **help exp** command typed in the Command window,

   (b) MATLAB Help Window.

2. Use the **lookfor** command to determine how to take the base-10 logarithm of a number in MATLAB. Then calculate **log10(2)**.

2.4.1.2 MATLAB Workspace

1. What is a workspace?

2. Create variables **x, u, velocity, height** and **v**

3. Use commands **who** and **whos** to see the variables in the workspace.

4. Clear variables **x, u** and **v**.

5. Clear all variables in the workspace.

6. Save selected and all variables.

7. Load variables.

2.4.1.3 Language: Variables and Expressions

1. Let $u = 2$ and $v = 3$. Evaluate the following expressions:

   (a) $\frac{4u}{3v}$

   (b) $\frac{2v^{-2}}{(u+v)^2}$

   (c) $\frac{u^3 v^2}{u^3 - v^2}$

   (d) $\frac{4}{3}\pi v^2$

```
>> u=2; v=3;
>> (4*u)/(3*v)
ans =
    0.8889

>> (2*v^(-2))/((u+v)^2)
ans =
    0.0089

>> (u^3*v^2)/((u+v)^2)
ans =
    2.8800

>> 4/3*pi*v^2
ans =
   37.6991
```

---

2. Distance traveled by a falling ball is given by the equation $x = x_0 + v_0 t + \frac{1}{2}at^2$. Let $x_0 = 10m, v_0 = 15m/s$ and $a = g = 9.81m/s^2$, calculate position of ball at time $t = 5s$.

```
>> x0=10; v0=15; a=9.81; t=5; x0+v0*t+1/2*a*t^2
ans =
    207.6250
```

3. Let $x = -5 + 9i$ and $y = 6 - 2i$, calculate $x + y, xy$ and x/y.

```
>> x=-5+9i; y=6-2i;
>> x+y
ans =
    1.0000 + 7.0000i

>> x*y
ans =
 -12.0000 +64.0000i

>> x/y
ans =
  -1.2000 + 1.1000i
```

2.4.1.4 Language: Basic Mathematical Functions

1. Let $x = 4.5$ and $y = 8$, show that $\ln(xy) = \ln x + \ln y$.

```
>> x=4.5; y=8; log(x*y)-log(x)-log(y)
ans =
    0
```

2. Let $x = 5 + 4i$ and $y = 6 - 8i$.

    (a) Find $z = x * y$.
    (b) Find real and imaginary parts of z.
    (c) Show that magnitude of z is equal to product of magnitudes of x and y, i.e. $|z| = |x||y|$.
    (d) Show that $\angle z = \angle x + \angle y$.

```
>> x=5+4i; y=6-8i;
>> z=x*y
z =
   62.0000 -16.0000i

>> real(z), imag(z)
ans =
    62
ans =
   -16

>> abs(z) - abs(x)*abs(y)
ans =
    0

>> angle(z)-(angle(x)+angle(y))
ans =
 -1.1102e-016
```

3. With $x = 0°, 45°, 90°, 180°, 270°, 360°$ show that $e^{xi} = \cos x + i \sin x$.

```
>> x=[0 45 90 180 270 360]; xrad = pi/180*x
xrad =
         0    0.7854    1.5708    3.1416    4.7124    6.2832

>> exp(i*xrad)-(cos(xrad)+i*sin(xrad))
ans =
     0     0     0     0     0     0
```

4. With $x = 0, 0.5, 1$ show that $\sin^{-1} x + \cos^{-1} x = \pi/2$.

```
>> x=[0 0.5 1]; pi/2, asin(x) + acos(x)
ans =
    1.5708
ans =
    1.5708    1.5708    1.5708
```

2.4.2   Arrays and Matrices, Subsect. 2.1.9

1. Enter given matrix in MATLAB and solve all given problems.

$$\begin{bmatrix} 3 & 7 & -4 & 12 \\ -5 & 9 & 10 & 2 \\ 6 & 13 & 8 & 11 \\ 15 & 5 & 4 & 1 \end{bmatrix}$$

```
>> A=[3 7 -4 12; -5 9 10 2; 6 13 8 11; 15 5 4 1]
A =
     3     7    -4    12
    -5     9    10     2
     6    13     8    11
    15     5     4     1
```

(a) Calculate A^{T}.

(b) Calculate $B = A + i * A$.

(c) Calculate B^{T}.

(d) Calculate B^{H}, conjugate transpose (Hermitian).

(e) Create vector v consisting of the elements of the 2nd column of A.

(f) Create vector w consisting of the elements of the 2nd row of A.

(g) Create a 4×3 array B consisting of all elements of the second to fourth columns of A.

(h) Create a 3×4 array C consisting of all elements of the second to fourth rows of A.

(i) Create a 2×3 array D consisting of the first two rows and the last three columns of A.

(j) Get the lenghts of v and w and sizes of A, B, C and D.

```
>> A'
ans =
     3    -5     6    15
     7     9    13     5
    -4    10     8     4
    12     2    11     1
```

```
>> B=A+i*A
B =
    3.0000 + 3.0000i    7.0000 + 7.0000i   -4.0000 - 4.0000i   12.0000 +12.0000i
   -5.0000 - 5.0000i    9.0000 + 9.0000i   10.0000 +10.0000i    2.0000 + 2.0000i
    6.0000 + 6.0000i   13.0000 +13.0000i    8.0000 + 8.0000i   11.0000 +11.0000i
   15.0000 +15.0000i    5.0000 + 5.0000i    4.0000 + 4.0000i    1.0000 + 1.0000i

>> B.' % transpose without conjugate for complex numbers
ans =
    3.0000 + 3.0000i   -5.0000 - 5.0000i    6.0000 + 6.0000i   15.0000 +15.0000i
    7.0000 + 7.0000i    9.0000 + 9.0000i   13.0000 +13.0000i    5.0000 + 5.0000i
   -4.0000 - 4.0000i   10.0000 +10.0000i    8.0000 + 8.0000i    4.0000 + 4.0000i
   12.0000 +12.0000i    2.0000 + 2.0000i   11.0000 +11.0000i    1.0000 + 1.0000i

>> B'
ans =
    3.0000 - 3.0000i   -5.0000 + 5.0000i    6.0000 - 6.0000i   15.0000 -15.0000i
    7.0000 - 7.0000i    9.0000 - 9.0000i   13.0000 -13.0000i    5.0000 - 5.0000i
   -4.0000 + 4.0000i   10.0000 -10.0000i    8.0000 - 8.0000i    4.0000 - 4.0000i
   12.0000 -12.0000i    2.0000 - 2.0000i   11.0000 -11.0000i    1.0000 - 1.0000i

>> v=A(:,2)
v =
    7
    9
   13
    5

>> w=A(2,:)
w =
   -5     9    10     2

>> B=A(:,2:4)
B =
    7    -4    12
    9    10     2
   13     8    11
    5     4     1

>> C=A(2:4,:)
C =
   -5     9    10     2
    6    13     8    11
   15     5     4     1

>> D=A([1:2],[2:4])
D =
    7    -4    12
    9    10     2

>> length(v), length(w)
ans =
    4
ans =
    4

>> size(A), size(B), size(C), size(D)
ans =
```

```
      4      4
ans =
      4      3
ans =
      3      4
ans =
      2      3
>>
```

2. Let

$$A = \begin{bmatrix} -7 & 16 \\ 4 & 9 \end{bmatrix} \quad B = \begin{bmatrix} 6 & -5 \\ 12 & -2 \end{bmatrix} \quad C = \begin{bmatrix} -3 & -9 \\ 6 & 8 \end{bmatrix}$$

(a) Calculate $A + B - C$.

(b) Verify associativity $(A + B) + C = A + (B + C)$.

(c) Calculate product of A and B using array product.

(d) Calculate A divided B using array division.

(e) Calculate B^3 element-wise.

```
>> A=[-7 16; 4 9]; B=[6 -5; 12 -2]; C=[-3 -9; 6 8];
>> A+B-C
ans =
      2     20
     10     -1

>> (A+B)+C, A+(B+C)
ans =
     -4      2
     22     15
ans =
     -4      2
     22     15

>> A.*B
ans =
    -42    -80
     48    -18

>> A./B
ans =
    -1.1667   -3.2000
     0.3333   -4.5000

>> B.^3
ans =
        216        -125
       1728          -8
```

3. Potential energy stored in a spring is kx^2, where k is spring constant and x is the compression of the spring (displacement). Forse, required to compress a spring is $F = kx$. Calculate compression x and potential energy for each value given in the table.

```
>> F=[11 7 8 10 9];     % F
>> k=[1000 800 900 1200 700];    % k
>> x=F./k
```

	1	2	3	4	5
F (N)	11	7	8	10	9
k (N/m)	1000	800	900	1200	700

```
x =
    0.0110    0.0088    0.0089    0.0083    0.0129

>> E=k.*x.^2/2
E =
    0.0605    0.0306    0.0356    0.0417    0.0579
```

4. Let

$$A = \begin{bmatrix} 3 & -6 & 2 \\ 2 & 8 & 3 \\ 1 & -2 & 5 \end{bmatrix} \quad B = \begin{bmatrix} 6 & 9 & -1 \\ 7 & 5 & 1 \\ -5 & 9 & 10 \end{bmatrix} \quad C = \begin{bmatrix} -7 & -5 & 2 \\ 10 & 6 & 1 \\ 3 & -9 & 8 \end{bmatrix}$$

be matrices. Apply matrix operations using MATLAB.

(a) Find AB.

(b) Find BA.

(c) Verify associativity $(AB)C = A(BC)$.

(d) Find A^3.

```
>> A=[3 -6 2; 2 8 3; 1 -2 5], B=[6 9 -1; 7 5 1; -5 9 10], C=[-7 -5 2; 10 6 1; 3 -9 8]
A =
     3    -6     2
     2     8     3
     1    -2     5
B =
     6     9    -1
     7     5     1
    -5     9    10
C =
    -7    -5     2
    10     6     1
     3    -9     8

>> A*B
ans =
   -34    15    11
    53    85    36
   -33    44    47

>> B*A
ans =
    35    38    34
    32    -4    34
    13    82    67

>> (A*B)*C - A*(B*C)
ans =
     0     0     0
     0     0     0
     0     0     0
```

```
>> A^3
ans =
   -145  -550  -222
    210   132   403
    -31  -322    17
```

2.4.3   Plots and Programming in MATLAB, Sect. 2.2 and 2.3

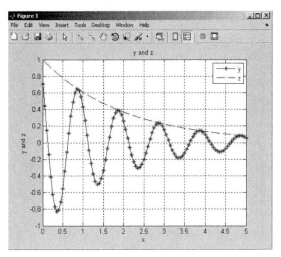

Figure 2.24: Figure for Problem 1

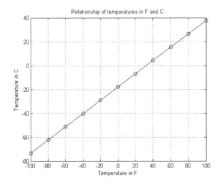

Figure 2.25: Figure for Problem 2

1. Create a script file that plots $y = e^{-x/2} \cos(2\pi x + \pi/4)$ and $z = e^{-x/2}$ in the same window for $x \in [0, 5]$ with step 0.05. Draw y with a solid blue line and a star on each data point, and z with a red dashed line. Set labels for x- and y-axes, add plot, turn on the grid and add title. Save x, y and z into MAT file with the same name as script with extension .mat. Run it and save graph with the same name, but with extensions .fig and .jpg.

```
% plot_pr_1.m
x=[0:0.05:5];
y=exp(-x/2).*cos(2*pi*x+pi/4);
z=exp(-x/2);
plot(x,y,'b-*');
hold on;
grid on;
plot(x,z,'r--');
legend('y','z');
xlabel('x');
ylabel('y and z');
title('y and z');
save plot_pr_1;                    % saving the workspace
saveas(gcf,'plot_pr_1.fig');       % saving the current figure
saveas(gcf,'plot_pr_1.jpg');       % saving the current figure
```

See figure in fig. 2.24.

2. Fahrenheit - Celsius converter.

   (a) Create function F2C.m that converts temperature T in Fahrenheits ($°F$) to temperature in degrees in Celcius ($°C$), where $T[°C] = \frac{5}{9}(T[°F] - 32)$.

   (b) Test it with $T = -100 \ldots 100°F$ with step $20°F$. Save results to file F2C.mat.

   (c) Plot it with Fahrenheits on x-axis and Celsius on y-axis. Set corresponding labels on axes, turn on the grid, put the title and save results to F2C.fig.

```
function Tc=F2C(Tf)
% F2C converts temperature in Fahrenheit to temperature in Celsius
Tc=5.*(Tf-32)./9;
end

function testF2C()
%testF2C test F2C

Tf = -100:20:100;
Tc = F2C(Tf);

for i=1:length(Tc)
    disp([num2str(Tf(i)), ' F = ', num2str(Tc(i)), ' C'])
end
end
```

```
save F2C Tc

plot(Tf, Tc, '-o');
grid on;
xlabel('Temperature in F');
ylabel('Temperature in C');
title('Relationship of temperatures in F and C');
saveas(gcf,'F2C.fig');
```

```
end
```

3. Create Celsius - Fahrenheit converter and perform the same actions with it. Follow steps of the previous problem.

2.4.4 Control Statements, Subsect. 2.3.2

1. Relational and Logical Operators.

(a) Let $a = 20, b = -2, c = 0$ and $d = 1$. Evaluate
   i. a>b,
   ii. b>d,
   iii. (a>b)&(c>d),
   iv. a&(b>c),
   v. (a&b)>c,
   vi. a==b,
   vii. a|(b&d).

```
>> a = 20; b=-2; c=0; d=1;
>> a>b, b>d
ans =
     1
ans =
     0

>> (a>b)&(c>d)
ans =
     0

>> a&(b>c)
ans =
     0

>> (a&b)>c
ans =
     1

>> a==b
ans =
     0

>> a|(b&d)
ans =
     1
```

(b) Fill the truth table using MATLAB (you can use vectors for variables).

```
>> x=[0 0 1 1]; y=[0 1 0 1];
>> x&y, x|y, xor(x,y), ~x
ans =
     0     0     0     1
ans =
     0     1     1     1
ans =
     0     1     1     0
```

x	y	x&y	x|y	xor(x,y)	!x
0	0				
0	1				
1	0				
1	1				

```
ans =
     1     1     0     0
```

2. Branching statements.

    (a) Use QuadraticEquation function to solve the following equations.

          i. $x^2 + 5x + 6 = 0$,

         ii. $x^2 + 4x + 4 = 0$,

       iii. $x^2 + 2x + 5 = 0$,

       iv. $2x + 5 = 0$.

```
>> a=1; b=5; c=6; [x1, x2] = QuadraticEquation(a, b, c)
x1 =
    -2
x2 =
    -3

>> a=1; b=4; c=4; [x1, x2] = QuadraticEquation(a, b, c)
x1 =
    -2
x2 =
    -2

>> a=1; b=2; c=5; [x1, x2] = QuadraticEquation(a, b, c)
x1 =
   -1.0000 + 2.0000i
x2 =
   -1.0000 - 2.0000i

>> a=0; b=2; c=5; [x1, x2] = QuadraticEquation(a, b, c)
??? Error using ==> QuadraticEquation at 7
a=0 - it is not a quadratic equation
```

    (b) Write a MATLAB program to evaluate $y(x) = \ln \frac{1}{1-x}$. Test it with $x = -2, 0, 1, 2$.

```
function y = fln( x )
%fln Summary of this function goes here

if x>=1
    error('x has to be smaller than 1');
else
    y=log(1./(1-x));
end

end

>> fln(-2)
```

```
ans =
  -1.0986

>> fln(0)
ans =
     0

>> fln(1)
??? Error using ==> fln at 5
x has to be smaller than 1

>> fln(2)
??? Error using ==> fln at 5
x has to be smaller than 1
```

(c) Write a MATLAB program to evaluate function

$$f(x,y) = \begin{cases} x+y, & x \geq 0 \text{ and } y \geq 0 \\ x+y^2, & x \geq 0 \text{ and } y < 0 \\ x^2+y, & x < 0 \text{ and } y \geq 0 \\ x^2+y^2 & x < 0 \text{ and } y < 0 \end{cases}$$

Test it with $(x, y) = (2, 3), (2, -3), (-2, 3)$ and $(-2, -3)$.

```
function fxy = funxy(x,y)
% funxy - complicated function with choices

if x>=0 && y>=0
    fxy=x+y;
elseif x>=0 && y<0
    fxy=x+y.^2;
elseif x<0 && y>=0
       fxy=x.^2+y;
else
       fxy=x.^2+y.^2;
end
end

>> x=2; y=3; funxy(x,y)
ans =
     5

>> x=2; y=-3; funxy(x,y)
ans =
    11

>> x=-2; y=3; funxy(x,y)
ans =
     7

>> x=-2; y=-3; funxy(x,y)
ans =
    13
```

3. Loop statements.

(a) Write a MATLAB program to evaluate equation $x^2 - 3x + 2 = 0$ for all values of x from

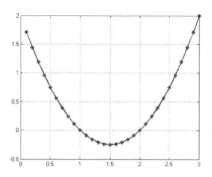

Figure 2.26: Figure for Problem 3

0.1 to 3 with step 0.1. Do it with `for` and array operations. Plot the resulting function using a red dashed line.

```
function y=polynomial_pr(x)
% polynomial_pr.m the polynomial of x^2-3x+2
    y=x.^2-3*x+2;
end
function y=polynomial_pr(x)
% polynomial_pr.m the polynomial of x^2-3x+2
    y=x.^2-3*x+2;
end

function test_polynomial_pr()
% test_polynomial_pr.m - tests polynomial_pr.m
% plots the figure of function y=x^2-3x+2
% in the range of x from 0.1 to 3 with step 0.1
% two methods applied

x=[0.1:0.1:3];
y=polynomial_pr(x);
plot(x,y,'-*','linewidth',2);
grid on;

% using 'for' loop to find the solution for y=0
disp('Method 1: Using for loop')
for i=1:length(x)
    if (abs(y(i))<1e-6)    % when y(i) is close to 0
        disp(x(i));        % x(i) is one of the roots
    end;
end;

% using array operation to find the solution
disp('Method 2: Using array operation')
subscripts = find(abs(y)<=1e-6);  % find the subscripts of all y close to 0
x(subscripts)

end
```

(b) Write a MATLAB program to generate 5×5 matrix A where $A_{m,n} = m + n$.

```
function A = A_mn(N)
% Amn.m  generates a N by N matrix with a(m,n)=m+n

A=zeros(N); % Initialising an all-zero matrix
for m=1:N
    for n=1:N
        A(m,n)=m+n;
    end
end
end

>> A_mn(5)
ans =
     2     3     4     5     6
     3     4     5     6     7
     4     5     6     7     8
     5     6     7     8     9
     6     7     8     9    10
```

(c) Write a MATLAB program with while loop, that allows the user to input a number at each iteration until a negative value is received. Calculate the average for all the input values between 40 and 80, inclusive. Test it with 29, 35, 65, 49, 38, 79, 93, 80, 28, 29, 58, -7.

```
function average = NonNegativeAverage()
% NonNegativeAverage.m - calculates average of non-negative inputs
% between 40 and 80 (inclusive)

sum=0;  % sum
N=0;    % number of inputs

% read in the first number
number = input('Please input the first number: ');
if number >= 0
    while number >= 0
        if number >= 40 && number <= 80
            sum = sum + number;
            N = N + 1;
        end
        number = input('Please input the next number: ');
    end
    disp('Finish');
else    % when the first number is negative
    disp('First number is negative!');
end

% when there were no valid input
if N==0 | sum==0
    disp('No valid input between 40 and 80.')
else
    disp('The average of the numbers is: ');
    average = sum / N;
end
end

>> NonNegativeAverage()
```

```
Please input the first number: 29
Please input the next number: 35
Please input the next number: 65
Please input the next number: 49
Please input the next number: 38
Please input the next number: 79
Please input the next number: 93
Please input the next number: 80
Please input the next number: 28
Please input the next number: 29
Please input the next number: 58
Please input the next number: -7
Finish
The average of the numbers is:

ans =
    66.2000
```

(d) Use `while` loop to determine how long in year it would take to accumulate €1000000 in a bank account, if you start with €10000, add €10000 in the middle of each year and the annual interest of 6% is paid at the end of each year. Set a breakpoint inside the `while` loop to trace each iteration. What is the resulting balance?

```
function BecomeMillionaire
% BecomeMillionaire.m - helps to determine, how to accumulate 1,000,000

deposit = 10000;
saving = 10000;
year = 0;

while deposit < 1000000
% the deposit at the end of the year is summation of
% the deposit at the beginning of the year +
% the annual interest of the deposit at the beginning of the year +
% the saving saved in the middle of the year
    deposit = deposit * (1 + 0.06) + saving;
    year=year+1;
end

sprintf('It takes %d year to accumulate 1,000,000', year)
sprintf('The final balance after %d years is %d', year, deposit)
end

>> BecomeMillionaire
ans =
It takes 33 year to accumulate 1,000,000
ans =
The final balance after 33 years is 1.041838e+006
```

2.4.5   Answers for Problems from Polynomials in MATLAB, Sect. 2.3.2.5

1. Perform the addition and substraction of $20x^3 - 7x^2 + 5x + 10$ and $4x^2 + 12x - 3$.

```
>> a=[20 -7 5 10], b=[0 4 12 -3]
a =
    20    -7     5    10
b =
```

```
      0     4    12    -3
>> a+b, a-b
ans =
     20    -3   17    7
ans =

     20   -11   -7    13
```

2. Find the product of $(20x^3 - 7x^2 + 5x + 10)(4x^2 + 12x - 3)$ and $(6x^3 + 4x^2 - 5)(12x^3 - 7x^2 + 3x + 9)$.

```
>> conv(a,b)
ans =
      0    80   212  -124   121   105   -30

>> c=[6 4 -5], d=[12 -7 3 9]
c =
      6     4    -5
d =
     12    -7     3     9

>> conv(c,d)
ans =
     72     6   -70   101    21   -45
```

3. Find the quotient and reminder of

$$\frac{20x^3 - 7x^2 + 5x + 10}{4x^2 + 12x - 3}$$

```
>> b=b(2:4)
b =
      4    12    -3

>> [q, r]=deconv(a,b)
q =
     5.0000  -16.7500
r =
          0        0  221.0000  -40.2500
```

4. Plot the polynomials obtained in the previous problems in the range $0 \geq x \geq 20$. Evaluate them at $x = 0, 2, 5, 10, 20$.

```
function plotPoly(poly, x, plot_title)
% plotPoly.m - plot polynomial in given interval with given title

y = polyval(poly, x);
plot(x, y);
grid on;
title(plot_title);

end

% plotting polynomials

x = 0:0.1:20; % interval
xx = [0 2 5 10 20];
```

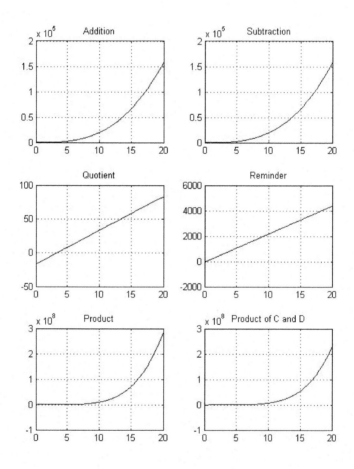

Figure 2.27: Plot of Polynomials

```
A=[20 -7 5 10];
B=[0 4 12 -3];

subplot(3,2,1)
sum = A + B;
sumAt = polyval(sum, xx)
plotPoly(sum, x, 'Addition');

subplot(3,2,2)
sub = A-B;
subAt = polyval(sub, xx)
plotPoly(sum, x, 'Subtraction');

subplot(3,2,3)
B=B(2:4);
[q, r] = deconv(A, B);
qAt = polyval(q, xx)
rAt = polyval(r, xx)
plotPoly(q, x, 'Quotient');

subplot(3,2,4)
plotPoly(r, x, 'Reminder');

subplot(3,2,5)
prod = conv(A, B)
prodAt = polyval(prod, xx)
plotPoly(prod, x, 'Product')


C=[6 4 -5];
D=[12 -7 3 9];

subplot(3,2,6)
prod2 = conv(C, D);
prod2At = polyval(prod2, xx)
plotPoly(prod2, x, 'Product of C and D');

>> plotPolys()
sumAt =
            7          189         2517        19877       159147
subAt =
           13          115         2203        18843       155473
qAt =
  -16.7500    -6.7500     8.2500    33.2500    83.2500
rAt =
  1.0e+003 *
   -0.0403     0.4018     1.0648     2.1698     4.3797
prod =
    80    212   -124    121    105    -30
prodAt =
          -30         5624       370520     10009120     288978470
prod2At =
          -45         2241       222585      7200265     230840775
```

See plots in fig. 2.27.

5. Find the roots of $x^3 + 6x^2 - 11x + 290$ and verify the solution.

```
>> A = [1 6 -11 290]; rt = cast(roots(A), 'single') % cast removes unneccesary tails
rt =
 -10.0000
   2.0000 + 5.0000i
   2.0000 - 5.0000i
>> polyval(A, rt)
ans =
   0
   0
   0
```

6. Find the roots of $36x^3 + 12x^2 - 5x + 10$ and verify the solution.

```
>> A = [36 12 -5 10]; rt = roots(A), polyval(A, rt)
rt =
  -0.8651
   0.2659 + 0.5004i
   0.2659 - 0.5004i
ans =
  1.0e-013 *
   0.0178
   0.1243 + 0.0178i
   0.1243 - 0.0178i
```

Due to float point representation and rounding errors we do not get zeros.

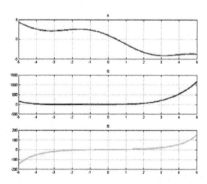

Figure 2.28: Figure for fzero demonstration

7. Plot equations $\cos x + \sin x = x$, $x^4 + 4x^3 + x^2 = -6$ and $e^x - e^{-x} = 1$ with a reasonable guess of x and solve them using fzero.

```
function y = f1_fzero(x)
% f1_fzero.m - cos(x) - sin(x) -x
y = cos(x) - sin(x) - x;
end

function y = f2_fzero(x)
```

```
% f2_fzero.m - x^4 + 4*x^3 +x^2 + 6
y = x.^4 + 4.*x.^3 +x.^2 + 6;
end

function y = f3_fzero(x)
% f3_fzero.m - e^x - e^{-x} = 1
y = exp(x) - exp(-x) - 1;
end

function y = FZeroDemo(x)
% FZeroDemo.m - a function for FZeroDemo

% main function which plots the
% functions and solving them
x=[-5:0.1:5];

subplot(3,1,1)
y1=f1_fzero(x);
plot(x,y1,'r','linewidth',3);
grid on; title('f1');

subplot(3,1,2)
y2=f2_fzero(x);
plot(x,y2,'b','linewidth',3);
grid on; title('f2');

subplot(3,1,3);
y3=f3_fzero(x);
plot(x,y3,'g','linewidth',3);
grid on; title('f3');

rt1=fzero('f1_fzero',0)

rt21=fzero('f2_fzero',-4)
rt22=fzero('f2_fzero',1)

rt3=fzero('f3_fzero',0)

end

rt1 =
    0.4566
rt21 =
    -3.5922
rt22 =
    -1.4820
rt3 =
    0.4812
```

See figures in fig. 2.8.

2.4.6 Answers for Problems from Linear Equations in MATLAB, Sect. 2.3.2.6

1. Solve

$$x + 10y = -6z + 5$$
$$3x + 2y + 4z = 4$$
$$4y + z = -3$$

```
>> A=[1 10 6; 3 2 4; 0 4 1];
>> b=[5; 4; -3];
>> x=A\b
x =
   -3.5000
   -1.8929
    4.5714
```

2. Find I_1, I_2 and I_3 for circuit depicted in fig. ?? when $V = 5V, V_1 = 5V, R_1 = 15\Omega, R_2 = 10\Omega$ and $R_3 = 5\Omega$.

Based on Kirchhoff's law we get

$$R_1 I_1 + R_2 I_2 \quad\quad = V$$
$$R_2 I_2 + R_3 I_3 = V_1$$
$$I_1 + \quad I_2 + \quad I_3 = 0$$

Replacing R_1, R_2 and V/V_1 by their values we get

```
>> A=[15 10 0; 0 10 -5; 1 -1 -1];
>> b=[10; 5; 0];
>> x=A\b
x =
    0.3636
    0.4545
   -0.0909
```

Bibliography

[1] Oracle and/or its affiliates. *Java Tutorials*, 2011. `http://java.sun.com/docs/books/tutorial/`.

[2] David J. Eck. *Introduction to Programming Using Java, Fifth Edition*, 2006. `http://math.hws.edu/javanotes/`.

[3] Marty Hall. *Java Programming Resource*, 2008. `http://www.apl.jhu.edu/~hall/java/`.

[4] S.T. Karris. *Introduction to Simulink with engineering applications*. Orchard Publications, 2008.

[5] T. Krilavičius. *Hybrid Techniques for Hybrid Systems*. PhD thesis, University of Twente, 2006.

[6] *MATLAB - The Language Of Technical Computing*. MATLAB web site.

[7] Wikipedia. *Java Programming Language*, 2011. `http://en.wikipedia.org/wiki/Java_programming_language`.